RELIGION AROUND BONO

RELIGION AROUND VOL. 7

PETER IVER KAUFMAN, *Founding Editor*

Books in the Religion Around series examine the religious forces surrounding
cultural icons. By bringing religious background into the foreground, these
studies give readers a greater understanding of and appreciation for individual
figures, their work, and their lasting influence.

RELIGION AROUND

BONO

Evangelical Enchantment and Neoliberal Capitalism

CHAD E. SEALES

THE PENNSYLVANIA STATE UNIVERSITY PRESS
UNIVERSITY PARK, PENNSYLVANIA

Parts of chapter 5 were previously published in "Love and Debt," *Cosmologics: A Magazine of Science, Religion, and Culture* (Summer 2016), http://cosmologics magazine.com/chadsealesloveanddebt, and they are reproduced here with the kind permission of *Cosmologics*, a magazine published by the Science, Religion, and Culture Program at Harvard Divinity School.

Library of Congress Cataloging-in-Publication Data

Names: Seales, Chad E., author.
Title: Religion around Bono : evangelical enchantment and neoliberal capitalism / Chad E. Seales.
Other titles: Religion around ; v. 7.
Description: University Park : The Pennsylvania State University Press, [2019] | Series: Religion around ; vol. 7 | Includes bibliographical references and index.
Summary: "Examines how the popular musician and public figure Bono represents the power of evangelicalism and promotes a religion of neoliberal capitalism"— Provided by publisher.
Identifiers: LCCN 2019027760 | ISBN 9780271084893 (cloth)
Subjects: LCSH: Bono, 1960—Religion. | Bono, 1960—Criticism and interpretation. | neoliberalism—Religious aspects—Christianity. | Evangelicalism.
Classification: LCC ML420.B6856 S43 2019 | DDC 782.42166092—dc23
LC record available at https://lccn.loc.gov/2019027760

The Pennsylvania State University Press is a member of the Association of University Presses.

It is the policy of The Pennsylvania State University Press to use acid-free paper. Publications on uncoated stock satisfy the minimum requirements of American National Standard for Information Sciences—Permanence of Paper for Printed Library Material, ANSI z39.48—1992.

To Mom and Dad

CONTENTS

ACKNOWLEDGMENTS

I wrote this book because Peter Iver Kaufman asked me to contribute to the Religion Around series. He suggested that I revisit ideas about religion and Bono that we had discussed years before. There are few academics more charismatic, more incisive, or more persuasive than Peter. I am grateful for his encouragement to pursue this project, which began when I was a graduate student in religious studies at the University of North Carolina at Chapel Hill. I also am thankful to Kathryn Lofton, who read drafts at every stage, from conference papers to final manuscript. As always, she helped clarify the concept. I also am appreciative of the staff at Penn State University Press, particularly Kathryn Yahner, who generously helped me think through how to make this a better book. Special thanks also to the anonymous reviewers for their insightful suggestions for improving the manuscript.

The University of Texas at Austin supported the completion of this project through a College Research Fellowship. I am grateful for my colleagues in religious studies at UT-Austin, who continually offer critical conversation: Oliver Freiberger, Virginia Garrard, Steve Friesen, Martha Newman, Joel Brereton, Alison Frazier, Jo Ann Hackett, Azfar Moin, Brent Landau, Geoff Smith, Jonathan Schofer, and John Traphagan. I am especially thankful to those in the Religion in the Americas Colloquium, including Jen Graber, Brent Crosson, Josh Urich, Michel Lee, Josefrayn Sanchez-Perry, and Megan Selander, who read chapters with a critical eye and helped me refine the argument. I also have benefited from conversations with former religious studies graduate students Mike Amoruso, Justin Doran, Elena Kravchenko, Brice Bongiovanni, and Brad King, who formatted the manuscript and prepared the index for this book; with current students Jaimie Gunderson and

James Henriques; and with colleagues in other departments at UT, particularly Randy Lewis, Sue Heinzelman, and Raj Patel.

Over the years, moving through institutional settings and conference gatherings, I have had a chance to gather insights from Jason Bivins, Tracy Fessenden, Shanny Luft, Mary Ellen O'Donnell, Jill DeTemple, Gary Laderman, Lucia Hulsether, Daniel Vaca, Kathryn Gin Lum, Heather Curtis, Tisa Wenger, Isaac Weiner, Kati Curts, Julie Byrne, David Shefferman, Evan Berry, Sue Ridgley, Randi Rashkover, Kevin O'Neill, Paul C. Johnson, Randall Stephens, Judith Weisenfeld, David Walker, Emily Clark, Susan Marks, Charles Wilson, Paul Harvey, Courtney Bender, Amy Koehlinger, Elijah Siegler, John Modern, and Chip Callahan.

Family and friends have been supportive throughout, many of them sending me the latest reports and articles on Bono's public engagements. Love and thanks to my mom, Faye, my dad, Gene, and my brother, Josh. To my wife, Emily, who is sunshine, love, and laughter, and whose practical idealism inspires me, and to our kids, Adlai, Emmett, and June, who wonder why it takes so long to write a book, when they can just come to my office and staple loose pages together. Done! To Carol and Mike Major, Laura and Kyle Lossen, and Madison and Sara Major. To friends at UUMC in Austin, especially John Elford, who helped me think through the theological limits of religious praise for U2, and Cade Patterson, who traveled to Houston to see a show from the Joshua Tree tour in 2017. And to those I grew up with in Florida, particularly my Baptist brothers and fellow fans, Mark Hinson and Jeff Baker.

INTRODUCTION

It's about feeling transcendent, forgiving the past, sharing a dream, together, in a moment. "It's not about politics, or religion, or the economy," Bono tells us in a promotional video for the 2010 FIFA World Cup in South Africa. We hear him and the music of U2, and we see images of communism, capitalism, socialism, Muslim women, processed poultry, gas masks, protests, global warming, all of it and more, a dreamlike sequence with the voice in your head saying, "it's not about those things." The song builds, Edge on guitar, Larry on drums, Adam on bass. You can't see them yet. Another flash of scenes, and there they are, in the stadium, as the pyrotechnics fire and Bono sings the hook, "Magnificent." This is it, he tells us, "the one month every four years that we all agree on one thing, thirty-two nations, one world watching."[1]

This book is about the evangelical enchantment of globalization. It is about a way of seeing the world as it is not. It is about the moral promise of economic elites to perpetually reform capitalism, to transcend its politics, its religions, and its economic facts. It is about an offer to solve the world's problems by democratizing capital and privatizing public services, to overcome poverty through microfinance and make new producers of new products for new consumers in new markets. It is about financial frontiers and the religious determination to conquer them, to hear the sounds of suffering and spread the shouts of good news. It is about a prophet with a band, a poet with a purpose. It is about a man with a message, for you, lost in the blur of media images, consumer products, and political reports, for you, who want to help but don't know how, for you, to tell you that you can, by just being yourself, just letting go, just listening and letting it wash over you, as you stand in the stream of commerce.

This book argues that Bono promotes, in popular culture and musical form, the religion of neoliberal capitalism. To be clear, Bono tries to overcome organized religion and he denounces neoliberal policies. He prefers to sing spiritual songs of global commerce, secular extractions of millennial capitalism, "a capitalism that presents itself as a gospel of salvation," write the anthropologists Jean Comaroff and John Comaroff, "a capitalism that, if rightly harnessed, is invested with the capacity wholly to transform the universe of the marginalized and disempowered."[2] Bono denies the categories of religion and capitalism and embraces the humanistic goal of reforming politics and economics to make them more about everyday people and less about institutional authority. Throughout the book, though, I contend that Bono's humanitarian work ultimately extends the power of evangelical Protestantism, including revival techniques, experiential piety, and life-or-death moral demands, along with the neoliberal practices of deregulation, privatization, and the expansion of free markets, into broader spheres of everyday life.

To see how this works, consider the difference between how Bono promoted the 2010 FIFA World Cup in South Africa and how the commercial event affected the lives of South Africans. In addition to the FIFA video, Bono and U2 created a series of music videos with the Soweto Gospel Choir for ESPN coverage of the 2010 World Cup. In one of the videos, Bono sings the gospel hymn "Amazing Grace" as the Soweto Gospel Choir walks into a stained-glass church. The video moves from shots of Bono onstage, to choir members in the city and choir members in the country, to young black South Africans holding the national flag. The arc of the video bends toward the idea of justice in a postapartheid nation, symbolized in an image of Nelson Mandela that appears as Bono sings, "I was blind, but now I see." The message is one of redemption and reconciliation, further symbolized in a Christian cross on a sunset horizon, as the music fades into the U2 standard "Where the Streets Have No Name."

Now consider the economic realities of Soweto at the same moment. In the year that Bono sang with the Soweto choir, the utility company Eskom, which provided electricity for the World Cup, continued to cut off the power of poor customers in Soweto who could not pay their bills. In one case, Eskom's action left a five-year-old boy with paralysis confined to his bed, without power for his wheelchair.[3] Residents of Soweto had protested such cutoffs for nearly a decade, forming a social movement, represented by the Soweto Electricity Crisis Committee (SECC), which organized protests and illegally reconnected electricity for residents.[4] In their public protests and for reconnecting residents' electricity, SECC activists risked being bullied, arrested, and even shot at. When frustrated, they tried to disconnect the electricity supply of politicians, to show them what it feels like to lose power. Such protests were met with fierce resistance. When activists tried to cut off power to the mayor of Johannesburg, shots were fired and eighty-seven people were arrested, including "elderly pensioners," according to one account. Global activists who supported the SECC declared its members "the first political prisoners of neoliberalism."[5] Bono was not among them.

The story of Eskom is the story of globalization in South Africa. In the late 1990s, the postapartheid African National Congress began the process of partially privatizing Eskom, the state-owned single supplier of electricity in South Africa. By 2002, according to Stephen Greenberg, a research fellow at the Institute for Poverty, Land and Agrarian Studies at the University of the Western Cape, Eskom had been "converted into a company, Eskom Holdings, and its regulated activities were separated from non-regulated activities." The result was that Eskom was no longer a "vertically integrated state monopoly supplier" but "just one amongst many energy companies operating in a competitive market."[6] These changes signaled a policy shift from a liberal, state-centered approach to a neoliberal, private-sector, market-driven approach.

This shift was intended to democratize access to electricity in the same way that microfinance was later promoted as democratizing access to capital. And, indeed, as a result of this shift, electricity became available to black households that had been excluded under apartheid. But once the market protections of the older liberal model were removed, Eskom began to suffer financial losses. The company responded by raising prices (rather than extending to all citizens the market protections afforded only to whites under the apartheid regime), and when poor customers, including many of the residents of Soweto, couldn't pay, the company cut off their power. According to Patrick Bond, the commercialization of Eskom "left 30,000 unemployed during the 1990s" and resulted in "disconnections of millions of people who fell into arrears on inflated bills."[7]

While Bono sang with the Soweto choir, Eskom promoted itself as "powering the 2010 FIFA World Cup South Africa," even trademarking the phrase. As part of its promotional campaign, it celebrated the new era of a postapartheid South Africa, developing "six universal principles" that represented "the hopes and aspiration of the country." These principles were "(1) a united, democratic and prosperous South Africa; (2) eradication of poverty and unemployment; (3) a thriving economy, connected to the world and integrated with the broader African continent; (4) a sustainable economy, not harmful to the environment and committed to [combatting] climate change; (5) enhancing the potential of each citizen; [and] (6) leveraging the role of state-owned enterprises for the economic development of the country."[8] Eskom's treatment of the low-income residents of Soweto clearly demonstrates its failure to uphold any of these principles. By 2018, analysts had declared Eskom "financially and environmentally unsustainable."[9]

This kind of bad news did not make it into the music video.[10] Bono religiously promoted a global event with the moral promise that it could deliver social salvation in the form of racial equality and economic development. He promoted the enchanting vision of a capitalism that could overcome violence, without recognizing the violence it produced. In this book, I explore the evangelical performance of that enchantment, its spiritual moods, biblical visions, and transcendent emotions, some of which are evident in the U2 promotional ads with the Soweto choir, from the gospel hymn "Amazing Grace," to the Christian cross on the horizon, to the more diffuse secular anthem "Where the Streets Have No Name." Like "Magnificent," another U2 song featured in a FIFA promotional video, "Streets" is filled with what fans refer to as secret biblical allusions. Those allusions don't necessarily make the songs or the ads an evangelical profession of faith. Rather, it is the cultural confluence of personal circumstances and providential force, of the history, politics, and economics around Bono, that delivers the promise of good news. To understand the ties that bind a sectarian Christian tradition to a universalizing economic philosophy, it takes a book. This is that book, a book about what isn't, a book about religion around Bono.

The first time I heard of U2, I was in the parking lot of a Southern Baptist church in the Florida panhandle. Wednesday evening service had just let out, and regular attendees hung around after the closing prayer, mingling in the aisles between the pews and loitering in the narthex before making their way to their cars. It was the same scene after each service; everyone came back to life after the final amen. Structured worship and hymns praising Jesus shifted instantly to camping plans, fishing reports, school gossip, talk of college football, ski boats, baseball games, or soccer tournaments. In a split second, that silent pause after the second syllable, we opened our eyes and there it was, the secular world. What would we do with it? How would we manage it? How would we enjoy it—but in a way that pleased God as much as it pleased us? It was a school night, so we moved more quickly than we would've on a Sunday. As we crossed the lot, two church moms were talking, one of them a good friend of my own mom's. "Faye, maybe you can help us," Mrs. Osborne said. "Have you heard of this band U2? Our kids have their album, *The Joshua Tree*."

I knew these kids, high schoolers, much cooler than me. I was entering sixth grade. They were way ahead. One of them wore bowling shoes all the time. I wasn't there when he walked out of the alley with them on his feet. But I heard about it. Some said he stole those shoes. But he insisted, so I heard him say, that it wasn't theft. He left behind his Converse high tops. He traded for them. "What do you think, Faye?" Mrs. Osborne asked my mom. "Do you think they are a Christian band?"

I stood outside this conversation looking in. I had no idea what they were talking about. I knew Bernice Osborne was an artist who signed her paintings "We," to acknowledge the divine source of her creativity and to signify that she alone was not the artist. God was with her, through the process and in her talent. One of her paintings hung in our house, a beach scene of waves crashing into rocks, sea oats in the background. And in the bottom right-hand corner was the brush-stroked "We."

I don't remember what my mom said to her friends. I remember her listening. But I can't remember how she answered the question. I do remember the sense of mystery around this band called U2. Were they or were they not Christian? And I remember, a few years later, when "I Still Haven't Found What I'm Looking For" came on the radio during a family road trip, that my mom decided that they must not be Christian, because if they were saved, they wouldn't need to keep looking. "Sounds like they are lost," she said.

Such parental clarity only made the band more compelling. For the churchgoing teenager, listening to U2 was an easy way to rebel. You didn't have to do or change anything. You didn't have to drink, or smoke, get a piercing, or dress differently. U2 made it cool *not* to do those things. They made it cool to stay the same. You didn't have to claim an Eastern religion or live like a bohemian. You didn't have to start Zen meditation and pretend you liked it, or read *The Dharma Bums*, or listen to the Lemon Drops and act like you understood it. Listening to U2 demanded very little, least of all the faux intellectual elitism of bright-eyed youth. Unlike my smart friends who listened to the Dead Milkmen and read Toni Morrison, I just didn't have to. I did, though. I read Dostoyevsky and Protagoras, Toni Morrison and Gwendolyn Brooks. I listened to Violent Femmes, Pearl Jam, Fugees, Led Zeppelin, and Nirvana. And I found them all compelling for different reasons. But none of these books and bands did church parents discuss in a church parking lot, reflecting on whether they were Christian. The answer was obvious. Nor were they ever topics of conversation in church youth group. There was no question. I once asked the youth minister, "What do you think about the idea that man is the measure of all things?" In response, I got a blank face, a long pause, and then a serious "God is the measure of all things." Church youth group was not a place to discuss humanism, or the symbolism of the dolls in *The Bluest Eye*. That was what you did in English class with Dr. Cunningham, who was no fan of bleached biblicism but who also glossed John Donne's biblical allusions, perhaps trying to sidestep the religious literalists in the class, whom she considered as unengaging as those who read CliffsNotes. I had a foot in both camps and wondered why. To answer that question required that two worlds collide—which was impossible, since biblical talk was met with secular silence at public school, and literary questions prompted distracted Tommy Boy impersonations at Bible study. In that latter religious space, to read and talk about anything that demanded inquisitive intellectual depth risked stepping out of the evangelical church and into the secular world, not as a missionary but as an unbeliever.

U2 was different. They were willing to step out but were able to come back. Bono discussed poetry and compared it to the Psalms. You could talk about U2 with church parents but still feel like they didn't understand. You couldn't do that with evangelical performers like Michael W. Smith. No one questioned whether he was Christian or not. And you could tell that your parents liked the music and wanted you to like it too. Bono was different. He was infinitely better *and* he said he didn't like church. But that didn't keep him from talking about biblical concerns. Bono was a rebel, but a rebel that hung around. U2 offered a way to feel like you were leaving your parents' religion without ever leaving it. They offered another way to be evangelical, not through restrictive doctrine but through expressive moralism. When I was in high school, I listened to *Rattle and Hum* enough to wear out the disk and to memorize Bono's speech about apartheid in South Africa: "This song was written in a hotel room in New York City." I would recite that speech at the oddest times, like during a church camping trip. No one knew what I was talking about, and they told me so. They may have listened to the songs, but they rarely paid attention to the words. And this all felt powerful, this feeling that you knew something that others should know, something you believed more morally Christian than the plan of salvation in the Roman Road. To really listen to U2 made you feel like a true rebel, because how could you be worried about personal sin, the litmus test of evangelical doctrine, when there were social sins so much worse? When there was apartheid out there somewhere, how could you care about whether someone was Christian or not, depending on whether they smoked, or drank, or did whatnot? How could you be so narrow? For the boy in the Baptist bubble, U2 offered the world.

But despite the fact that Bono spoke sincerely, using the bullhorn of Christian reform, I ultimately found the quieter voices of skeptics and sophists more compelling. In college, I switched majors from engineering to philosophy. This change was unrelated to U2. But it put me on a path that led to this book, as I went on to graduate school to study American religious history, took a class in globalization theory, and realized that Bono stood at the intersection of both. I also learned during that time how to use historical approaches, critical race theory, and studies on religion and popular culture to deconstruct the evangelical world that had shaped my identity as a white male. Some of that thinking and reflection focused on the popular tradition of blackface minstrelsy, which I discuss in the last chapter of this book, where I work through Bono's racial and gendered performances of his muscular Irishness.[11] It is this Irishness that Bono cites as an ethnic marker of outsider status within colonial empires. I technically share some of that ethnicity, as I am of roughly half-Irish and half-Dutch descent. But I'm not sure how much that hidden genetic history really matters compared to the cultural conditions that present white males as divinely sanctioned political protectors of spiritual transcendence, which in evangelical cultures is embodied in white feminine counterparts. In retrospect, I can better understand why I was drawn to Bono's gendered performance of white male sovereignty in *Rattle and Hum*, his overly confident and exuberant, even godlike, claim to a universal knowledge of right and wrong. His confidence emerged from loss and claimed to conquer it; it was an expression of a desire to protect mothers, "the women and children," that was also a desire to transgress the limits of those who claimed to protect them. For Bono, confidence conquered supremacy, of religion and race, even as evangelical whiteness remained the medium of U2's love supreme.

While I was phenotypically like Bono the Irishman, a white male, I wanted to be more lyrically like Bono the rock star, a prophetic figure who sang for justice as if he were a racial outsider. This desire to preach freedom as a social outcast is part of the story of evangelicalism. But it is a story that is entangled with the racialized and gendered histories of blackface performances, which express love for those marked as different and a desire to transgress the boundaries that divide, but which ultimately maintain the solidity of racial and gender distinctions. Blackface is a ritual technique used to control the beloved, without being changed by the act of love.[12] Bono is confident that he can love Africa, that he can transgress the colonial difference and still be the same, that he can be Irish in the present and African in the past, that he is now, and has always been, an outsider. I'm less certain.

While I give some attention to race and gender, this book focuses more on class distinctions. It focuses less on Bono than on the religion around Bono, a religion that names a place where the good news of evangelicalism and the moral promise of millennial capitalism meet. Plenty of evangelical apologists focus on the theological meaning of Bono's lyrics and speeches but ignore the economic impact of his neoliberal promotions. And plenty of secular critics size up those who benefit from the system that Bono promotes but do not consider the religion that organizes it. *Religion Around Bono* describes a rock star in relation to an evangelical history and criticizes the religion around him that reconciles the spiritual meaning of church tradition with the present promise that free markets and for-profits will bring justice and freedom to the world's poor.

This book contributes to the Religion Around series by detailing the historical influence of evangelical Christianity on Bono as an iconic musical and political figure of the late twentieth and early twenty-first centuries, while also considering the cultural role Bono has played in the secular promotion of evangelical spirituality as a consumer practice of *neoliberal religion*. The book examines the neoliberal religion around Bono as a cultural system that lyrically and politically carries the political ideals of consumer citizenship and free-market economies. As a cultural carrier of neoliberalism, Bono employs the language and emotion of spirituality, reforming religion in the image of personal choice, in order to make it compatible with the economic demands of a democratic capitalist world polity. From within this polity, economic elites promote the expansion of free markets as necessary for the full realization of human rights. Bono's role in this political process is that of the prophetic agent, in this case the modern evangelical revivalist, who binds earthly sovereigns to the spiritual calling of divine love. *Religion Around Bono* examines the cultural system that makes meaningful this religious imagination.

Focusing on the cultural system of neoliberal religion around Bono, this book differs in method and approach from the journalistic coverage afforded rock stars and popular bands like U2—the magazine stories, in-depth interviews, and eclectic biographies—along with the more recent monographs and articles that make up the subfield of U2 studies. In 2009, Scott Calhoun, a professor of English at Cedarville University, a Christian university in Ohio, organized the first "U2 Conference," in Raleigh, North Carolina, which was presented as an academic conference with an advertised call for papers and a program of more than fifty presenters, many of them university professors. The conference met again in 2013 and 2018. Professor Calhoun has also developed a "U2 studies network" of scholars and journalists, and a "U2 studies bibliography" that lists close to one hundred published books and essays on Bono and U2. While *Religion Around Bono* will eventually be added to that list (my article "Burned Over Bono" is already included in that bibliography), it will be distinguished by its cultural studies approach to the subject of religion *around* Bono. That is, "U2 studies" consists primarily of the work of a collection of scholars who support Bono and U2's humanitarian mission. Many U2 studies scholars, though not all, are progressive Christians; Bono delivers his religious message in a way that resonates with both confessional churchgoers and moral secularists. Almost all, however, share the religious tenet that Calhoun expresses as "I believe in U2."[13]

Taking up the intellectual charge of the Religion Around series, this book examines the cultural system, in the words of Clifford Geertz, that makes the "moods and motivations," or the feeling of sincere belief, surrounding Bono and U2, seem "uniquely realistic." *Religion Around Bono* is not a biography. It includes biographical details about Bono and the band only as they relate to the overarching story of religion around. The book does not attempt to uncover hidden theological messages and biblical allusions in the lyrics of U2 or in interviews with Bono. Rather, it uses such attempts by academics and journalists as evidence for the cultural practice of neoliberal religion. Nor does the book attempt to construct a practical theology or prescribe a set of spiritual disciplines for congregational practice based on the U2 lyrics or Bono's public statements. Again, it is concerned with the cultural construction of such attempts.

What the book does do is consider Bono as a cultural icon of neoliberal religion. It argues that Bono promotes the cultural practice of neoliberal religion as the secular consumption of a particular kind of spiritual affect—the feeling that personal choice has salvific consequences and that with this choice the consumer transcends the moral limits of traditional religion. This spiritual feeling has been ritually cultivated in the revival tradition of evangelical Protestantism. Bono emerges out of this historical tradition and extends it beyond doctrinal or sectarian definitions of evangelical Protestantism and into the popular culture of rock concerts and product branding.[14] Throughout the book, I use the term *neoliberal religion* to describe the cultural system within which we come to understand the economic meaning of social order and personal choice. Neoliberal religion is not just a revelatory response to the philosophical question about the meaning of life—the question *why am I here?*—but it is a social solution to the existential problem of the meaning of consumer freedom—an answer to not just *what* but also *why* we should buy. In its answer, neoliberal religion offers an economic theodicy, an explanation for why we have purchasing power and why others don't, not yet. Neoliberal religion is defined by its millennial promise that those who don't, the poor, will one day be like the rich, and will be able to buy. But they will only be able to do this tomorrow—and only if those who *are* able to buy today will do so in order to help those who face the prospect of death survive until tomorrow. Neoliberal religion makes it seem as if the survival of the poor depends on the very class distinction that marks them as not rich, since that class distinction makes it possible for the wealthy to create the economic possibility of financial salvation through their consumer purchase and humanitarian will. To dissolve the class distinction would negate that soteriological promise. Neoliberal religion supports the cultural system of class distinctions between those with economic power in the present and those with economic potential in the future. It persists in these collectivities, of congregants, fans, citizens, and brands, as defined in relation to a lower economic class set apart.

Religion organizes individuals into collectives in relationship to things set apart as sacred. Religion is never just about the doctrine I believe, or the album I buy, or the song I sing, because religion transforms the *I* into the *we*. The philosophical problem of true belief that motivates Bono is a social problem, because without society, there is no true or false, no right or wrong, no good or bad, and no religion. But neoliberalism makes it seem that religion as spirituality is just about *you*, as if religion as spirituality were just a philosophical idea, a transcendent feeling—and it is your idea, your feeling. Neoliberalism organizes individuals into collectives while promising the dissolution of collectivity and the triumph of individuality. Neoliberalism is an economic philosophy, and neoliberal religion is the social practice of that economic philosophy, the making of the world in relation to the political promise of individual freedom through free markets. Neoliberalism names the absence of religion in the economy, even as the economic order is its religious manifestation. This very act of naming *what isn't* in relation to *what is* makes sense only within a particular cultural system. To see how Bono is part of this cultural system, we must understand his relationship to evangelicalism, and evangelicalism's relationship to popular culture.

To put it more concretely, when Mrs. Osborne asked my mom if U2 was a Christian band, she was participating in a cultural system that connected what she considered Christian—her Protestant church—to what she would normally have considered not religion—a rock band. At the time, I was fascinated by Mrs. Osborne's problem, which was how her evangelical faith related to her (or her kids') secular choice—not just what we should believe, but how I choose the right music based on what we believe. Mrs. Osborne's problem was religious because the *I* was transformed into a *we* through her relationship to the moral community of her church. But her solution to this problem appeared secular because the *we* was transformed into an *I* through her consumption, her purchase of a U2 album. She wanted to know if it was okay to be a member of her Christian community and also enjoy being a secular fan. Using a commonsense approach to religion, as Bono does, Mrs. Osborne's problem could be solved rather simply. The organizing force of her life, her religion, needs to be reformed, if not abandoned, so that she can find the spiritual freedom to seek truth within the secular marketplace of art, ideas, and commerce.

My methodological approach to the study of religion around Bono is necessarily critical because I use the term *religion* differently than my subject does. By religion Bono means the institutional structures of Christian churches, though he also invokes the term to describe traditions that resemble those structures. Religions, for Bono, have distinct clergy, elites, or other authorities who define and explain scripture, doctrine, and ritual. For Bono, what institutional religions try to do is organize your life. And he says that he doesn't like someone trying to tell him what to believe or profess, what to read and what it means, how to pray or what to say, how much to give and whom to pay. Bono doesn't like organized religion. And, like evangelicals, he believes that you can escape religion, that you can transcend it, and that you can get to a higher place without it. In academic tension with that view, I maintain that you can't make that promise without making religion, as a cultural system. For the very cultural system within which Mrs. Osborne and Bono call the world religious or not religious is itself religion, in that it is another form of social classification, of setting apart in relation to things, persons, or ideas made sacred.

Taking a critical approach to the study of religion around Bono doesn't necessarily mean that you can't like his music. When it comes to the performance, I'm not a disgruntled fan. The sound remains the same; the message is what it is. You can study religion critically while recognizing its power to shape our moods, our emotions, to hit us in the gut, whether we believe in it or not. I don't believe in the religion around Bono, but I am still moved by the transcendent promise of his prophetic performance. I mean, wouldn't it be nice to escape the limits of tradition, to end poverty, to dissolve racism, to flash the peace sign and make it happen? What U2 fan doesn't feel like all of that can happen? For how we feel is not our choice. To put it another way, I am not a huge fan of the Americana duo Shovels & Rope, but their song "Birmingham" gets me every time. It's the hook, based on the eighteenth-century hymn lyric "Rock of Ages, cleft for me / Let me hide myself in thee." When I hear those words, I can see my dad's mother, a sharecropper's daughter from southern Mississippi, standing stout in the kitchen, frying chicken in a cast iron skillet, half-humming, half-singing the same lyric. And I remember being a kid in her living room. A kid with a toy box and a kid in a Landmark Missionary Baptist church, singing "Rock of Ages" from the hymnal in the family pew. But it's not just that. It's not just the distant echoes of childhood memories. It's the way the hook in "Birmingham" becomes a way to make meaning of a human story about two tough-luck artists trying to make it on their own, outside the walls of the church. There is spiritual power in the story of human struggle to overcome religion, and Bono sings with that power as the Edge searches for the secret chord.

Overcoming religion while claiming spirituality is a disposition that Bono shares with evangelicals, who, as I note throughout this book, have a history of saying that what they have is faith, and that what they do is not religious. When studying evangelicals, most scholars wink at their antireligious professions and focus instead on the archival realism of their organized churches and doctrinal statements. Evangelicals may say they don't have religion, these scholars note, but they keep meeting on Sunday and they keep talking about God and Jesus and personal salvation. Historians in particular emphasize the theological impulse of Protestant evangelicals to resist the institutional traditions of their Roman Catholic predecessors, as they foreground personal relationships with God and fellow humans (and, I would add, private property rights) above all things they consider too Catholic, from liturgical commissions to worker cooperatives. Historian Mark Noll argues that evangelicalism is expressed as "a multifaceted protest against ecclesiastical formalism and an urgent appeal for living religion of the heart."[15] For Noll and other historians, evangelicals have sustained their anti-institutional appeals to the religion of the heart, or experiential piety, through revivalism from sixteenth-century Europe to twenty-first-century America and beyond.

The problem with this historical approach, however, is that it includes a wide range of Protestants who may or may not claim to be evangelicals. For this reason, sociologists of religion prefer to use evangelicals' self-identification when studying them.[16] This method is straightforward. If someone says they are evangelical, then they are. But this approach also has its drawbacks. Evangelicals, or those who share a common appeal to experiential piety, go by many names. They may call themselves followers of Jesus, or just Christians. The term *evangelical* was highly politicized in the 1980s, with the rise of the religious Right in the United States. Since then, evangelicalism has been associated with fundamentalist biblical interpretation and strident political moralism. Some members of evangelical churches that developed out of the revival traditions that historians use to define evangelicalism, such as those within reconciling congregations in the United Methodist Church, for example, may no longer claim the label, since their views on social issues differ significantly from those of the "moral majority." To take their self-identification at face value would mean forgetting the religious histories they share with their post-1980s evangelical counterparts.

But self-identification is still important, because saying you are not something is a political statement. What all of those Protestant practitioners share, regardless of whether they identify themselves as evangelical, is a persistent parceling of the world into religion and not-religion, followed by an attempt to transcend the very binary they ritually produce by offering an alternative classification of sacred practice, whether as personal faith or spiritual experience. Studying religion around Bono requires both methodological approaches, in order to write a history of subjects who deny their own history to make it anew. One of the goals of this book is to demonstrate the historical continuities between evangelical Protestantism and popular culture, by showing how Bono extends evangelical principles of experiential piety and revival traditions into the popular realm of rock concerts and humanitarian concern. In this way, the book tells a secularizing story of religion persisting in modern life, as evangelical "church" values are over time diffused into popular culture.[17] But I also want to tell this story in a way that does not assume that the secular present is just another name for past religion, or that a particular consumer practice today is just the latest iteration of a sixteenth-century Protestant ethic.[18] It may be that, but it is not only that, because to tell the story of secularization requires a particular religious imagination, one not all that different from the popular practice of extracting spirituality from religion, a practice that Bono promotes.

To tell the story of religion around Bono in the historical framework of change over time requires an arbitrary starting point. My starting point in this book is evangelical Protestantism and its revival traditions. I want to make clear, though, that I use the terms *evangelical* and *revival* as heuristic placeholders for broader cultural patterns. That is, I use the terms to indicate emotional states and affective traits that move across the very boundaries between religion and not-religion that Bono and U2 fans maintain. These states and traits can be classified with the terms noted above, *spirituality* being the most popular among them. I have chosen the terms *evangelical* and *revival* to signify the process of this setting apart, to highlight historical continuities of religious affect and mood that historians and practitioners have identified as evangelical, in order, ultimately, to show how Bono emerged from such evangelical communities and how he has carried on their emotional commitments, while resisting the limits of their collectivity. He has taken from evangelicalism a spirit of protest and a spirit of setting apart. But he has made it seem that he reverses the order in which evangelicals do the same thing. He presents an image of himself not as an evangelical protesting the world, but as an artist in the world protesting evangelicals in the church, and setting himself apart from them in order to make a space, to invoke a place, without categorical limits, a place where the streets have no name. By calling Bono a cultural icon of neoliberal religion, I am trying to present the ritual extraction of consumer spirituality from evangelical Protestantism as a historical process.

To locate a "spirit" in history that connects religious ideas to secular habits, as Max Weber did in *The Protestant Ethic and the Spirit of Capitalism*, requires a categorical setting apart of a particular strand of religion back then from a secular cultural practice right now. For much of human history, it was unnecessary, redundant, even impossible to describe religion as something set apart as a distinct source of social organization, because religion was inextricably woven into all spheres of life. When we talk about religion in modernity, we often think of it as an external organizing force, something outside our daily routines, that has the power and authority, based on its connection to a divine source, usually from a God or gods, to tell us how to live. The organizing force we call religion, though, has always been part of our daily routine, part of our work, our play, our cultivation, and our commerce. Religion names the idea of society.[19] We have only recognized it as such since roughly the nineteenth century, when philosophers and social theorists identified religion as both a problem and a solution for the division of labor in modern civilization.

To isolate a particular strand of religion back then, such as evangelical revivals in eighteenth- and nineteenth-century North America, and say that they diffused religious values of experiential piety and personal conversion into the popular culture of a U2 rock concert tells only one side of the story, as it looks from the inside out of church history.[20] Again, part of this book tells that story. But the book does more than just describe evangelicalism around Bono; it also critically examines the neoliberal religion that locates both evangelicalism and Bono within the same market economy. It does this while acknowledging that academic labor also is performed within and in relation to this market.[21] Scholars often study evangelicals as *in* but not *of* the world, which is consistent with how evangelicals describe themselves. Academics often treat evangelicals as solely religious subjects who carry their religiosity, expressed as personal piety, with them from the church into the world. This kind of approach keeps the focus on the church, whether as a physical space, or as a history of doctrine and belief, or as another name for networks of denominational institutions, as the defining religious limit of evangelicalism in contrast with the secular world beyond that limit. This approach is not much different from Mrs. Osborne's. On the surface, it might seem commonsensical to describe evangelicalism as evangelicals describe it. But this invites the possibility of accepting the world as evangelicals see it, which is to filter the past through the promise of good news. Consider, for example, that when the historian Donald G. Mathews argued that lynching in the American South was a religious rite, the majority of historians of southern religion and American evangelicalism disagreed.[22] And the reason they disagreed, they said, was that lynchings occurred outside the church and were not part of church doctrine. Even though Mathews demonstrated that lynchings occurred in the counties with the highest rates of church attendance, and that participants in lynch mobs praised God, other historians found the argument too circumstantial, too indirect. I cite this example to illustrate how telling the story of evangelicals as evangelicals tell it themselves shares a potential affinity with neoliberal ideals, as it leaves open the possibility of remaking good religion by recovering lost moral essences in new popular forms. In the case of lynching, it leaves open the option that the church can religiously reform a cultural practice by renewing its historical claim to true Christian doctrine. Such stories begin with a generation that has lost its way, a generation that has lost the religion of its fathers and mothers to the advance of secular culture, a generation in need of being rescued by its prophetic and progressive sons and daughters. In the case of economic development in Africa, such an approach to the study of evangelicalism tells a story of one generation of evangelicals who lost their true religion by making a political pact with the Republican Party to govern America, and of the next generation of evangelicals' finding good religion again through a moral compact with an Irish rock star to save Africans. In such stories, good religion is the connective thread that runs through a normative history, a history that is morally redeemed through generational cycles of evangelical revivals. This book says yes, that story has to some extent happened. Bono and many of his fans see themselves as recovering something spiritual lost to traditional religion. But the book also asks what it means, in the terms of neoliberal religion, if we tell that story as good and redemptive.

"What the facts are telling us," Bono claims in a 2013 TED talk titled "The Good News on Poverty (Yes, There's Good News)," "is that the long slow journey, humanity's long slow journey of equality, is actually speeding up."[23] Bono tells us the good news on poverty with big charts citing the historical decline of extreme poverty, defined as a personal income of less than $1.25 a day, with a projected virtual elimination of poverty by 2028. This is the good news, the moral promise of millennial capitalism. But what does it mean to end extreme poverty when prices keep going up, and what does it mean to employ the poor when, like many of the residents in Soweto, they still can't pay for what should be public services? What does it mean to sing the good news and claim that it is not about politics or religion or the economy when it is about all of those things? What does it mean if we tell the story of religion around Bono as it is told to us, as good news? What does it mean if we believe in the moral sincerity of a celebrity icon while denying the religious source of our belief? What does it mean if we feel spiritually connected to that celebrity without asking how he profits from that feeling? What does it mean if we believe in our moral agency to change the world through our product purchase, without recognizing the religion we consume, the religion that consumes us?

To answer these questions, the book travels an arc from historical description to critical reflection. Chapter 1, "Evangelicalism Around," situates Bono's message, and his delivery techniques, in an evangelical history of American revivalism. This chapter argues that Bono empties out the radical elements of the prophets he references, and through that emptying out continues a religious tradition of muscular white evangelical revivalists, who promised free-market capitalism and believed in the idea of racial difference. He maintains the very tradition of white evangelicalism that he appears to break from, as he makes listeners feel that they are rejecting or overcoming the unjust racial and economic limits of traditional religion. Chapter 2, "Around Bono," describes how fans receive that message and how self-identified evangelicals hear the Gospel message in the music of U2. These two chapters set a descriptive tone of cultural evangelicalism around Bono that builds into a sustained critique of neoliberal religion around evangelicals *and* Bono in the next three chapters.

This critique of neoliberal religion begins in chapter 3, "Neoliberalism Around," with a more confrontational tone than may be necessary, in order to resist the consensus that the moral problems of life and death, as presented by Bono and by his economic mentor, the Harvard economist Jeffrey Sachs, seem to demand. But there are alternative forms of social organization. There are other arguments that do not take private property rights and free-market principles as self-evident universal truths. One of the goals of this book is to help the reader understand how neoliberal religion as a cultural system keeps us from seeing other economic possibilities by making us think that there is no alternative. This feeling of inevitability signals the religious power of neoliberalism. Chapter 4, "Around Africa," shows how Bono and Sachs wield that religious power, as representatives of political and economic interests in Africa, in their response to public criticism of their neoliberal policies, even when that criticism is directed more at the problem of external control than at the underlying economic principles.

And chapter 5, "Love and Debt," shows how Bono's cultural promotion of neoliberal religion depends upon an essentialist view of racial difference and musical expression that connects him to an American history of blackface minstrelsy. This chapter concludes by reflecting on the economic function of Bono's minstrel act, which is to increase the personal debt of Western consumers by making them feel as if they are relieving the debt of others. This chapter reflects on how Bono makes it feel as though he has reversed the minstrel rules of popular culture, now giving to, rather than stealing from, Africans, and how he offers this feeling to consumers in the branded image of Africa in need that is the Product Red campaign.

EVANGELICALISM AROUND

Bono is a self-identified Christian who has an antagonistic relationship with religion. For Bono, religion is a negative. It is a lack. An absence. Religion is something to keep at a distance, something to stand outside and shout back at. Religion for Bono, as for any prophet, is the bureaucratic habit of the lost way.

A prophet is a charismatic individual who gives the people what they want: a big idea that can change the world. The authority of the prophet is based on his revolutionary promise that change is near; that the way things are today will be different tomorrow, if they believe. Prophetic authority depends on the ability and the willingness of the people to recognize the idea, and to believe in it. Without the people, without an audience of fans, without their consent, the prophet's message is mere noise. With them, he is their voice. The power of the prophet is his revolutionary promise, but that power is irrational and unstable. Charisma is heart over mind. It is the feeling of connection, and feelings are fleeting. They are in the moment, and the moment must end. So the prophet must keep gathering his audience, to take them to the place where he shows them the horizon. Unlike the priest, who meets his congregants in relation to the institution that guarantees him, the prophet stands alone before the crowd. And because of this, the prophet must always be great, or else his authority will fail. If he is less than that, his people can walk away, to find another. He must keep bringing them back, to him, to hear his message.[1]

Bono is a modern prophet of the secular age. His celebrity is his charisma. His music is his medium. And his message is a personal offer of spiritual transcendence, a secularized soteriology—a public prescription for soul salvation unbounded by a religious institution. This message Bono distributes through the rock band U2, selling it on records, performing it to audiences in live concerts, and explaining it face to face with music journalists. Since the late 1990s, when he began his advocacy work on behalf of Africa, Bono has also worked beyond his rock 'n' roll venues, politically circulating in the lobbying arena, the talk circuit, and the world of the corporate brand. In this chapter, I focus on how Bono formulates a prophetic message of spiritual transcendence and human liberation. I argue that as a prophetic type, Bono identifies religion as a spiritual problem (he says, for example, that "religion gets in the way of God"), he connects that spiritual problem to a moral crisis (such as violent conflict in Ireland, or U.S. military involvement in Central America), and he offers the feeling of transcendent experience (sung as the refrain "in the name of love") as a secular solution to these crises.

All prophets come from somewhere, even if they appear, and may claim, to come out of nowhere. They emerge from the religion around them, even as they claim to break from it. Siddhartha came from Vedic traditions, Jesus from Jewish traditions, Luther from Catholic traditions . . . and Bono from evangelical Protestant traditions. Such comparison immediately invites a host of contradictions. Siddhartha, Jesus, and Martin Luther sparked religious reform movements that over time grew into new religious traditions. This, at least, is how they appear to us now. By our common sense, we think of each of these men as a religious figure. They lived long enough ago that they seem different from us, and we look back and remember them as exceptional, inspired, and innovative in a religious way. But Bono is not at first glance obviously religious. He is the energetic rock star who, unlike average rock stars, insists on removing the distance between himself and us. He wants to be the song in our head. He sings from the stage but moves among the crowd, crossing the divide to pull us back, to his side. "My idea of a performer," he says, "is one that is not comfortable with the distance between the stage and the audience. My idea of a performer is one that might leave the stage and you might find them in your lap, in your life, following you home, mugging you in the alley, making you tea, whatever it is. That comfortable distance we've always tried to attack as a band. Between an audience and the stage. We do it with technology now. But back then [referring to Live Aid] we just did it physically. We went into the audience."[2] Such proximate performance belies the need for mediated connection. Bono lives in the moment, as if in constant contact with his fans. And while those who practice Buddhism, or Catholicism, or Lutheranism may remember their prophets walking with or talking to the people, they remember them through their traditions, their stories, their scriptures, and their liturgies. Which is another way to say that a prophet may be recognized in the present but more often is recognized after the fact, after he is sufficiently gone. For it takes a collective to make a prophet, to recognize his message, and to remember his life. But Bono has yet to leave the moment, the stage, the promotional video. He keeps mugging you, making you tea, whatever. He is recognized in the present, but will he be remembered forty years, one hundred years . . . twenty-five hundred years from now?

What distinguishes Bono from the prophets of old is his modern moment, a moment when the powerful forces of neoliberal economies organize collectives. Bono is a different kind of prophet, a modern prophet, who by way of mass communication can distribute his message and gather his collective rapidly, repeatedly, and with global reach. This collective is the religion around him, the confessional moral community of evangelical Protestants from which Bono emerges and the nonconfessional moral community of U2 fans to whom he speaks. Religion around Bono begins with evangelical Protestantism. It is the background to the more visible rock star image.

Bono is Irish, and Ireland has been religiously dominated by Roman Catholicism and politically shadowed by violent conflict between

Protestants and Catholics. In the mid-twentieth century, Ireland was divided into two regions. Southern Ireland became the Republic of Ireland in 1949, gaining independence from British rule. Northern Ireland remained part of the United Kingdom, which historically, through British colonialism, had promoted its state religion, the Anglican Communion, throughout its territories. The Church of Ireland is a legacy of such actions, and was Protestant only because of the strange historical circumstances that surrounded Henry VIII in the sixteenth century. Henry, a Roman Catholic, was unable to produce a male heir through his first marriage to the Spanish princess Catherine of Aragon, also a Roman Catholic. Blaming Catherine for the failure, he sought an annulment from the pope. When the pope refused, Henry, as king of England (and Ireland), broke with Rome and declared the establishment of the Church of England (which included the Church of Ireland), of which he appointed himself the head. He then annulled his marriage to Catherine and married Anne Boleyn, who, also failing to bear a son, was later executed on false charges. Anne did give birth to a daughter, Elizabeth, who became queen of England, but only by remaining loyal to the Protestant Church of England, which legitimated her claim to the throne, a claim challenged by Henry's Catholic daughter by Catherine, Mary. The religious battles in England between Protestants and Catholics determined who ruled the United Kingdom and thus spilled over into Ireland, England's colonized territory. The colonial demand for political and religious loyalty to the sovereign claims of England produced the lingering religious divisions in Ireland.[3]

After the regional division of Ireland in the mid-twentieth century, political fractures manifested themselves in two major groups. Nationalists, also known as Republicans, most of them Catholic, did not want to live under British rule; they wanted to be part of an independent Irish state. Loyalists, also referred to as Unionists, most of them Protestant, wanted Northern Ireland to remain part of the United Kingdom. During "the Troubles," a period lasting from the late 1960s through the 1990s, violence between the two camps escalated, and British troops were sent to Northern Ireland for the professed purpose of protecting Catholics. The presence of troops sparked more violent protests from resistance groups like the Irish Republican Army (IRA), which saw itself as defending its territory from British occupation. In 1998, after thirty years of fighting, the Good Friday Agreement ended the conflict for all intents and purposes. As part of the agreement, a new legislative body was organized, the Northern Ireland Assembly, with the purpose of providing political representation for all citizens. The assembly was composed of several political parties, including those affiliated with Unionists and Nationalists, who were forced to share power in the new government. In 2017, however, the assembly was suspended because of unresolved political disagreements.[4]

Bono grew up in Ireland during the violence of the 1970s that was associated with the "the Troubles," but he was shielded from its direct impact, bunkered in what he describes as the "suburban blank" of Dublin. The son of a Roman Catholic father and an Anglican mother, Bono often claims to understand the political and religious conflict in Ireland. His parents' interreligious marriage was taboo, and Bono describes their relationship as one of love that transcended politics. "Both my mother and my father didn't take religion seriously," remembered Bono. "They saw the absurdity of the fuss made over their union, though my mother used to bring us to chapel on Sundays and my father would wait outside. I have to accept that one of the things I picked up from my father and mother was a sense that religion often gets in the way of God."[5] Citing the influence of his parents, who refused to pick a side in Ireland's defining conflict, Bono rejected religion in favor of evangelicalism, a much more radical form of Protestantism than the Anglican state church. With its emphasis on experiential piety and spiritual spontaneity, evangelicalism resists the liturgical formalism of both Catholicism and Anglicanism. Bono's religious path through evangelicalism took him away from the religious limits of Irish ethnicity and toward a more global, heartfelt, expressive form of cultural Irishness.

Evangelicalism accounts for a tiny demographic slice of the religious pie in Ireland. Ireland has the lowest percentage of evangelicals in the English-speaking world, at roughly 1.5 percent of the population, with the overall number of Protestants at about 5 percent and Catholics at 85 percent.[6] Compare that to the United States, where evangelicals make up 25 percent of the population, with the overall number of Protestants at 49 percent and Catholics at 21 percent.[7] These numbers don't tell the whole story, as Catholics and Anglicans may share emotionally expressive traits with evangelicals. Movements such as the Charismatic Renewal in the Roman Catholic Church and the U2charist communion service in the Anglican Church, which I discuss in more detail in chapter 2, illustrate this point. These movements, though, were intended to renew the spiritual life and global witness of their respective religious institutions. Bono, however, rejects the social idea of a religious institution, favoring instead loose assemblies of evangelical organizations—which is another way to say that you can be a Catholic or an Anglican and still attend a U2 concert. Just know that Bono isn't going to attend your service. He's not going to be a regular attendee in your church. The only services he ever attended with any regularity were with evangelicals who didn't consider them services at all, and he only did that briefly.

In the religious history of Ireland, modern evangelicalism was a decoupling force, connecting its small gatherings of believers to a much more American model of religious participation based on voluntary association, sincere belief, and nondenominational revivalism.[8] To see this decoupling in action, consider how Bono can offer a poem for evangelical revivalist Billy Graham, let the pope wear his sunglasses, and hear the archbishop of Canterbury quote his statement "I'm not into religion. I am completely anti-religious. Religion is a term for a collection, a denomination. I am interested in personal experience of God."[9] Bono's religious path through evangelicalism sent him outward into a spiritual future beyond Ireland and beyond the categorical limits of its religious denominations. That journey would ultimately return him, as a brand, as an idea, to the very collections that he spurned. As he became a cultural icon for a spiritual but not religious movement, denominational leaders and organizers sought to reincorporate his prophetic charisma in order to reinvigorate their institutions.

Bono's encounters with evangelicalism began in school. Bono attended Mount Temple Comprehensive School in Dublin in the late 1970s. Steve Stockman describes it as a "nondenominational school" and a "progressive experiment." "The school," he says, "had a more open view [than traditional parochial schools] of Church things and some of [its students] had a free and serious commitment to Christian faith." What Stockman describes is a charismatic and experiential culture, where "prayer meetings were taking place every morning, and at lunchtime, upward of one hundred students would meet for praise."[10]

In 1976, as a student at Mount Temple, Bono experienced a "Christian conversion."[11] This was the same year that Bono joined Larry Mullen Jr., the Edge (David Howell Evans), and Adam Clayton to form the band later named U2. It also was just two years after Bono lost his mother, Iris Hewson, who collapsed while attending her own father's funeral and died four days later. Bono was fourteen. He has spoken of the loss of his mother as the origin of his "whole creative life" and a source of "fear" and "rage" that he has lived with ever since.[12] The principal expression of Bono's creative life is the music of U2, though he often mentions his love of painting and recalls the times he has painted with his good friend Derek Rowan, whom he calls "Guggi."[13] Bono likes to be respected as an artist, and his most recognized artistic expression consists of his authentic mode of spiritual transcendence. His mother, he says, is the source of his aesthetic spirituality. Commentators have tracked references to her in U2 lyrics, particularly those on the album *October*, the band's most overtly Christian album.[14]

In the 1970s, evangelicalism was in the culture around Bono. The evangelical organizations World Vision and Campus Crusade for Christ "began to actively evangelise in the streets and campuses of Irish cities."[15] When he experienced his Christian conversion in 1976, Bono became part of an intentional evangelical community that promised peace. He joined Shalom Christian Fellowship in Dublin in 1978.[16] Dennis Sheedy, whom Bono met by happenstance at a McDonald's, introduced him to the group. Sheedy was at a table reading a Bible, engaged in an animated conversation with a Hare Krishna. Bono stepped in to see what was happening and took Sheedy's side, defending his Christian position.[17] After that encounter, Bono began attending Shalom with the Edge and Larry Mullen Jr. Commentators have described Shalom as a "charismatic home-church" and an "evangelical Christian group." Bono was baptized in the sea, along with the Edge, and attended Shalom twice a week, getting up as early as 5:00 A.M. for Bible study and prayer. He also reportedly "experimented with speaking in tongues."[18]

Shalom was an otherworldly ascetic sect whose members wanted to retreat from the world in order to purify themselves. Bono said of Shalom, "They were a kind of inner-city group living life like it was the first century A.D. They were expectant of signs and wonders; lived a kind of early-church religion. It was a commune. People who had cash shared it."[19] "They were devoted," Bono recalled, "to the idea of Christ as a commitment to social justice, and having no possessions."[20] Committed to an ascetic otherworldly ethic, several members of Shalom considered the musical aspirations of U2 as outside the bounds of Christian devotion. Members of Shalom tried to persuade Bono, the Edge, and Larry to quit the band. But manager Paul McGuinness famously convinced them to stick together, and they eventually broke from Shalom. Bono explained, "In the end, I realized it was bullshit, that what these people were getting close to with this idea was denial, rather than willful surrender."[21] Even after the break, though, Bono still told reporters, "I believe that Jesus is the son of God. I do believe that, odd as it sounds."[22] In some cases, reporters didn't know what to make of such professions. Bill Graham, a writer for *Hot Press* magazine and an early supporter of U2, decided not to print Bono's 1979 statement about Lypton Village (an imagined community that included Bono, Guggi, the Edge, and others)—"One thing you should know . . . we're all Christians"—worrying that it might hurt their reputation.[23]

Since the earliest days of his career, Bono spoke as a confessional Christian, in the language of experiential piety familiar to evangelicals. He described his relationship with God as "not belief in God, more an experiential sense of GOD." As a cultural movement, evangelicalism emphasizes experience over belief. Evangelicals share a common concern that belief alone is not enough, claiming that even the devil may believe that God is real; he just believes him to be an enemy. Belief for evangelicals can be true or false, and true belief they consider grounded in a direct experience of God. This is the cultural connection that evangelicals share with Bono. But the religious history of evangelicalism is also a story of denominational divisions that corporately prescribe the doctrinal terms of personal belief. Bono resists this institutional incorporation of religion. Like evangelical revivalists who work across denominational lines, gathering whomever might come into the shared space of spiritual experience, Bono insists on disaffiliation. For him, "words and music," not "religious argument," are the path to an "experiential sense of GOD."[24]

Bono delivers his prophetic message using revival techniques developed within the transatlantic history of evangelical Protestantism. From a broad vantage point, historians consider evangelicalism best identified in its connections to eighteenth- and nineteenth-century revival movements that began in western Europe and spread to North America.[25] Some trace American religious history through episodic widespread revivals, or "awakenings," arguing that each revival had a cultural impact as a social organizing force.[26] Historian Nathan Hatch, for example, has argued that the First Great Awakening of the 1730s–40s was a cultural force behind the American Revolution, because it consolidated geographically dispersed colonists by providing them with a shared religious experience.[27] What Bono has done as a rock 'n' roll performer is akin to what revivalists like George Whitefield did during the First Great Awakening. Whitefield was a traveling performer during the colonial period who toured the countryside, holding open-air gatherings where he stirred up emotional fervor and ecstatic experience in his listeners through his spoken word.[28] Like Whitefield, Bono's musical performances united otherwise disconnected people in a common cultural movement by way of shared religious experience.

Historians point to the Second Great Awakening of the early nineteenth century as marking the advent of modern revivalism, because it routinized the spontaneity of earlier revivals. In 1830, a series of revivals broke out in upstate New York, an area referred to as the "burned-over district" because of its sweeping religious fervor. This was where Mormon founder Joseph Smith spoke of golden plates, and where evangelist Charles Finney declared that "God has made man a moral free agent." The common theme of the Second Great Awakening was an emphasis on human moral ability, the idea that with God's help, believers could make a new religious future. Historian Paul E. Johnson argues that Finney's revival work signaled a revolution in American religious thought and practice, a turn away from divine providence to human agency.[29] Finney led revivals that were part of a larger cultural and theological shift, one predicated on the premise that humans played a role in personal and collective salvation. This is why revivals were so important for Finney: they were necessary vehicles of Christian conversion, regeneration, and social purification.

For Finney, the prosperity of the church depended upon revivals, and he asserted that "no doctrine is more dangerous" than the Calvinist notion that revivals were a miracle, and as such beyond "the ordinary rules of cause and effect."[30] It was not enough, as Jonathan Edwards had done in the First Great Awakening, to preach the word and leave it to God to sort through the sinners. Finney compared the revivalist to a farmer, someone who must sow the seeds and, with the help of God, harvest a crop. In contrast to miracles, Finney argued, revivals made "the *right* use of appropriate means." Like tending crops, making revivals required methodical action and followed set "stages of conviction, repentance, and reformation." At each revival meeting, Finney employed a repertoire of rhetorical and material techniques, including his famous "anxious bench," where seekers were called to the front of the crowd to sit and ponder their eternal souls in full view of all gathered there.

With his "modern revival techniques," Finney overcame the dominant Calvinist theology preached in the Protestant churches of his day. Initially, he stood outside those churches, rebuking them with prophetic voice. His opponents, in turn, denounced Finney's excessive emotional approach and his disregard for God's providence. But eventually he converted a number of his critics, including Lyman Beecher, a Presbyterian minister in Boston and a sworn enemy of Finney. Beecher, who had once vowed to "call out the artillerymen" if Finney ever came to Boston, welcomed him into his pulpit in 1831.[31] The Second Great Awakening, which lasted from the 1780s to the 1830s, was both an industrializing and a nationalizing force in America. The impact of Finney's preaching, felt in churches from Boston, to Rochester, to Philadelphia, illustrates the institutional connections between revivals and congregations. Finney's revival meetings brought new converts into existing congregations, helped create new churches, and extended evangelicalism beyond the walls of those churches and into the popular culture of America.

Historian Donald Mathews put it simply, stating, "one cannot have a revival without churches." According to Mathews, these revivals helped organize a geographically dispersed group of people into a national body through the formation of "thousands of [similar] local organizations that helped to create 'a common world of experience.'"[32] Revivals brought the principles of democracy, individualism, and self-governance to the people through the church. Preachers, the voices of the popular church, "fanned the flames of religious ecstasy" from the pulpit and were accompanied by "rousing gospel singing." From the dawn of America as a political idea, revivals democratized Christianity, as Hatch puts it, and were "the very incarnation of the church into popular culture."[33]

Bono's methods of advocacy and his techniques of political conversion resemble the revival techniques of American evangelists. Like his evangelical counterparts after Finney, from D. L. Moody to Billy Graham, Bono has toured both sides of the Atlantic and traveled the globe preaching his message of debt forgiveness for Africa. In terms of form and effect, Bono is in the close company of American revivalists. Like them, he has used his physicality to circulate his spiritual message, though his physicality is of a different kind.[34] Many of the earlier revivalists, like Billy Sunday, were athletic and dapper, disciplined in their bodily performance. Bono, by contrast, presents the image of an out-of-control rock star, even if he is equally choreographed and repetitious in his showmanship.

For an example of Bono's revival techniques, consider how, on U2's Vertigo Tour, Bono wore a headband in concert that included the major symbols of Islam, Judaism, and Christianity—a crescent, the Star of David, and the cross—within the word "coexist." Bono donned the headband while performing "Love and Peace or Else" and kept it on for other songs, including "Miss Sarajevo," a song that asks, "Is there a time for first communion? Is there a time for synagogue? Is there a time to turn to Mecca, beauty queen before God?" Bono concluded by reflecting, "Is there a time for shared values . . . a time for human rights?" As one fan recounted in an online blog, during "Bullet the Blue Sky," Bono "slips his rock messiah bandana over his eyes and gets down on his knees with his hands over his head. . . . I think he's trying to make a point about Abu Ghraib and Guantanamo Bay."[35] And in what some fans refer to as the "We are all children of Father Abraham" sermon, Bono explains the significance of the headband by pointing to

each symbol while delivering the line in cadence, "Jesus, Jew, Muhammad; it's true, all sons of Abraham."[36]

Bono's performance of "Bullet the Blue Sky" was one of his earliest
sermons to America. During a break in the song, Bono would launch
into a prophetic homily, as he did in the 1980s on the *Rattle and Hum*
album and tour. Back then, it was about American militarism or, in
other songs, apartheid and South Africa. Later, at the turn of the new
millennium, on the Elevation Tour, it was about the ethical emptiness
of consumer materialism, the failure of the European Union, or the
AIDS crisis in Africa. On the Vertigo Tour, the homily was about the
post-9/11 message of religious transcendence, and on the Joshua Tree
Tour in 2017, it was about returning to the spiritual landscape of the
1980s album as a refuge from the political chaos, from which to gain
strength and resist the Trump moment. In each case, the message
was reproduced, packaged, and delivered in a routinized fashion. The
content changed, but the method stayed the same. The lights dim, a
spotlight roves around a packed stadium. Bono breaks out his "messiah headband." He calls out visiting politicians seated in a luxury box.
He runs around a heart-shaped stage. These are performance techniques of a rock show that resemble the modern revival techniques of
nineteenth-century American evangelists.

Through his political advocacy for Africa, Bono has continued
an evangelical Protestant tradition of diffusing church into culture,
distributing emotional revivalism through his public promotions of
secular humanitarianism. Just as Finney connected the evangelical
principle of individual agency with the labor demands of the industrial
economy of his day, Bono connects evangelical religious principles to
the needs of an expanding global economy. Working with NGOs, and
in concerts and speaking engagements, Bono promotes "democracy,
individualism, and self-governance," the values that, historians argue,
evangelical revivals made "incarnate in popular culture."[37] Bono distributes his secular message through personal conversion, from his
concert antics to rhetorical tropes that resemble those of Finney and
later evangelists, such as D. L. Moody, Sam Jones, and Billy Sunday.[38]
Like those revivalists, Bono is out to make converts. In 2004, he told
the Labour Party Conference in Brighton, England, "If you're already

converted, you don't need me preaching at you. Though I must admit I enjoy it."[39]

To get a better sense of Bono's conversion techniques, let's look at his 2001 concert at the Meadowlands in New Jersey.[40] The front section of the wraparound upper deck of the Continental Airlines Arena is lined with advertisement boards. Bono stands at the apex of the heart-shaped walkway that extends from the stage. U2 is in the middle of "Bullet the Blue Sky," and Bono grabs a spotlight. In the darkened arena, he shines it across the advertisement boards and cries out against self-interested corporations. He chides America for hoarding its wealth and ignoring the AIDS crisis in Africa. The homily ends. The refrain begins. The Edge summons fighter planes from his guitar and Bono announces that Bill Clinton and a United Nations representative are in the house, along with the Beastie Boys. Bono praises them for their humanitarian work, and he calls for more funding for AIDS research and more aid to Third World countries.[41] This is Bono's luxury-box version of Finney's anxious bench. When Bono gives a shout out to politicians attending his concerts, he puts them under the political gaze of his audience until they convert to his cause.

In terms of conversion tactics, Bono is comparable to Finney, who believed that after conversion at a revival, a new believer "will be filled with a tender and burning love for souls. They will be in agony for individuals whom they want to have saved; their friends, relations, enemies. They will not only be urging them to give their hearts to God, but they will carry them to God in the arms of faith, and with strong crying and tears beseech God to have mercy on them, and save their souls from endless burnings."[42] Finney moved believers spiritually and emotionally toward conversion. Bono has had a similar effect on his political converts, among them Jesse Helms, the long-time North Carolina senator known for his staunch conservatism. After attending a U2 concert and meeting Bono in person, Helms reportedly was moved to tears and later became a strong supporter of the fight against AIDS in Africa.[43]

In each revival, Finney tried to bring his audience closer to God, giving them a taste of heaven, to induce repentance and conversion. Finney described the effect of this technique: "A revival breaks the power of the world and of sin over Christians. It brings them to such vantage ground that they get a fresh impulse towards heaven. They have a new foretaste of heaven, and new desires after union to God; and the charm of the world is broken, and the power of sin overcome."[44] After showing the purity of the divine, Finney then called Christians, both old and new, to clean themselves up, both body and soul, and go out and convert others. If they were diligent in their task, together they could usher in the millennium in a few short months. Comparatively, Bono elevates his audience, lifting them to a place "where the streets have no name." On the Elevation Tour in 2001, Bono proclaimed, "The goal is soul!" and encouraged the audience to "turn this song into a prayer."[45]

Bono's political work is comparable to Finney's religious work because both accomplish similar tasks; they organize individuals religiously and integrate them economically into larger bodies. Finney's revivals were a religious solution to the moral dilemma presented by free labor in an industrializing society. According to historian Paul E. Johnson, the moral dilemma and political impasse of free labor in mid-1820s New York state "prepared the ground" for Finney. Business leaders and factory owners needed more workers, and more efficient workers. Finney's revivals "healed divisions within the middle class and turned businessmen and masters into an active and united missionary army."[46] This is why Johnson describes the 1830s revivals in the burned-over district as part of a "shopkeeper's millennium." The revivals did not benefit society as a whole but served the interests of an industrialist class.

The way Bono delivers religious messages in concerts also resembles the methods of revivalists like Dwight L. Moody, who incorporated gospel singing into his revivals. Song leader Ira D. Sankey almost always accompanied Moody on his itinerant tours, first in Great Britain and later throughout the United States. Sankey worked from his own songbook, the *Sankey-Moody Hymnbook*, which a *New York Times* reporter who attended a Moody revival in 1875 described as "the best for congregational use ever printed. Its words are full of the Gospel, its tunes express the thoughts they are allied to, and are so simple and yet positive in character that anyone can sing them after once hearing them."[47] The U2 catalog is the evangelical hymnbook for secular humanitarians, including gospel anthems like "Pride (In the Name of Love)" and "I Still Haven't Found What I'm Looking For," recorded with the Harlem Gospel Choir. Bono distances his music from contemporary Christian "praise and worship" songs, what he calls "happy clappy," yet still confesses that his songs "proclaim Christ." Referencing the biblical description of creation as a natural reflection of the divine, Bono asserts that U2's music has its "own proclamations" of God.[48] In concert, then, Bono often performs the dual role of gospel song leader and lead preacher, a rock 'n' roll Moody and Sankey in one.

In addition to musical and rhetorical techniques, one of the most striking similarities between Bono and American revivalists is Bono's persistent effort to overcome organized religion. His emphasis on the individual relationship with the divine is what makes his work so similar to that of evangelical revivalists. Like those revivalists, Bono preaches a message of individual faith over institutional sacraments. In Protestant fashion, Bono "protests" against clergy, those "staring at the sun." His suspicion of organized religion echoes the words of Billy Sunday's sermons: "faith in Jesus saves you, not faith in the Church."[49] For Sunday, Jesus is the only way. For Bono, Jesus is his way but not the only way; it is up to the individual to find a personal spiritual path. Bono's soteriological prescriptions are secular because, for him, religious individuals, not church institutions, are sites of spiritual transformation and soul salvation.

To put it another way, in the Roman Catholic Church, the Eucharist is a vehicle of salvation; it is made sacred as "real presence" through the charisma of the office, not the individual.[50] The priest has power because of his relationship to the church, through apostolic succession. Bono protests the priestly authority of the church, opting for individual choice over institutional obligation. In the song "Acrobat," recorded on *Achtung Baby*, Bono quips, "Yeah, I'd break bread and wine if there was a church I could receive in." In concerts, Bono has called church life "claustrophobic," preferring instead his own rock congregation. Singing "I Still Haven't Found What I'm Looking For," Bono tells his audience, "Take it to church, that's right, you're in church."[51]

Bono sounds like a revivalist, saying "take it to church," but he does so in a secularizing way that makes a morally conservative form of evangelicalism feel socially liberating and politically progressive.

Bono's revivalism aims to break down traditional church limits, rather than restore the church's theological center, by bringing more people within its doctrinal boundaries. Bono presents his rock star image as not limited to evangelicalism as doctrinally defined by what historian David Bebbington identifies as its four characteristics of *"conversionism*, the belief that lives need to be changed; *activism*, the expression of the gospel in effort; *biblicism*, a particular regard for the Bible; and what may be called *crucicentrism*, a stress on the sacrifice of Christ on the cross."[52] When he describes his personal beliefs, Bono will say things that sound similar to nineteenth-century evangelical exhortations. But he always resists the religious limitations that he thinks such professions of faith imply. He believes that lives need to be changed yet does not say that there is only one way to change them. He preaches a gospel message of liberty to the captives but does not proclaim that Christianity is the only gospel. He has a particular regard for the Bible, as evidenced, for example, in his conversations with Eugene Peterson about the Psalms, but he is not concerned with defining orthodox interpretation. He believes that Jesus is the Son of God and died on a cross, but he does not preach that his blood sacrifice alone makes personal salvation possible. Bono talks like an evangelical but never *as* an evangelical.

Bono appears more secular than traditional evangelists who fit Bebbington's doctrinal definition because he is more likely to invoke the name of Martin Luther King than he is the name of Jesus, and he is more likely to invite you to help save someone else's life than to save your own soul, to buy a branded product rather than say a sinner's prayer. Where revivalists like Billy Graham used the name of Jesus as the theological medium of personal salvation, Bono uses the name of Dr. King, who spoke in the name of Jesus, as a spiritual proxy for that religious claim. Bono renders King a religious resource for spiritual transcendence, without recognizing him as a secular source for economic critique. Bono meets King at the religious threshold, to prophesy a moral vision of the American dream. And Bono portrays himself as carrying Dr. King's message onward, into the secular world of consumer freedom. With this performance of progressivism, Bono empties out the radical elements of the prophets he references, and through that emptying out, he continues a religious tradition of muscular white evangelical revivalism preached by men who promised free-market capitalism and believed in the idea of racial difference. He maintains the very tradition that he appears to break from, as he makes listeners feel that they are rejecting or overcoming the unjust racial and economic limits of traditional religion.

This emptying out of economic critique from evangelical revivalism makes Bono's message more palatable, more marketable, to a wider rock audience. U2 found its musical success in the United States when younger Americans were increasingly engaged in popular culture, outside their parents' churches, as a way to create new forms of religious belonging, a trend that began in the 1960s. Scholars have examined such meaning making in popular culture, arguing that fandom, whether of music or of film, can be studied as religion.[53] Viewed from within the interpretive framework of religious studies, rock concerts can be seen as cultural sites for the production and performance of religious experience and moral belonging. The image that Bono creates of himself, though, denies the religiosity of U2 shows. Bono consistently says that he is not making *religion*, preferring instead to emphasize the *spiritual* dimensions of U2's music. But things get confusing, because Bono also tells his fans, during concerts, that they are at "church," and he describes the musical performance as "worship." Bono creates an image of a rock star who rejects religion but uses terms that many fans recognize as religious. Evangelical fans are more likely than others to recognize this language, given their history of saying that they are not religious but believers, that they have faith, not religion.

Bono borrows from evangelical revival techniques to project the image of a rock star who cares for people in need and sings for justice, and who transforms a rock concert into a church that scorns the name of religion. He stands with one foot in secular fandom and the other in evangelicalism, but he is never fully within either camp. He must stand among them but not as one of them, in order to maintain his image as a prophetic voice that can speak to both traditions.

Maintaining this proximate distance is a secularizing strategy, one that Bono uses with prophetic effect. U2 offered a path to salvation that spurned both the new religious movements that began the 1960s and the conservative religious evangelicalism of the 1980s.[54] Bono extracted from the 1960s the *feeling* of social protest, and he used that feeling to resist the evangelical moralism of the religious Right in the United States, which, under the leadership of Jerry Falwell, Pat Robertson, and Ralph Reed, strategically conflated the term *evangelicalism* with the fundamentalist Protestantism that was directly associated with the Republican Party.[55] Prior to the 1980s, evangelicals were much less consolidated into a political bloc. Self-identified evangelicals might vote for a Democratic or Republican candidate, depending on the election year.[56] Theological differences were also generally more varied, though such things are always difficult to measure.[57] Scholars debate the historical importance of the religious Right, noting that evangelicals were politically involved, though not as visibly, before the 1980s.[58] What is clear, though, is that during the same period that U2 emerged as a global rock band, the term *evangelicalism* was highly politicized in a particular way. And Bono and U2 set their brand in opposition to the politicized religious moralism of the religious Right.

At the same moment that Bono was distancing himself from the Republican image of American evangelicals, he was directly associating himself with African American blues traditions and the image of Africa in need. This is important to recognize, because Bono's brand of secular evangelism is intimately connected with religious *and* racial difference. Bono derives his prophetic power from his political rejection of evangelical religion and his public embrace of black religiosity. Yet he ultimately distances himself from both religious traditions, claiming not to be an evangelical and acknowledging that he is not black. Thus Bono presents a self-image in which he sings with B. B. King or the Harlem Gospel Choir, and cares about the welfare of Africans, while using black and African religiosity as a musical medium through which to transcend religion in the name of love, or universal spirituality.

Using a secularizing strategy that specifically names racial and religious others, while also claiming to transcend and mediate the particular differences of this otherness (in the name of love and in a place where the streets have no name), Bono achieved the mainstream success that eluded evangelical Christian singers of the era. Larry Norman, for example, was one of the key representatives of the "new Jesus music" produced in the United States in the early 1970s, a genre that Larry Eskridge describes as a "musical mix that included country and both Southern white and black gospel artists who were representatives of the new Jesus music."[59] Norman claims that his records influenced U2, and listening to his 1972 album, *Only Visiting This Planet*, you can hear why. Norman addressed themes of spiritual emptiness in secular political and consumer life that resonated with U2's songs. You can hear echoes of Norman's song "I've Got to Learn to Live Without You" in the affect and phrasing of "With or Without You," and the airplane and bombs motif of Norman's "I Am the Six O'Clock News" in U2's "Bullet the Blue Sky." You can also hear the apocalyptic portrayal of secular news in that Norman track in Bono's line "I can't believe the news today" on U2's "Sunday Bloody Sunday," and in Bono's speech in "Bullet the Blue Sky," which includes the line "I can't tell the difference between ABC News, Hill Street Blues, and the Old Time Gospel Hour."

Norman's music had a cultural, evangelical influence on Bono and U2. Bono met Norman in 2002, and he respected him enough to send flowers when he died in 2008.[60] But, unlike Norman, Bono publicly disassociated himself from confessional evangelicalism, claiming instead a nonsectarian brand of Christian spirituality. "I never really accepted the whole 'born again' tag," Bono said in the late 1980s. To explain this distance, he expressed his desire to keep religion out of politics, as he did with respect to the religious conflict in Ireland, saying that in America in the 1980s, the term *born again* "had been raped of its real meaning, of its spiritual significance, and instead a political significance was left."[61]

In discussing his musical influences, Bono consistently dismisses the notion that his work is influenced by particular religious traditions, instead emphasizing spiritual connection. But his evasiveness on the subject belies the evangelical specificity of Bono's spirituality. Deane Galbraith has observed that "U2 publicly identify with only *certain forms* of Christian spirituality (especially, for example, Black American churches, Watchman Nee—who Bono refers to as a Chinese "mystic"— and Bishop Tutu.) Similarly, U2 repeatedly distinguish 'spirituality' (presented as a positive) from 'religion' (presented as a negative), all the while obscuring that what they are vaguely referring to as their 'spirituality' is in fact charismatic evangelical Christianity."[62]

What appears on its shiny surface to the secular consumer and music fan as a universal expression of spirituality is a market gloss for what is particularly religious at the core. The religious influences on U2's music are well documented, and Galbraith identifies several of them. The U2 song "Magnificent" was modeled on Bach's Magnificat from the Gospel of Luke, and it takes Bach's "suspended chords" to create what Bono calls that "happy-sad feeling" of "agony and ecstasy."[63] Many of U2's songs, like "40," "Gloria," "Love Rescue Me," and "Wake Up Dead Man," allude to the Psalms. And the song "No Line on the Horizon," as Galbraith explains, is "punctuated with occasional melodies and words that the band has uplifted from traditional Christian hymns."[64] By alluding to religion without being part of it, Bono keeps a distance that allows him to claim what he sees as the spiritual essence of the Christian tradition without being captive to its institutional history. Bono can steal and borrow without having to belong.

Bono's refusal to admit the religiousness of his spirituality is a public secret. Bono never hides his spiritual claim to God or to Jesus as Christ, but he persistently denies the doctrinal limits of those claims. The same goes for U2, which everyone knows is a Christian rock band— this is no secret—but which is presented as if it is *not that kind* of Christian rock band, yet is the most transcendently successful of all rock bands. The U2 brand is built on the premise that spirituality, rather than religion, is the only transcendent mode of popular consumption and market success. Bono sees "secular society" as permeated with "religious instinct" that "comes out as gambling, as horoscope reading, as yoga." Such practices Bono lumps together with "superstitious" dispositions that include petitionary prayer for physical healing. The religious instinct, he says, is "not that far from the surface. We've gone two hundred years since the Enlightenment, but science is starting to bow again."[65] The implication is that religion persists, and its refusal to go away suggests that Enlightenment rationalists, and the scientists who are their heirs, got it wrong. What they got wrong, though, is not the critique of the institution, but the disbelief in what the institution corrupts. For Bono, religious instinct points to the spiritual essence of human experience. And for him, the marketplace, not the church, is where spirituality will surface over and above the traditional limits of religion. In the marketplace, spirituality competes with religion, as Bono does with the televangelist, and spiritual feeling, he declares, is the only authentic nonreligious religious experience.

Such persistent obfuscations are essential to the success of U2, and Bono positions himself as the prophetic mediator standing above history and speaking for those trapped within it. This is his claim to a secular spiritual position. Rather than own up to specific evangelical musical influences like Larry Norman, Bono and the Edge emphasize the influence of secular icons like Elvis Presley, Bob Dylan, Johnny Cash, and Roy Orbison. Bono uses the language of spirituality to connect to secular musicians, speaking in biblical terms of generic Christianity. For example, when asked in a 2017 interview with Zane Lowe about meeting Bob Dylan, Bono included in his reply a reference to the "biblical way": "Part of the sort of biblical way is the passing of a blessing, the laying on of hands, you know, so you think of, you know, Abraham laying on his hands on Isaac. So this bestowing of ancient wisdom, and we always had a reverence for older, wiser, troubadours. Johnny Cash is eternally cool . . . we wanted to learn from Johnny Cash [in the 1980s]. That's more believable than going after Bob, although Bob will always turn everything on its head." Bono's embrace of Johnny Cash, contrasted with his ambivalent relationship with Bob Dylan, signals the brand of spiritual sincerity that he promotes. Dylan is the fox to Bono's magpie, with cunning tongue, sly grin, and clever disguise, ever moving, difficult to define, and always, as Bono puts it, turning "everything on its head."[66] What Bono is after in his musical associations is the feeling of transparency, of authenticity, of a steady hand on the shoulder. Bob could be faking. But not Johnny Cash.

Cash, though, unlike Bono, was willing to call himself an evangelical. But Cash was more private about his evangelicalism than Larry Norman was, which made it easier for Bono to acknowledge his influence. While Bono finds spiritual kinship with both Norman and Cash, he is more willing to claim Cash openly, not only because he is an American icon but also because his private belief and his cautious proselytizing make him more easily adapted to a secular spiritual audience than

Norman is. Allen Flemming, a friend of Norman's, remembered that "Larry's initial reaction to U2 was that they did not talk about Jesus openly enough."[67] By contrast, Cash, who said, "I don't compromise my religion," also said, "If I'm with someone who doesn't want to talk about it, I don't talk about it. I don't impose myself on anybody in any way, including religion. . . . Although I am evangelical, and I'll give the message to anyone that wants to hear it, or anybody that is willing to listen. But if they let me know that they don't want to hear it, they ain't never going to hear it from me."[68] Bono shares with Cash an unwillingness to demand conversion to a specific sectarian set of beliefs. As early as 1987, reporters described U2 in such general terms as "The band shares a kind of ecumenical, nonspecific spirituality."[69] Bono, like Cash and Norman, will say, "I believe that Jesus is the son of God." But of the three, only Norman was committed to that statement as an exclusive doctrine. To illustrate the difference, consider how Norman's album *Only Visiting This Planet* is more theologically specific than any U2 album. The track "I Wish We'd All Been Ready" is a dispensational-ist standard, directly expressing a fundamentalist evangelical premi-llennial view of the end times, when true Christians will be raptured, or taken up to heaven, with everyone else left behind to suffer the tribulation that is to precede the second coming of Christ. Bono, by contrast, qualifies his professions with statements like "I don't accept the fundamentalist concept [that Jesus is the only way and that other religions are false]."[70]

Bono's rejection of religion and his embrace of spirituality enable him to separate the feeling and mood of evangelicalism from its doc-trinal and sectarian particularities, secularize it, and diffuse it into popular culture. This move went a step beyond what Cash and other mainstream evangelical-influenced musicians were doing in the 1970s and 1980s, which was merely expressing their beliefs in a private way that did not attempt to put any sort of public pressure on a listener's personal beliefs. Bono continued the pattern of removing theologi-cal demands on the listener to adhere to a religiously defined doc-trine, and offered instead the spiritual freedom to listeners to make their own meaning, of the lyrics, of the sound, of the message. In the offer of new spiritual freedom, Bono extended the political impact of evangelicalism further into popular culture, detaching the end-of-the-world anarchism of his evangelical predecessors from any doctrinal particularity, removing their public demands for personal salvation, and reattaching that moral demand to secular causes that anyone could support, regardless of what they believed about religion. Whether you claimed Krishna, Buddha, Jesus, or Muhammad, it didn't matter, so long as you agreed that Africans need our help, and that buying the album, listening to the music, and purchasing the right products—that's how you save lives. Over time, Bono rebranded the apolitical anarchism of the evangelical subculture as the political spirituality of consumer consciousness. To see what that evangelical subculture looked like before Bono, consider that Norman's song "I Wish We'd All Been Ready" was featured in Donald Thompson's 1972 rapture film *A Thief in the Night*, which tells the story of a woman left behind in a world where the United Nations is a vehicle of the Antichrist and liberal Protestants preach to the unsaved. The political message of the film is that national governments and global coalitions cannot be trusted. Norman's music and Thompson's film both express an anarchist streak that scholars have identified as a characteristic of the Jesus movement, the label used to describe the evangelical hippie subculture of the late 1960s and 1970s that influenced musicians from Dylan to Bono.

That subculture was most expressive in California, but its practitioners saw connections abroad. T Bone Burnett, who was a supporting musician on tour with Dylan at the time, said of the era, "There was a spiritual movement, beginning in 1976, something happened all across the world. It happened to Bono and The Edge and Larry Mullen in Ireland. It happened to Michael Hutchence in Australia, and it happened here in Los Angeles."[71] Speaking of the movement in broad spiritual terms, Burnett and others in the 1970s rock scene distanced themselves from the doctrinal specificity of evangelicalism. Political scientist Jeff Taylor and historian Chad Israelson argue that, like Dylan, Bono "imbibed Jesus Movement–inspired Christian anarchism in the late 1970s–early 1980s."[72] Unlike Norman, though, Bono's anarchist musical streak was generically Christian, without any denominational particularity, and thus more amenable to a broader range of political views on social issues.

Bono distances himself from doctrinal evangelicals who postpone claims of justice and judgment to the next life. Instead, he takes a stance that would have been familiar to liberal Protestant proponents of the Social Gospel in the nineteenth century. He has said, for example, "I don't expect this pie in the sky when you die stuff. My favorite line in the Lord's Prayer is, 'Thy kingdom come, thy will be done on earth as it is in heaven.' I want it all, and I want it now. Heaven on earth—now—let's have a bit of that."[73] Heaven on earth is exactly what postmillennial proponents of the Social Gospel wanted, for they thought peace on earth was a prerequisite for the second coming of Christ. Premillennial evangelicals, like Norman and Thompson, believed instead that peace would only come when Christ returned, and this world would only get worse before he did. In the United States, that theological difference translated into competing political opinions on the role of the federal government, with liberals wanting a greater institutional and structural role, and conservatives wanting less.

Bono, in his public professions, comes much closer to a liberal religious view of social justice as focused on this world, and not the next, though it is important to recognize that Bono does not embrace more radical forms of liberal Protestantism that criticized capitalism and called for a greater role of government in regulating markets and providing public goods. In a 2016 interview with Charlie Rose, when discussing the power of rock 'n' roll as an "act of defiance" in the context of a question about how to respond to terrorism, Bono reminded Rose that "our music was always wrapped around social justice." Bono perpetually presents himself as a voice of justice, emphasizing justice's universal spirituality while downplaying any religious particularity. "Music is the language of the spirit," he says. It is "another kind of talking . . . our spiritual life, or whatever you want to call it." His conversation with Rose, like many of his interviews, shows the influence of Bono's evangelical experiences during his youth. As noted earlier, Bono reportedly experimented with speaking in tongues while part of Shalom Christian Fellowship. He has described his style of writing songs as beginning with sounds or utterances before forming concepts into words. But he has never fully embraced the doctrinal notion of glossolalia (speaking in tongues) that defines Pentecostalism. Instead, he speaks in the generic secular terms of music as a language of the spirit, saying that "all music is worship."[74]

Bono uses the language of spirit and spirituality to infuse popular culture with a feeling of nonreligious transcendence. He claims to capture the ideal essences of human experience, of love, freedom, justice, and joy, that he believes misguided clerics and televangelists falsely moralize about in the name of a judgmental God. His act of defiance is to speak in the name of love rather than in the name of religion. To Rose, he said, "There is nothing more romantic in the world than defiance. It's kind of the essence of romance. And joy, you know, is the ultimate act of defiance. If you think of music, the Beatles, whether it's Mozart or Beethoven. Irish people, we can surrender to melancholy any day of the week and cry into the beer, but what I'm really attracted to, U2 was formed on that idea of pure joy as an act of defiance." Pure joy, love, romance, defiance—all, for Bono, are wrapped up in the music, for music "connects us with our spirit, our spiritual life," and all music is worship of some kind. "If you don't believe in God," he told Rose, "it can be anything. It can be a woman. It can be a lot of bad things. But it's worship."

Again, worship for Bono is not religious in the sense of liturgy or church tradition. Rather, Bono recasts worship as connecting to an idea that transcends the limits of human experience and bureaucratic institutions. Bono sings songs in order to let the spirit speak through the melodies. But it is up to his audience to hear the ideas of love and justice in the music. Without making any religious demands on his listeners, he says, "I reach for what you might call God."[75] This style of giving an account of one's personal spiritual experience and granting the audience the freedom to interpret that experience in their own way follows the prophetic pattern in which the listener must recognize the message—with one major exception. Most prophets call for the upending of the social order in the name of justice. Sociologist Max Weber located the defining feature of the prophet in his promise to break from the established order.[76] Bono promises a spiritual break from institutional religion, but never a material break from the established social order of capitalism, or the idea that class differences and racial essences are natural and harmonious with divine agency.

In 2019, Bono declared at Davos that "capitalism is not immoral—it's amoral. It requires our instruction."[77] The religious instruction that Bono offers, which he says can change the course of capitalism, advocates working for spiritual connection and moral reform from within the system. Bono believes that millennial capitalism, what he refers to as the globalization of the "wide end" of capitalism, or as the spread of "conscious commerce" through business entrepreneurship, is the best economic system for the realization of God's purpose and plan on earth, which for Bono is manifest in the "journey of equality" and the decline of extreme poverty.[78]

To see the continuity between Bono's spiritual message and his capitalist practice is to recognize that his prophetic brand is the spiritual individualism of moral sincerity, not the social collectivism of economic critique. This is how Bono is able to declare allegiance to the prophetic voices of Martin Luther King Jr. and Gustavo Gutiérrez in order to claim a spiritual message of racial equality and justice for the poor and oppressed. But he does so without recognizing King's and Gutiérrez's radical break from capitalism. King was a socialist and Gutiérrez a Marxist. While Gutiérrez's liberation theology was the backdrop for Bono's visit to Central America in the 1980s, and while it informs the political attitude of the song "Bullet the Blue Sky," which was written to capture that visit, it is King to whom Bono refers most often in lyrics, concerts, and interviews. And it is King who warned, channeling James Baldwin's prophetic voice, of the danger of being "integrated into a burning house," where "racism, economic exploitation and militarism are all tied together."[79] King also supported organized labor, something antithetical to Bono's neoliberal view of economic markets. On the eve of his assassination, King was supporting a labor strike among sanitation workers in Memphis, Tennessee. Bono memorializes King's assassination in song, but he never mentions one of King's major concerns, workers' rights and the organization of labor.

Unlike Dr. King, Bono does not critique the economic relations that produce poverty and inequality. He promotes a defiant idea of Christian love professed by the religious prophets of the modern age. But he decouples their ideas from any form of structural economic critique. Bono expresses his spiritual sincerity in his desire to care for the world's poor, to help those in need, especially women and children. "I'm representing the poor and wretched in this world," he says.[80] But the mechanism by which he offers this care is the thing he sells, his music. Bono prefaced his comment to Charlie Rose that "our music was always wrapped around social justice" by saying that the "music gives me the currency . . . the music has given me the life, has given us the life." And later in that interview he added, "I see melodies and ideas as being the same thing. Even little businesses, startups, they're like melody lines to me. A great melody and a great idea have a lot in common." For Bono, there is no difference between good melodies, good ideas, and good business. Bono insists that his role as the leader of U2 and his advocacy work against global poverty and AIDS in Africa are different parts of a harmonious whole. On the symmetry of melodies and ideas, he added, "There is a sort of arc, a beautiful arc, a certain inevitability, you feel you know where it's going, though you've never seen one before. I feel like that about a song. I feel like that about the ONE campaign, or RED, or anything I do."[81] Bono describes his business enterprises as he does his evangelical spirituality. Both share the same melodies: an antiauthoritarian attitude that stands against institutional religion, and a neoliberal belief in the liberating power of free-market entrepreneurial capitalism. Bono, more than any other evangelical spokesperson, has been able to harmonize the religious and economic strands of evangelicalism and neoliberalism and unite them in the practice of popular consumption.

To sell music to the largest number of fans, to be the biggest rock band ever, requires relating to as many people as possible in a language that they can understand and in a way that does not radically change their worldview, even as it appears to challenge it. Thus the details of social justice—what it actually means, how to actually get there—are burdensome for Bono. He would rather think in macro terms, following the melody lines that draw the biggest crowds. When asked in 1989 why he doesn't focus on "abortion, Israel and the Palestinians, the death penalty, AIDS, gay rights," issues that might divide and alienate fans, Bono replied, "I will admit that we are attracted to issues that unify people rather than divide them." When asked about homophobia and why he did not speak out in favor of gay rights, Bono said:

OK. My bottom line on any sexuality is that love is the most important thing. That love is it. Any way people want to love each other is OK by me. That's different from abuse, be it homosexual or heterosexual.

But your question is, why don't we write about those issues? The reason is that there aren't enough minutes in the day, or days in the year, for us to approach every abuse of human rights, and because, in the end, that isn't our job anyway. Our own way of dealing with it is to try to get at what is essentially behind all abuse of human rights, to go to the heart of the problem, to the kernel rather than the husk.

And that, of course, will always bring me back to the idea of love. Spirituality. That God is love. That love is not a flowers-in-the-hair situation. That it is something you have to make happen. It has to be made concrete. . . .

You see, [with] problems like Belfast's in Northern Ireland, or racism in the Southern states here in America, you're dealing with entrenched communities. When you're dealing with illogical views, the hells that are just deeper, the answer is not argument, often. They're not problems of the intellect. . . .

That is why I will always look not to the flesh of the situation, but the spirit. These are spiritual conditions, malaise. You know hatred is beyond reason. Love is an antidote to that. . . .

I find myself going away from the specific, and even more towards the universal, more towards that one point, which I call "liberation."[82]

Throughout his career, Bono has offered a spiritual solution to social crises. He claims a universal human spirituality that transcends personal or cultural particularities. Yet he delivers his message in the same mode used by the muscular evangelical revivalists who preceded him. His dismissal of the idea that love is a "flowers-in-the-hair" kind of thing is just one of many examples. Bono says that he's "always been more mannish than boyish," and prefers Johnny Cash to the "effete rock 'n' roll figure." He has repeatedly rejected "hippie" Christianity. "There's nothing hippie about my picture of Christ," he says. "The Gospels paint a picture of a very demanding, sometimes divisive love, but love it is."[83] When confronted with the specific historical tradition from which his prophetic voice emerged, Bono always responds with generalizations amenable to a culture of mass consumption and in a universalizing manner that is unlikely to divide his audience. In this way he projects a sense or feeling that he is above religion, all the while working within the moral limits of evangelical Christianity. He expresses a message of love as a universal ideal. But he projects this message through a particular performance of masculine action, of mannish incarnation, of a modern prophet in black steel-toed boots.

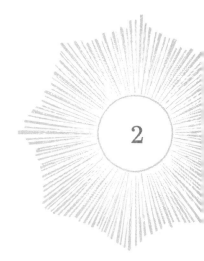

AROUND BONO

The prophet must be recognized.[1] On the first Sunday of each month in 1987, a gathering of U2 fans, nearly 250 of them, met at the Lhasa Club in Hollywood. There was a suggested donation of five dollars per person to cover costs; any leftover money was donated to Amnesty International and World Vision, an evangelical humanitarian charity. When reporter Steve Hochman visited the club while working on a story for *Rolling Stone* magazine, a Lhasa co-director explained, "We're definitely a secular club. We have no affiliation with any church or religion or value system, although World Vision is a Christian-based organization. I see a bunch of middle-class kids with middle-class values, and if those are Christian then, yeah, that's what you might see." The goal of the club, this person said, was to change the world, to "go down to McDonald's and find a homeless person and buy him food and change his life for one day. That's the idealism we believe in. That's what U2 said all along. This is right. This is true."[2]

This snapshot from the 1980s captures the patterns of religious reception around Bono. The U2 fan base was composed of white, middle-class kids with middle-class values. Their class status was signaled in the fact that they, or their parents, had enough money to buy a concert ticket, and enough money to feel that they could buy someone else a meal at McDonald's. Their parents were the products of the post–World War II economic boom in the United States, a time of religious restructuring and institutional remolding. "Institutions powerfully shaped the character and understanding of the middle class during the time of the great postwar boom and subsequently," wrote the authors of *The Good Society*.[3] The mores of the middle-class parents of U2 fans were shaped by where they went to school, where they worked, and how they spent their leisure time, in addition to their commitments at home and in church. U2 fans grew up in an era in which secular institutions were as powerful as religious institutions were—sometimes more so—in shaping moral values.

The values of U2 fans at the Lhasa Club blended secular and religious moral traditions within a shared humanitarianism. Take, for example, the two organizations the fan club supported. Amnesty International claims no ideology or religion, whereas World Vision is the "largest evangelical agency" and "largest Christian humanitarian organization in the world."[4] Culturally ecumenical, the U2 club was a place where fans could associate with either or both of these organizations, without being limited by competing doctrinal claims on their identity. Sectarian affiliation was a personal option, not an institutional demand. "The idea of letting go as we know it is, for U2, essential to any non-proselytizing form of morality or ethics and to any real social change," writes an affirming commentator.[5] Club members found common ground in their shared cultural consumption of the U2 spiritual brand of social change. And in the descriptions of their fandom, they spoke a common language, expressing humanitarian concerns in spiritual terms that signaled their common values.[6]

Thirty years later, U2 continues to attract middle-class fans with middle-class values that include a shared sense of humanitarian spirituality. In 2017, U2 returned to the place where many fans first discovered them, with a revived, thirtieth-anniversary version of the 1987 Joshua Tree Tour. For three decades, fans kept coming back to the shows, to hear Bono protest injustice, to hear the band evoke spiritual landscapes, and to feel connected to something larger than themselves, something transcendent. U2 fans consistently speak of their fandom as a type of protest and a source of good feelings. For them, the U2 experience is more than just the ecstatic experience of rock 'n' roll anger. It is spiritually redemptive, recognizable in the personal feeling of emotional uplift. U2 concerts transform political anger (at political leaders, from Reagan to Trump) into righteous indignation (symbolized by the human rights activists referenced by name or presented onscreen). This transformed rock aggression is expressed as righteous love for the fearfully angry, a distinction often measured in the generational relationship of enlightened child to narrow-minded parents. From that dialectical tension between generations past and present emerges a future-oriented feeling of spiritual ascent. This is, many fans say, a better experience, a more positive emotion, than anything they ever felt in church.

This chapter outlines the range of religious reception around Bono, arguing that regardless of perceived differences of religious self-identification, whether nonconfessional or evangelical, U2 fans are members of the same class: they are all cultural consumers of secular spirituality. In later chapters, I examine the economic aspects of the consumerist religion around Bono. Here, I track the cultural language of secular spirituality expressed in the written accounts of U2 fans, including those published by scholars, to show how they recognize Bono as a prophetic voice and how confessional evangelical fans reintegrate Bono's professed secular spirituality back into their self-identified Christian worlds, reversing the very process he promotes.[7]

Since the 1980s, American Christians have increasingly sought spiritual experience beyond their participation in a church. They have taken part in a "spiritual but not religious" cultural movement that emphasizes the creative power of individuals to select beliefs and rituals from religious and secular traditions and mix them together to create their own spiritual meaning in harmony with their personal life journeys. Sociologists have identified this spiritual but not religious mindset in their suspicion of institutional religion and their preference for individual spirituality. This cultural expression of personal preference has coincided with a structural shift in American religions since the 1960s in which the significance of denominational identities has declined.[8] Americans are increasingly less likely to call themselves

Baptists, Methodists, or Presbyterians than they are to identify as Christian or, even more broadly, as spiritual but not religious.[9]

Historians have argued that such expressions are part of a much longer history of religious experimentation in America.[10] Disclaiming institutional religion is an American cultural tradition. Some scholars worry that this tradition has eroded voluntary organizations, especially mainline churches, that cultivate the very middle-class values that spark the kind of spiritual search for moral goodness expressed by U2 fans. Such concern was crystalized in Robert Bellah's normative description, in the late 1980s, of "Sheilaism," the term that a woman named Sheila Larson used to describe her own personal religion. Bellah wagered that if there was a religion of Sheila, then there could be millions of personal religions, one for every American. And if everyone had his or her own religion, then how, he wondered, would we collectively judge right from wrong, without any shared beliefs or values. For Bellah, the logical outcome of Sheilaism was an antinomian crisis, in which there would be no social basis for ethical claims and we would all be isolated, atomized individuals following our emotional whims and listening to our inner voices.[11]

Scholars have since argued that such spiritual individualism is rarely so disparate or chaotic, but is in fact happily homogenous and strikingly predictable, despite the appearance of endless variety and diversity. What is presented as a personalized critique of organized religion, they observe, is actually another expression of religious belief and practice.[12] This is the case for U2 fans, whether they identify themselves as evangelical Christians or not, who see themselves as like Bono, as critical of religion, but who speak a shared language of spirituality that signals how broader cultural forces are organizing individual meaning making—external organizing forces that in this case are connected to the economic forces of neoliberal corporatism. Economic values promoted by profit-driven corporate entities foster an ethical system of missionary philanthropy and multicultural cosmopolitanism that U2 fans share. "Cosmopolitanism," says Alan McPherson, professor of Latin American history at the University of Oklahoma, "embraces the struggle for a universal moral order—a U2 precept if there ever was one."[13]

U2 fans are inspired by Bono's moral message to promote social action on a global scale. At Saint Mary's College of California, for example, Marshall Welch organized a "community engagement service-learning course that used the musical and spiritually-based activism of the rock group, U2, as an alternative approach and example of engaged spirituality using activism and advocacy." This course combined what it called the activism approach of U2, modeled in ONE.org, with the "tenets of Catholic Social Thought." One student commented at the end of the course, "Personally, I think we're on the brink of something. ONE.ORG taught me that just your voice, instead of money, can make a difference." Another added, "I've done my share of volunteering and other beneficial events. But I could never help feeling that I was only treating symptoms of the problem, not solving the issue at its core. . . . This class really served as an eye-opening experience for me in that I can now see the difference I can make both as an individual and as part of an organization like ONE.ORG."[14] The organization of the Saint Mary's class and the student comments show how U2 fans are moved by Bono's message and U2's music to try to make the world a better place.

This model for social activism is corporately mediated, for the ONE Campaign, discussed in more detail in later chapters, is closely tied to multinational companies directly associated with the Bill and Melinda Gates Foundation, which has worked with Monsanto, for example, on agricultural reform in Africa. Within a neoliberal economic framework, such mediation is neither ironic nor hypocritical, since for-profit corporations are promoted as economic engines of prosperity and catalysts of social justice. The Saint Mary's class invokes a model of social justice that is led by financial elites and mediated by transnational corporations. That this economic model can be advanced in a religious institution that promotes Catholic social teaching, which advocates social and economic justice for all, suggests the prophetic power of the myth and mystique of Bono as good-hearted rock star. Many commentators focus on Bono's earnestness and good intentions, rather than on the economic implications of his message. Catholic thinker Stephen Catanzarite, for example, says, "Pry away all the pop glamour and artifice the band deftly employed on *Achtung Baby* to obscure its more obvious intentions, and you will find U2's traditional pose: furrow-browed earnestness."[15] And Theodore Trost, a religious studies scholar at the University of Alabama, argues that "*Pop* stands as a theological assertion, namely that the commercial realm is also God's realm."[16] Whether you are confessional or not, whether you are at a private religious college or a public secular university, economic details are less important than whether you recognize Bono as a prophetic voice for social justice and commercial sincerity.

U2 fans recognize Bono as a prophetic voice by consuming his cultural message, but not his economic philosophy or business practice. Fans with a desire to do good are often persuaded by his pitch, believing that he stands fast against the sin of "corporate greed" and in solidarity with liberation theologians who call for the redistribution of wealth.[17] They may see Bono the performer who protests human suffering, but not Bono the businessman who writes a *New York Times* op-ed on selling pollution rights on the free market, in which he tells the reader to "trust in capitalism—we'll find a way."[18] That op-ed was written in 2010, calling for new markets, financed in new ways, in the midst of a global financial crisis. Fans might also fail to see Bono the investor, who as managing director and co-founder of Elevation Partners purchased 40 percent of Forbes Media and then immediately froze Forbes employees' pension plans. This is the same Bono who speaks as a pacifist and anti-war activist but invests with his business partners in video war games.[19]

Many U2 fans are spiritual seekers who look to Bono and U2 for personal inspiration. They are consumers of a spiritual brand of popular culture. They may desire spiritual freedom, unrestrained by any official church, but this does not mean that they create their own expressive medium. Again, the dissolution of traditional church authority does not necessarily mean an antinomian crisis. Rather, fans choose from the soundtrack presented to them. And within these limits, they often make a common choice. The anthem for spiritual seekers, according to biblical studies scholar Deane Galbraith, is "I Still Haven't Found What I'm Looking For." The song is their secular hymn. "If you're willing to construe the term 'hymn' liberally," writes another scholar, "then the most heard, most successful hymn of the last few decades could be 'I Still Haven't Found What I'm Looking For,' by U2."[20] That secular spirituality can produce a hymn, one that spent two weeks in the number-one spot on Billboard's Top 100, suggests another expression of religious organization, one with more authority, not less, in everyday life, measured here in the ability to influence consumer behavior and shape economic choices.[21]

I highlight the attractiveness of spiritual beliefs in popular culture in order to make three points. First, despite the logical possibility of endless individual creative expressions, "spiritual but not religious" movements trend toward similarity and sameness. Second, Bono is a celebrity catalyst for the convergence of spiritualism and consumption. His celebrity is the moral brand that his fans consume. Third, most nonconfessional fans are probably content to find their personal spirituality in their concert experiences and fan communities. By contrast, confessional fans tend to use Bono and U2 as a cultural vehicle through which to integrate their vision of Christian church with what they see as the secular world, and they may even try to reintegrate the consumerist spirituality that Bono offers back into their religious communities.

Recognized as a prophetic voice by spiritual consumers, Bono is the revealer of messianic secrets. As noted earlier, he will ask his concert audience, "Have you been to church?" and then respond, "This is church!"[22] Bono claims to break from church traditions and to find "church" in the secular. He says, with the secularizing spirit of a dissenting evangelical, that the signage is wrong—that church is not over there, set apart by steeple and marquee, but here, in the arena or the stadium, or wherever the spirit enters and God is in the house. J. Heath Atchley argues that the "defining mark of the secular" is its "inability to speak, the lack of promise of revelation."[23] By this definition, Bono constantly interrupts his secular silences during concerts. He claims the role of a secular performer resisting the confessionals of the pastor and priest, yet he ritually reveals his spiritual message using religious means.

Bono's version of evangelical secularism is filled with biblical allusions, meant not as doctrinal concepts but rather as emotional evocations. Bono acknowledges his deliberate attempt to convey theological statements that are not obviously religious. He refers to this as "drawing fish in the sand," which is itself a biblical allusion. Of this style, he says, "It's there for people who are interested. It shouldn't be there for people who aren't."[24] Fans who are interested in seeking the underlying Christian meanings can easily find them. Galbraith observes that

> the charismatic-evangelical members of rock band U2 double code their lyrics in such a manner that Christian references are hidden from mainstream listeners and media while being readily recognizable to their Christian fans. The device of allusion is especially amenable to this end, as the meaning of an allusion can only be considered by a reader or listener who possesses the requisite competency in respect of the evoked text(s). Through their utilization of biblical allusions, U2 therefore construct two different, perhaps even irreconcilable, groups of listeners—a knowledgeable Christian in-group and an unknowledgeable non-Christian out-group.[25]

The hidden Christianity of U2 is an open secret. And in the secular game of popular culture, open secrets are the most popular secrets. As fans circulate them, they create new forms of quasi-religious community. Don't you know, says the evangelical believer to her uncommitted counterpart, that the song "40" is really a Psalm?

Biblical studies scholars have also worked to uncover the hidden scriptural references in U2 songs. In an essay titled "The Bible Under the Joshua Tree: Biblical Imagery in the Music of U2," posted to the Society of Biblical Literature online forum in January 2009, Andrew Davies of Mattersey Hall, a Christian college in England, argued:

> Bono wanted to be biblically inspired, motivated, and guided in his social critique, and actually he sought even more than that, for he explains: "I wanted something biblical. My understanding of the scriptures were the psalms of David and the lyricism of the King James Bible and I tried to bring that in, to give it a religiosity." It is almost, then, as if he felt he wanted to *write* scripture in the process of rereading it—to deliver a new psalter for his generation that combined the pathos of lament with prophetic

fury to rage against (what he saw as) the injustice endemic in *God's own country*.

Davies described Bono as a "new epic biblical poet" and went on to track the allusions, the hidden translation of biblical text into lyrical expression, in the tracks on the *Joshua Tree* album.

Nonconfessional fans often respond to such religious intrigue with reserve or detachment, holding out for a more free-form spirituality. Galbraith describes how fans debate religious versus nonreligious interpretations online on U2 fan forums, how, for example, "the covert language of 'Magnificent' facilitates quite opposing interpretations. Fans alternatively interpret 'Magnificent' as the Christian God, or as a non-specific spirituality, or in an entirely non-religious way."[26] Nonconfessional fans often resist the theological interpretations of lyrical biblicism, focusing less on close readings of the text and more on the sonic tone. Journalist Matt Snow writes, "The Edge's guitar playing creates enormous space and vast landscapes. It is thrilling and a heartbreaking sound that hangs over you like the unsettled sky. In the turf it stakes out, it is inherently spiritual. It is grace and it is a gift."[27] Nonconfessional fans prefer the language of the spiritual, while confessional fans understand that language as biblical.

The music industry has promoted the spiritual brand of U2. From the band's earliest days, critics have used the terms of nonspecific spirituality that appeal to non-Christian fans, but have still claimed that the music is Christian, as Neil McCormick did in 1981:

> "October" is an LP of exciting, emotional, spiritually inclined rock. . . . It is a Christian LP that avoids all the pedantic puritanism associated with most Christian rock, avoids the old world emotional fascism of organized religion. . . . It is fortunate that the main spiritual issues dealt with can be related to a wider frame of reference than Christianity: man's struggle to know and control himself and his own nature is something that comes to everyone in some guise. And its celebratory sound has the same positive touch as gospel music, it rejoices, and that feels good.[28]

The good feelings, the celebratory sound, the rejoicing—all describe the evangelical humanism of Bono that begins with Christianity but does not stay there.[29] Bono moves beyond the old constraints of religious sectarianism and into the new world of secular cosmopolitanism, where fans can relate to spiritual issues regardless of their religious persuasion.

Confessional fans use what is presented as a spiritual but not religious message to try to persuade the unaffiliated around them to join their religion. They see these fans as drawn to the spirituality of the music without having yet realized its true religious source, so they invite all fans to travel with them and follow where the music leads, which for them is back to Jesus. Robert Vagacs, at the end of his book *Religious Nuts, Political Fanatics: U2 in Theological Perspective*, asks, "Where to now? How is this book applicable to the reader?" His answer: "Well, that depends. It depends on which stream you may belong to. According to my limited math, there are four possible groups to which you, the reader, could belong."

    A. You are neither a U2 fan nor a Christ follower.
    B. You are a U2 fan with no real connection to Jesus
       Christ.
    C. You are a Christian with no connection to U2.
    D. You are both a U2 fan and a Christ follower.

After listing these options, Vagacs suggests some further reading. For those in group B, the seekers whom he sees as the most likely converts, he recommends Steve Stockman's *Walk On: The Spiritual Journey of U2*, Raewynne J. Whiteley and Beth Maynard's *Get Up Off Your Knees: Preaching the U2 Catalog*, and *The Message*, Eugene Peterson's contemporary translation of the Bible.[30] Vagacs intends this reading list to be used as the evangelist uses tract literature, in the hope that it will lead the spiritual seeker to personal salvation and ultimately into Christian fellowship.

Confessional fans debate what that fellowship looks like in relation to the limits of traditional church. Some self-identified evangelicals argue that God may use Bono, but that does not mean Bono is a committed Christian, because he stubbornly stays outside the church, refusing to belong to any particular congregation.[31] Most Christian fans, though, see in U2 an opportunity to rethink the organizational structure of church. This is especially the case for white, middle-class evangelicals in the emerging church movement, which is an attempt to find new ways for evangelical faith to engage with secular culture. Those associated with the movement often meet in coffee shops and individual homes, rather than in recognizable churches. They often include popular music in their devotional practices, and they often are willing to consider Christianity a conversation open to question rather than a dogmatic sermon with specific instruction.[32] These fans seek theological meaning behind pop surfaces, claiming to see what the "shallow souls on Christian and secular fronts" can't see, which is the true meaning of U2 songs. These fans call themselves "thoughtful evangelicals," identifying themselves as the kind of Christians "who had a rightful place in their hearts for Martin Luther King and Archbishop Oscar Romero's self-giving martyrdoms."[33]

Self-professed Christian fans of U2 consider Bono a prophet who makes possible the arrival of the spirit of Jesus in secular culture. Eugene H. Peterson, professor emeritus of spiritual theology at Regent College in Vancouver and the author of *The Message*, mentioned above, describes how listening to U2 connects non-Christians to Christian community:

> A friend recently invited some of his friends to invite all the friends they knew who loved the songs of U2 for an evening of "Jesus and Bono." Most of the people gathered were not followers of Jesus—they would have been embarrassed to be identified that way—but they were unembarrassed followers of U2. . . . Bono had engaged them at some level of spirit. . . . Is U2 a prophetic voice? I rather think so. And many of my friends think so. If they do not explicitly proclaim the Kingdom, they certainly prepare the way for that proclamation in much the same way that John the Baptist prepared the way for the kerygma of Jesus. . . . What prophets do, the good ones, is purge our imaginations of the

culture's assumptions on what counts in life and how life is lived. . . . Prophets train us in discerning the difference between the ways of the world and the ways of the Gospel, keeping us present to the Presence of God.[34]

For Peterson, whose vernacular translation of the Bible is influential among evangelicals, Bono is not just *like* a prophet—he *is* a prophet. Peterson considers Bono comparable in his role, if not equal in historical significance, to John the Baptist. He is a good prophet. And Peterson recognizes this goodness in Bono's sincerity. Reflecting on a three-hour conversation with Bono, he said, "I was really taken by the simplicity of his life, of who he was, who he is. There was no pretension to him. So at that point, I felt like he was a companion in the faith."[35]

For many evangelicals, Bono is a good prophet who promotes good causes, like fighting the AIDS crisis in Africa. Jennifer Dyer, a scholar of evangelicalism who worked as the national faith outreach director for the DATA Foundation, argues that "Bono played the role of the 'prophet' among American evangelical conservatives, to reignite a zealous advocate for those dying of infectious diseases, albeit a world away."[36] For pastor, theologian, and sociologist Christian Scharen, U2 is a "spiritual companion." "I've always felt a spiritual kinship with them," he writes, "as though they seem to know my soul and put words to thoughts I've had. This is true during times when I've felt at home in a traditional church but even more so during times when I've felt frustrated with the church." Like other Christian fans, Scharen finds in U2 a source of prophetic criticism, a context for new forms of Christian community. Bono, he says, speaks with the "voice of prophecy, not in some sense of knowing the future, but in the sense of portraying grief-filled anger at what has been in order to make space for other visions."[37]

For many Christian fans of U2, this means finding a faith community in the everyday forms of popular culture, beyond what is for them the typical Sunday service. Brian McLaren, one of the "twenty-five most influential evangelicals in America," according to *Time* magazine, a Christian pastor and proponent of the emerging church movement, describes an experience at a music-listening party with friends. Someone played the U2 song "Stuck in a Moment," and after it ended the group talked about how great it is to be alive when U2 is "creating—not only their extraordinary music but also a movement of concern for global problems, especially in Africa." For McLaren, Bono is "creating a different way of relating to people, not dividing the world into liberals and conservatives, but bringing together everyone he can from across the cultural/political spectrum for joint commitment to worthy goals. . . . We might even say he is pioneering a different identity for being a Christian."[38] In this commentary, notice the emphasis on Bono's sincere concern and the belief in Bono's ability to create spiritual music, political change, and a new way to be Christian. McLaren considers Bono a creative force. And he feels that those at the listening party are lucky enough to live in the historical moment of his prophetic witness.

Others feel the same. In *We Get to Carry Each Other: The Gospel According to U2* (for which McLaren wrote the preface), Professor Greg Garrett works through the biblical allusions and theological lessons of Bono and the band. When he first saw them perform in 1982, he recognized their "almost painful sincerity" as signaling, in retrospect, a call to transform a rock venue into "a place of worship." Garrett later saw U2 as breaking from "traditional church," while offering, in their "close fellowship," a "powerful model of how a community of faith ought to look and act." Garrett says U2 "are doing theology." Citing commentary from the *Christian Century*, he sees in U2 a spiritual message delivered in "parables" that offer a "discourse about the soul for those with ears to hear." For Garrett, it is this soul-level spiritual humanism that gives U2 "almost universal appeal." It is the emotional sincerity that appeals to all fans, like Garrett's friend Zane Wilemon, who attended a U2 show in 2001, right after Bono lost his father, and said that "the honesty and heart-wrenching transparency that Bono poured out that night elevated us all through music and our shared humanity to a place beyond a concert and deeper than church."[39] It is this quality, this "essential honesty," Niall Stokes reflected in 1979, that "underlies U2's existence."[40]

Fans consistently say that U2 concerts take them to a place better than church. That place, they say, echoing Bono, is what church should be. In 1999, Michelle Perez, the co-leader of a U2 fan club, wrote in her foreword to Dianne Ebertt Beeaff's *A Grand Madness: Ten Years on the Road with U2*, a diary account of Beeaff's experience of following U2, "What being a U2 fan has done for me is simple—it's enriched my soul and made me happy." Perez added, "it's different for every fan . . . but in nearly all cases, it's about finding your kindred spirit [in U2] and giving back some of what they've given you."[41] Dianne Beeaff herself described this kindred spirit in the language of spiritual freedom. In her entry for November 13, 1997, she wrote, "What church should be in my view, it [the song "Where the Streets Have No Name"] highlights the enormous difference between religion and spirituality. Religion is exclusive, excluding people based on dogma and a 'chosen few.' Spirituality is inclusive, including people based on the concept of 'many paths up the mountain.' I believe in God. I just don't trust many people who work for him."[42] Perez and Beeaff, like many fans, feel their souls moved at a U2 show. They feel that U2 creates an experience of church without religion, a feeling of moral community and spiritual connection without religious salesmen or untrustworthy clerics. Alan McPherson, the history professor and U2 fan quoted earlier, describes the band's concerts in similar terms. "I attended their show at the Montreal Forum in 1985 and was hooked," he says. "Like many fans, I liked their records just fine, but the live experience was something else altogether. Its feeling of social consciousness, community, and transcendence proved more powerful than any church had ever filled me with. . . . U2 was the soundtrack of earnestness. . . . Bono's sincerity . . . never seemed in doubt." Like other fans, McPherson felt something at a U2 concert that he had not felt with such power and force at church. He likewise recognized Bono as an authentic messenger of social consciousness by virtue of his earnestness and sincerity. Another fan, whom McPherson quotes, said the same thing, recalling, "The first time I saw U2, I would say I had a spiritual experience. I go to church and I love the people in my church, but seeing U2 feels more like a church."[43]

The experience of U2 concerts felt so much like church to confessional fans that some churches tried to replicate it. In his theological interpretation of U2 as a model for Christian community, Greg Garrett credited Brian McLaren's call to Christian song leaders to learn from U2 with influencing evangelicalism toward a more socially oriented message.[44] Music incorporated into meetings of the emerging church movement included U2 songs. At a typical meeting, those gathered might "join together in a cappella and acoustic guitar-led songs of petition and praise—from St. Bernard to Charles Wesley to U2."[45]

In 2011, one self-identified Christian fan of U2 wrote an entry for the *Thinking Worship* blog that outlined why Bono and the band were "some of the best worship leaders of our time." They had everything a worship leader should have: faith, preparation, connection, attentiveness, and response.[46] Another fan, and a worship leader, Aaron Niequist, who has worked at some of the largest and most influential evangelical churches in the United States, including Mars Hill Bible Church in Grandville, Michigan, and Willow Creek Community Church in Chicago, wrote in a 2017 article for the journal *Liturgy* about how, a decade earlier, he had tried to re-create the experience of U2 concerts in his worship services, explaining that he had learned from Bono everything he knew about leading worship. Niequist was compelled by Bono's ability to "harness the energy of a stadium upward," his clear understanding of the "nature of praise," and his "relentless call to action on behalf of the poor." He felt that U2 "offered the ultimate example of worship" and that the band should be a "model for modern-day worship leaders." Niequist's enthusiasm was tempered over time, though. Ten years later, he still felt that U2 performances offered that "mountaintop experience," but he no longer thought the U2 model for worship was sustainable Sunday after Sunday. Niequist compared attempts to make every service a U2-like "epic worship experience" with trying to live in Disney World. It was one thing to visit such a place, but to live there would be exhausting.[47]

From Niequist's reflections we can glean the impact of Bono's performative style on evangelical worship services, as well as the revivalist qualities of U2 concerts. As discussed earlier, traditional evangelical revivals are not intended as routine experiences, even if their presentation is highly routinized. The revival itself is ritualized and repetitive. But it rarely occurs in the same place for an extended period of time. It is a traveling show.

Other churches have held U2-inspired revivalist services that are less frequent but more directly imitative. These services, promoted as

"U2charist"—a ritual reenactment of U2 shows as Eucharist—structure the liturgy around U2 songs that are either played from one of their albums, sung collectively by the congregation, with the lyrics projected on a screen, or performed by a live band (or some combination of the three). The idea for U2charist services came from Sarah Dylan Breuer, a graduate of Episcopal Divinity School in Cambridge, Massachusetts, who also contributed several essays to the 2003 volume *Get Up Off Your Knees: Preaching the U2 Catalog.* In April 2004, Breuer organized a U2charist service at an Episcopal church in Baltimore.[48] The following year, the Episcopal Diocese of Maryland held a U2charist service at its October conference. And the year after that, Reverend Paige Blair officiated at a U2charist service at St. George's Episcopal Church. By 2006, the U2charist movement had garnered national media attention in the United States, when the ABC *Nightline* program reported on a service at All Saint's Episcopal Church in Briarcliff, New York. It was the second time the church had hosted a U2charist service, and the rector described how it drew new people to the congregation; at the first service, he did not recognize 70 percent of the people in the pews. The *Nightline* segment shows him telling the congregation that Bono lives out his faith better than most Christians do. And it cites the $1,700 donated during the service for poverty relief. U2charist services had quickly become a trend and were being held throughout the world, including in Mexico, the Netherlands, Australia, Italy, and the UK.

Like the fans who gathered at the Lhasa Club in Hollywood in 1987, attendees at U2charist services were there for the music and the message of Bono and the band. What began outside the church in the 1980s, with spiritual seekers leaving their parents' congregations and experiencing in U2 concerts what they felt church was supposed to be, came full circle in the early 2000s, as religious institutions sought to reclaim secular culture. As Greg Garrett puts it, "The current phenomenon of U2charists . . . [is] just the formal manifestations of U2's engagement with the divine."[49] Or, as a contributor to the blog *U2charist/U2 Eucharist* writes, "As a Christian, I love the fact that U2 addresses spiritual issues—and that much of it demonstrates a clear understanding of God's love for us. Some of U2's songs are—as the U2-Charist shows—modern-day worship songs."[50] If Bono's evangelical spirituality is a public secret—fans have been talking about U2 songs and concerts as carriers of spiritual meaning and experience since the band first arrived in the 1980s—then the ritual innovation of the U2charist is an attempt to reveal that secret as truly and sincerely religious. This is the secular tension with Christian faith that Bono circulates, the desire to claim popular culture as a source of divine revelation.

Think of the fan club in Hollywood. It did not matter whether you were confessional or not, religious or secular. What mattered was that you shared the same devotional icon—in this case, an Irish rock star. An analysis of forty short essays posted on a U2 fan site found that fans relate to Bono as an icon, as an image that has the "function of a chan-nel, a mediation, of divine presence, grace or activity." In those essays, fans consistently reported a "genuine reassurance, healing, [and] well-being" through the "public persona" of Bono as iconic.[51] Nonconfes-sional fans attach spiritual meaning to Bono as icon, while confessional fans attach biblical truth. Both attachments share the same moral con-cern. Think again of how both Amnesty International and World Vision coexisted within the same U2 humanitarian club. This is how Bono the rock icon is also Bono the moral brand.

"It's a certain moral authority," says Bono of representing a con-stituency of Africans, "that's way beyond your own life and capabilities. The punch you throw is not your own. It has the force of a much bigger issue."[52] Throughout his career, Bono has been a spokesman for Afri-can social causes, his activism becoming more intense after 9/11. The moral practice of asking others to help meet African need, to intervene in order to overcome poverty and ill health, defines Bono's consumer brand. Bono sells his moral message through music and speeches in the same way that Oprah Winfrey promotes her spiritual practice through products and interviews. Both celebrities share a spiritual vision that is a secularized version of evangelical mission. In the nineteenth century, evangelical missionaries traveled from North America and Europe to Africa and beyond. They were motivated to leave their home for foreign lands by a religious calling to save souls and Christianize the world. But they also functioned as ambassadors of the political and economic interests of a modern West. In his history of modern Africa, Richard Reid writes that nineteenth-century "missionaries were so often at the moral frontier of empire."[53] In the nineteenth century, empire entailed the expansion of nation-state territorial control and economic interest. By the end of the twentieth century, new consolidations of global power had emerged in relation to the nation-state. These included media empires of global celebrity, built on a nonsectarian missionary impulse of consumption-based spirituality. "What matters to understanding what makes *Oprah*," says religious studies scholar Kathryn Lofton, "is that this explicitly missionary maneuver to help people was her empire's ascent."[54]

Whatever the epoch, empire cannot maintain its sovereignty without missionaries. In the twentieth century, modern empires were restructured, as the sovereignty of nation-states was reconsolidated in relation to an emerging global polity of multinational corporations. In the postcolonial period that followed World War II, nation-states remained important, as they guaranteed military force and legal systems used to police and protect corporate interests within political borders.[55] But multinational corporations increasingly transgressed those regulations and borders, as they moved capital to dark corners of banking houses and created new economies through investment and speculation, all structural moves that demanded resource extraction and compelled human migration.[56] That Bono was named in the "Paradise Papers," the "leaked papers revealing investments in tax havens by the world's wealthy," in 2017, just shows that he acts as a multinational corporation acts, as an empire within empire.[57] "The concept of Empire," argue political philosophers Michael Hardt and Antonio Negri, "is characterized fundamentally by a lack of boundaries: Empire's rule has no limits."[58] Bono is Irish and claims his Irishness, but, as his tax controversies show, he does not live within the legal limits of Ireland but within the economic spaces of global empire. When Bono justifies his tax decisions, he defends both his economic self-interest and a particular corporate consolidation of political empire that enables the financial pursuit of that self-interest.

It is helpful, perhaps, to think of Bono and U2 as Irish citizens of a global empire of millennial capitalism, rather than as citizens of a particular nation called the Republic of Ireland. In deregulated transnational economic markets, nation-states still matter, but the way in which they matter has changed. Rather than constituting a political sovereignty that regulates a geographic territory, a nation-state is now a diasporic brand within a global economy. The ethnic and regional particularity of that brand locates it within a market, to be bought and sold, but it does not protect it from the governing forces of the market itself. Just consider the financial collapse of the Irish economy in 2007–8. During the Celtic Tiger era of the 1990s and 2000s, the economy flourished, as money flowed into Ireland. Credit was cheap, regulation was lax, and property values soared. The Irish bought Ireland, as author Michael Lewis puts it, and global investors gave them the cash to do it. When the global financial crisis hit in 2007, it took three years to transform a budget surplus into a budget deficit of 32 percent of GDP, which, writes Lewis, was "the highest by far in the history of the euro zone."[59]

As Ireland's economy was downgraded to Third World status, Bono and U2 were traveling the globe for the U2 360° Tour, which included a stop in Johannesburg, South Africa, where Bono sang a revised version of the song "In the Name of Love" with the lyrics, "February 13, 1990 / Word rings out in a Jo'burg sky, / Free at last to live your life, / The Lion of Africa and his pride."[60] Two days later, Bono participated in a discussion hosted by the ONE Campaign about the role of "transparency and technology in driving economic development" in Africa. As part of the publicity surrounding the event, Bono told reporters an African story of global investment in a continent with vast economic potential. "If the right economic plans are made and civic society can keep the vision honest," he said, "it will make our interest irrelevant. I never felt so good to feel so useless. These African lions will put us out of business."[61] Within two months, the entertainment company Live Nation, which promotes U2 shows, reported that the U2 360° Tour was the highest-grossing concert tour in history, with ticket sales exceeding $700 million.[62] Meanwhile, Ireland was trying to recover from its economic recession, and was considering restructuring its "sovereign debt to lower interest payments or extend the maturity of its borrowing as the economy contracts again."[63]

In the shadow of globalized financial markets, both nation-states and corporations need new missionaries. Both need new forms of religious representation, and to this need Bono offers his moral celebrity brand, as well as his nonpartisan nonprofit, the ONE Campaign. In the global empire of neoliberal capitalism, celebrity is a cultural commodity with political currency, and sovereignty is restructured through NGOs and venture capital.[64] And these new consolidations of power rival the existing heads of state. In 1956, C. Wright Mills observed that "the institutional elite must now compete with and borrow prestige from these professionals in the world of the celebrity."[65] Bono is to the political power of neoliberalism as Billy Graham was to the foreign policies of the Cold War. Both men are evangelical celebrities who justify political positions as legitimately righteous. Politicians needed Graham's approval, as Graham needed to be publicly associated with their power and influence. Bono's public persona is made in that prophetic image, though he, like Oprah, uses it within the secular framework of spiritual nonsectarianism. Graham asked his audience to accept the Gospel message of his Jesus. Bono just wants you to buy the product stamped with his moral brand. Transcending the secularizing shift from confessional particularity to generic spirituality, Bono shares with Graham the celebrification of moral value. The celebrity gains value as he circulates. His is the well-known name. He can be incorporated into an enterprise, a business, or a media empire. Bono speaks of himself, as the lead singer of U2, as the front man of a corporation, "We like to say our band is a gang of four, but a corporation of five. I understand brands. I can understand corporate America. I can understand economics." Bono understands the business of celebrity, and he uses it for a purpose. All of this knowledge, he says, is what helps "get your message across," and that message is "the moral weight of an argument," an argument about Africa that "we can't lose."[66]

But just as the prophet must be recognized, the people must hear the message. Any value attached to celebrity is value added by the believer or the fan. Lofton argues that the religious celebrity "doesn't speak for you. You've just made him be the one that you want; you've made him the one that you want to see because you see him everywhere."[67] In their reception of Bono, fans repeatedly see two things: his celebrity brand and his advocacy for moral causes, which begin and end with Africa. And because they believe in one, the sincerity of the celebrity, they often believe in the other, the missionary call. U2 fans want to believe in something good, and Bono sells them that something. Fans believe that Bono speaks for goodness, because he speaks of a moral imperative to either help people live or let them die. The religious seriousness of this moral dilemma, which leaves no other economic alternative, even as fans see new spiritual possibilities, is a source of political power. Bono:

> I don't have any real power, but the people I represent do. The reason why politicians let me in the door, and the reason why people will take my call is because I represent quite a large constituency of people. Now, I do not control that constituency, but I represent them in a certain sense, even without them asking me to, in the minds of the people whose doors I knock upon. That constituency is a very powerful one, because it is a constituency of people from eighteen to thirty, who are the floating vote. They have not yet made their mind up which way they're going to vote. They're the most open-minded, and that's why politicians pay attention to what's going on in contemporary culture and what a rock star might have to do with all of this: because of the people I represent.[68]

What Mills observed in 1956 holds true for celebrity more than half a century later. Politicians let Bono in the door because they need the votes of the people they imagine he speaks for. Bill Clinton, George W. Bush, and Tony Blair all associated with Bono, knowing that he speaks for a segment of voters concerned with a particular set of moral causes. Corporations also associate with Bono because it is good business. He speaks for consumers as he does for voters, consumers who choose products just as they choose politicians, on the basis of their moral brand. According to one commentator, "Bono was pioneering new ground within the realm of celebrity activism, moving from the former archetypal celebrity-as-fundraiser to the realm of celebrity-as-lobbyist (for corporate wealth, not people power)."[69] Bono, however, sees his activist work with Jeffrey Sachs, George Soros, and global corporate executives a bit differently. To his mind, these are the people who get things done, for themselves *and* for the people. For Bono, to sit back and criticize the pursuit of wealth is the equivalent of navel gazing: a self-occupied exercise, akin to therapy, that may yield some insights but is debilitating if totalizing. Thus Bono says of U2, we "were never dumb in business . . . we don't sit around wondering about world peace all day long. We're not sitting around like a bunch of hippies. We're from punk rock, and we're on top of it." Bono claims to be self-aware, says he knows he is playing a political game, but believes that any compromise he makes is in the name of a higher cause. "The moral force, finally," he says, "I do believe in the weight of it. But the apparatus is not moral. The route through it is a very cynical one."[70]

When the world is measured in terms of life and death, as Bono measures it in African lives, it is difficult to quantify the tradeoff between the moral cause and the cynical route. Bono has called the AIDS crisis in Africa "the defining moral issue of our time. Two and a half million Africans are going to die next year because they can't get hold of drugs we take for granted. We have these drugs that simply aren't getting to them. If you remember the story of the Good Samaritan, well, when it comes to Africa, we're not just crossing the road to avoid the man who needs help, we're catching a bus in the other direction."[71] Notice how the celebrity Bono frames the political issue of moral crisis. Within that framework, he defines the measures. The celebrity personalizes politics. Riina Yrjölä says of celebrities like Bono that they "do not only have a central function in the legitimisation of capitalist economies: they are also an essential part of the personalized Western politics, where political authority is increasingly constructed through emotional appeals, management of symbols, affections and imaginaries of being and becoming."[72] As cultural consumers, citizens of the West measure political authority through the emotional, symbolic, affective, and imaginative appeals presented by the celebrity voice. Who wants to be on the bus going in the wrong direction? By these measures, fans as citizens evaluate Bono and his causes, along with the politicians he supports or who support his cause.

As he performs the celebrity role of political advocate, Bono increasingly speaks as an intellectual authority on economic policy and global health initiatives. Health geographers, for example, have decided that "some celebrities such as Bono are becoming *de facto* public intellectuals, among the few people who seem able to effectively deliver messages—particularly those containing bad news—and challenge large audiences."[73] They insist, though, that such figures have to know their facts and find ways to connect with academics. Bono is the rare celebrity who appears to have that ability. And commentators often recognize and praise that ability. Sociologist Douglas Hicks, for example, may question the sustainability of celebrity leadership; he asks whether prophetic charisma can be institutionalized. But he does not question the prophetic message, or what Bono the celebrity signifies:

> Bono may well prove to be the most successful celebrity-leader of our time. . . . Yet celebrity-leadership can take us only so far. What happens, for instance, when the celebrity fades? . . . Bono's success as a leader will hinge on the extent to which he can create and maintain an enduring institutional and international effort to reduce poverty, through organizations such as DATA and the ONE Campaign and through lasting political changes in foreign development assistance. . . . Through international mechanisms like the United Nations Millennium Development Goals, the nations of the world have already pledged to act. The bottleneck is the moral and political will to realize those promises. In that context, Bono as celebrity leader makes a notable contribution that stands as a challenge to citizens to press our political leaders into doing their part.[74]

Hicks sees Bono as an aspirational model. If only other famous people could be like him, and we could bottle and broadcast his message more widely, the world would be a better place. In an issue in which Bono graced the cover as one of three "Persons of the Year," *Time* magazine declared that "Bono's great gift is to take what has made him famous—charm, clarity of voice, and ability to touch people in their secret heart—combine those traits with a keen grasp of the political game and obsessive attention to detail, and channel it all toward getting everyone, from world leaders to music lovers, to engage with something overwhelming in its complexity." Bono is not just a famous guy who makes you feel "like you're in the living room with your buddy," as George Clooney described him. He's not just a humble rock star. He knows his facts, and "the fact is," the *Time* writer tells us, "Bono gets results."[75]

The results of celebrity advocacy are presented as quantifiably measurable in monetary terms. In the *Time* magazine piece, Gleneagles, Scotland, is the reference point, "where Bono and his policy-and advocacy body, DATA, met with five of the eight heads of state at the summit—the G-8 approved an unprecedented $50 billion aid package—including $25 billion for Africa—and pledged near universal access to antiretroviral drugs for almost 10 million impoverished people with HIV."[76] By what instrument, though, does the fan measure those numbers, if not by celebrity? Theologian Greg Garrett calls Bono "the most important activist in the world." Journalist J. Traub declares Bono "the most politically effective figure in the recent history of popular culture." U2 scholar Scott Calhoun claims that "U2's fans know that things have changed for the better because of U2."[77]

But how do they know? And how do U2 fans respond to criticism of Bono and the band? The editor of a U2 fan website, responding to Dave Marsh's review of Harry Browne's book *The Frontman*, a review that supports Browne's critical stance on U2, wrote:

> As U2 fans, we have a choice whether or not to engage with criticism like this. Some choose to ignore it; others take a defensive stance. My perspective has always been one taken from Bono's lyrical playbook: "Stand up to rock stars." Or put another way, practice critical fandom. Despite what others say, he's neither saint nor messiah and is worthy of constructive pushback, especially if it comes from a good place. I definitely don't see Bono as an uber-capitalist "lapdog for neoliberals" as he's been called, and at the same time, I don't think we need to be lapdogs or sycophants for Bono or U2. . . .
> I don't know how I feel about liberalism or capitalism beyond the degree to which I participate in both by

necessity. But I do know what I perceive as the source of my activism and Bono's: Jesus and the Bible; spirituality and scriptures; the new commandments of radical love and service taught by the carpenter from Nazareth. What's been called the preferential option for the poor. Bono's lack of economic literacy, or worse, allegiance to wrong-headed economic mentors, may make me and others uncomfortable and may play into the hands of the problem-creators rather than the problem-solvers, yet Bono's biblical, musical, and poetic literacy remain on target in my eyes and heart.[78]

By what measure does this fan assess criticism of Bono? By whether or not it comes from a *good* place. By what measure does this fan judge Bono? By his *biblical* message. Is the world complicated? Yes, says this fan. Is it difficult to tell who is right and who is wrong, who gives and who takes, who helps and who harms? Yes. How, then, does the moral collective decide what to do and how to act? In a world of economic uncertainties, when it is impossible to grasp the unseen forces of neoliberal capitalism, this fan does what many other U2 fans have done; he finds religious certainty in Bono's biblical literacy and heartfelt spirituality. This is how evangelicals measure moral celebrity.

In the religious terms of American revivalism, evangelicals developed the theological instrument of the individual heart to ascertain correct doctrine and right action.[79] Billy Graham was the greatest celebrity of that tradition in modern times. Like Graham, Bono speaks within the religious framework of evangelicalism, of heartfelt personal sincerity. But Bono, unlike Graham, detached the moral message from its religious context. Bono embodies the secular presentation of evangelical celebrity. He has translated the religious language of the heart into the cultural language of spiritually transcendent morality. In both the religious and the cultural expression, celebrity is the measure. Whereas Graham's moral celebrity was used to measure the Christian superiority of U.S. foreign policy in the Cold War, Bono's moral celebrity is used to measure the spiritual legitimacy of neoliberal Western contracts with developing nations. The economic rules of empire have changed, and so have its missionaries. How we see the changes depends upon the moral community to which we belong. U2 fans, whether they are confessional evangelicals or spiritual but not religious, almost always, at least in the United States, see Bono in the same light, as a good-hearted rock star, taking the stage for a morally righteous cause.

NEOLIBERALISM AROUND

In February 2006, Bono gave the keynote speech at the National Prayer Breakfast in Washington, D.C., an event organized by a fundamentalist evangelical Christian foundation.[1] After admitting to a crowd of more than three thousand people, including President George W. Bush, members of Congress, and a sampling of world leaders, that "there's something unnatural, something even unseemly about rock stars mounting the pulpit and preaching at presidents," Bono gave a homily (his term) on the virtues of aiding the sick and the poor in Africa. Appealing to "higher laws," he called on politicians worldwide to move beyond religion, because it "often gets in the way of God," and embrace the "era of grace" that began with the new millennium, the year of jubilee. Progressive evangelical Jim Wallis called it "his best sermon yet."[2] At the close of the speech, Bono made a direct plea for U.S. funding to African nations, saying, "To give one percent more is right. It's smart. And it's blessed. There is a continent—Africa—being consumed by flames. I truly believe that when the history books are written, our age will be remembered for three things: the war on terror, the digital revolution, and what we did—or did not do—to put the fire out in Africa."[3]

Neoliberalism is both a descriptive term and a normative claim, and it deeply informs our understanding of the religion around Bono. Neoliberalism emerged in the 1980s as a political promise that freeing labor and finance from government regulation, privatizing public services, opening markets, and expanding global trade would bring greater financial prosperity for all and expand human rights around the world.[4] The advancement of neoliberalism is most directly associated with the political and economic policies of Ronald Reagan in the United States and Margaret Thatcher in the United Kingdom.[5] Cultural geographer David Harvey describes it as "a theory of political economic practices that proposes that human well-being can best be advanced by liberating individual entrepreneurial freedoms and skills within an institutional framework characterized by strong private property rights, free markets, and free trade. The role of the state is to create and preserve an institutional framework appropriate to such practices."[6] This is neoliberalism as economic theory and political policy. Neoliberal religion uses the moral crises of life and death to justify that theory and policy, to call on the state to protect private property rights, free markets, and free trade, and to intervene in times of crisis, but only for the purpose of restoring individual freedoms, not to impose regulation or oversight.

The religious culture of neoliberalism is made in its political cycles of moral crises and economic solutions, where the dire prospect of human death (which the system itself generates) demands the intervention of the state to redeem the failures of free-market capitalism.[7] The requisite economic response of market deregulation is demanded within a moral framework that makes it appear that "there is no alternative."[8] This TINA doctrine can be seen as a religious formulation, if we think of religion as signaled in the stress responses to life-and-death situations.[9] In terms of a post-1980s evangelical America, consider that the moral crises of abortion and the death penalty, two politically divisive issues, are directly concerned with life and death. Both issues involve economic considerations. A pro-life voter, for example, is likely to oppose universal health care, because he does not want to fund what he sees as the murder of the innocent. A voter who supports the death penalty is likely to support the prison industry, as she sees punishment, not rehabilitation, as the primary reason for incarceration. But these are complicated moral issues with oblique economic connections. Their life-and-death importance is rarely linked directly to financial concerns. To put it another way, these two moral issues might determine a political election, but they alone are not enough to justify a global economic intervention. Neoliberalism is defined by its political consensus, not its partisan politics.

To generate political consensus, Bono invokes an image of Africa in need. He uses the moral concern for life and death in Africa to leverage neoliberal economic policies. He is not the only figure to do this, but he's one of the most visible, and perhaps the most influential. African need provides Bono with his moral claim to economic justice. Bono professes a secular Christian spiritual calling to end poverty. "Aside from redemption," he says, "the second theme of the entire scriptures is poverty. It's the only time that Christ speaks of judgment, is how we treat the poor."[10] Bono plans to end poverty, though, not by helping the poor but by creating the market conditions within which the poor can help themselves. This is the vision he shares with neoliberal economists who see Africa as home to the poorest of the world's poor. From the earliest years of his career, Bono has located himself in relation to Africa as a biblical source of moral judgment. And that moral judgment is the defining feature of his neoliberal brand.

Bono's speech at the prayer breakfast in 2006 was just one example of his political advocacy for Africa. In 1999, Bono joined Pope John Paul II and others in the Jubilee 2000 movement, or Drop the Debt Campaign. Invoking the Levitical tradition of a jubilee year, when debt was forgiven without penalty, these religious leaders called First World nations to forgive the debts of poor Third World countries. Bono has continued this movement in the new millennium. In 2002, he founded DATA, the NGO that advocated for debt relief on behalf of African nations. In 2007, DATA merged with ONE, a "campaigning and advocacy organization of more than eight million people around the world taking action to end extreme poverty and preventable disease, particularly in Africa."[11] Bono continues to promote ONE, even as the organization was accused in 2018 of fostering an "atmosphere of bullying, abuse and, in one case, attempted sexual coercion in its Johannesburg operation," according to the *New York Times*. In this particular case, Bono said he had heard about "low morale and poor management in this office [in Johannesburg]" but did not know of anything "along the lines of what emerged recently." In response to that news, Bono pleaded institutional distance, saying that "the head office [in Washington, D.C.] failed to protect those employees and I need to take some responsibility for that. In fact, if they would agree, I would like to meet them and apologize in person." This has been a pattern throughout Bono's career—not this particular kind of accusation, but this type of response to the moral failings of social institutions with which he is involved. Bono's response is to meet in person, face to face, and then return to his higher, more distant, calling. "The poorest people in the poorest places being bullied by their circumstance is the reason we set up ONE," Bono explained. "So to discover last November that there were serious and multiple allegations of bullying in our office in Johannesburg left me and the ONE board reeling and furious. You question the whole reason you're doing this."[12] These rhythms of distant crisis, moral outrage, self-reflection, personal encounter, and transcendent resolution have defined neoliberal religion around Bono since the earliest days of his career.

"Dislocate. Surrender." Bono sings "Bad," the second of what was supposed to be a three-song set at the Live Aid concert in Wembley Stadium on July 13, 1985. "We're an Irish band. We come from Dublin City, Ireland," he tells the world. In full mullet, against a white canvas backdrop with two black silhouettes of the African continent, with a guitar neck extending north from each and "LIVE AID" in block letters across the necks, Bono begins the iconic twelve minutes that launched U2 onto the global music scene. At the halfway point, he drops the mic and starts to wander. He heads toward the audience. A barricaded section blocks the way. From the elevated stage he looks down. He motions for someone to come out of the crowd. No one can. Everyone watches, him, waving, pacing. Some 72,000 people in the stadium, 1.4 billion people tuned in to the MTV broadcast.[13] He keeps pointing at someone. Is it her? Or her? He keeps motioning for that person to come forward. But she can't. So everyone waits, and watches, and the Edge and Larry and Adam keep playing, and the music starts to feel more anxious, and everyone wonders what is happening—was this planned?

Then he jumps and points at her. And the security staff drags her over the last barricade. And he holds her, dances with her, slowly. His eyes closed. Kisses her on the forehead. Then climbs back onstage. Hugs two more women along the way. Where did they come from? Then kisses another, catches the mic, which someone has tossed in his direction, and finishes the song, "wide awake, I'm not sleeping." But he doesn't finish, instead segueing into an impromptu call-and-response with the audience: "goodbye, Ruby Tuesday . . . Pleased to meet you, I hope you guess my name . . . doo, doo, doo, doo, doo, doo, doo . . . Holly came from Miami F.L.A., hitchhiked her way across the U.S.A., she could hear the satellite coming down, pretty soon she was in London Town, Wembley Stadium, and all the people went . . . doo, doo, doo, doo, doo, doo, doo . . . thank you, God bless you." And he was gone.

That 1985 performance was the grand metaphor of Bono's career as artist, activist, and opportunist. Bono *was* Live Aid. He was ready—to make history, to try something, anything, to get your attention. Bono crosses the barrier, retreats, crosses it again, retreats, but you know he will always return. Such is the ritual repetition of the concert specialist. And there were plenty of those there that day, at the event organized by his fellow Irishman Bob Geldof to raise money to help relieve famine in Ethiopia. Rock stars. Pop stars. Folk stars. Rap stars. They were there in London and in Philadelphia: Mick Jagger, Keith Richards, Phil Collins, Madonna, Paul McCartney, David Bowie, Sting, Freddie Mercury, Bob Dylan, Joan Baez, Elvis Costello, Run-DMC, and many more. They were there, broadcast to the world. But Bono was the only one the world remembered, thirty years later, for not just leaving the stage but leaping off it. He took the risk. He was seen. And more than anything, he hasn't stopped talking about what happened to him, onstage and in Africa, ever since.

"Everyone was very annoyed with me, I mean, very annoyed." In the first hours and days after the moment, Bono was depressed. His mates were angry. "Larry told me he was going to stop playing. This was a big show for our band, there were a billion people watching, and we didn't do our big song." It took him a week, as Bono tells the story, to realize he had done the right thing. That everyone thought it was great. That when he got back to Dublin, "I met this sculptor, in Wexford, a little town in Ireland, and he was working on a piece, and it was a guy jumping, and he said, 'It's called the leap.' And he said, 'It's you.' 'You see,' he said, 'you made a leap of faith that day.'"[14] As commentators tallied the reports and reporters compiled the stories, "U2's Live Aid performance in 1985" would be remembered as "one of the band's greatest marketing moments."[15] Those who saw it happen remembered it happening. The account of the moment, of the leap, of the embrace, became a staple of Bono's interview scripts. But as always, the story felt spontaneous, self-reflective, and monumental. "I didn't know that when I was holding her I'd be holding on to the rest of the world."[16]

Bono's journey to Africa, to the metaphorical embrace, went through Bob Geldof. In 1984, Geldof put together a benefit single, "Do They Know It's Christmas?," to raise money for famine relief in Ethiopia. This was the precursor celebrity project to the Live Aid event. Among the many voices featured, Bono sang the line, "Tonight, thank God, it's them instead of you." According to Bono, the financial success of the song, which raised a reported $8 million for famine relief, surprised Geldof, but not him. "For Bob Geldof, the sight of little bits of black plastic actually saving lives was a bit of a shock," Bono recalled. "He had always thought of pop music as something wonderful in itself but nothing more than that. But I wasn't quite as taken aback by the success of it all. The 1960s music that inspired me was part of a movement that helped to stop the Vietnam War and there is no reason why contemporary music cannot have a similar importance."[17] What Bono found in his relationship with Geldof was something he claimed to know already, which is that music can change the world in a particular way. And the part of the world that most needed changing was the African continent.

From Geldof and other Irish influences, Bono learned to set Africa apart as a moral problem. "What I'm telling you is, being Irish, I wasn't exposed to Africa as a cultural force, more as a moral dilemma," he told an interviewer. Bono describes his connection to Africa through his Irishness, an ongoing theme throughout his career. On his interest in the 1985 Live Aid concert, he noted, "Ireland has a lot of ties with Africa, because of Catholic missions: nuns, priests. Ireland is very Africa-conscious because, I suppose, as a country, it had its own famine not that long ago . . . maybe it's folk memory, maybe it's just a shared colonial past."[18] There is a long history of Irish Catholic missionary work in Africa.[19] Bono's link to Africa, though, was forged not so much through Catholicism as it was through evangelical Protestantism. The Catholic Church provided institutional resources and religious motivation for the Jubilee 2000 movement and Drop the Debt Campaign, but evangelical Protestantism was Bono's bridge to Africa. In 1985, Bono took a trip to Ethiopia with his wife, Ali, a trip arranged, according to Harry Browne, by "World Vision, a California-based evangelical charity that has come in for criticism over the years for its marketing of 'child-sponsorship' as a means of fundraising."[20] World Vision programs have functioned as political extensions of U.S. global interests. In the Americas, for example, child-sponsorship programs were a religious strategy of soft security promoted by the U.S. government, a strategy that used cultural influences, such as religious leaders and organizations, rather than direct governmental influence through military intervention, in the name of fighting gang violence.[21] Bono's interest in Africa as a place in need of outside help reinforces the missionary motivation of organizations like World Vision, which supports Western intervention in African nations while it works to convert a region to Protestant Christianity.[22]

Evangelicalism is well suited to the economic demands of a neoliberal world. As a religious system, evangelicalism helps those disaffected by globalization make sense of their suffering in a way that gives them a feeling of agency, but in doing so places the blame for their own suffering on their individual actions, abilities, drives, will, and thoughts, more than on a structurally limiting social reality. This is why, many scholars have argued, evangelicalism has flourished globally since the 1960s. The cultural power of evangelicalism is evident in how it dislocates individuals from their surroundings in order to promise a new world in their hearts, homes, and families, while compelling the converted to surrender to the world as it is, outside their personal enclaves. Evangelicalism was the religious medium for Bono's personal connection with Africa, experienced through the expansive evangelical networks that connected global politics to individual hearts, rather than through the traditional Irish routes of Catholic institutions.

Bono came to the world through Live Aid, which was Geldof's big idea. And Geldof got the idea for Live Aid from evangelical missionaries in Africa. In 1984, the BBC broadcast a seven-minute report on famine in Ethiopia. This was the report that, according to independent researcher Michael Barker, "fueled Bob Geldof's initial humanitarian efforts in the region." "The two reporters who filed the BBC report (Mo Amin and Michael Buerk)," Barker notes, "were working under the auspices of World Vision—a well-publicized, right-wing, evangelical Christian organization." This, Barker explains, is why the report invoked the religious terms of "biblical famine" and depicted Ethiopia as the "closest thing to hell on earth." The surprise here, for Barker, was not that evangelicals would use such terms but that the secular press took them as true, without trying to "explain the root causes of the famine." Emerging from an evangelical missionary vision of Africa, Live Aid was the media spectacle that Geldof used to promote his humanitarian efforts. To question the motives behind the continental silhouettes, to ask why the bands were there, and why we should help Africa, would require more than seeing the show and swaying to the music. To find the answers to those questions, Barker argues, the mainstream media would have had "to challenge the dominant developmentalist narrative upon which NGOs in the aid industry then relied—and continue to rely."[23] In the last two decades of the twentieth century, that narrative was rarely challenged in mainstream media. And while critical voices grew louder in the opening years of the twenty-first century, that narrative persisted by evolving into new models of economic development, including the privatization of public services and the corporate sponsorship of agrarian reform, which I discuss in more detail in chapter 4.

One of the reasons why this narrative persists is that Bono's fusion of rock 'n' roll and evangelical revivalism involves more than just merging music and religion. It is also an ideological imagining of the politically and economically integrative promises of neoliberalism. In his work with DATA, Bono advocates the inclusion of African nations within an emerging U.S.-led world polity. Africa's inclusion is predicated on the global expansion of democratic governing structures and capitalist markets. Bono's promotion of world polity theory is an example of what sociologists have called "ideological globalization from above."[24]

Bono's attempt to integrate African nations into this imagined world polity is part of a modern secular project that assumes that nation-states are sovereign (that they can regulate defined borders) and that their sovereignty is based on Enlightenment rationalism, not religious tradition or practice. Sociologist of religion José Casanova argues that the modern global public sphere, or world polity, that emerged in the late twentieth century has exhibited a rational Enlightenment impulse. In order to participate in this polity, nation-states and NGOs must adapt to the demands of modernity born of this impulse. For Casanova, this holds for religion as well. He argues "that only a religion which has incorporated as its own the central aspects of the Enlightenment critique of religion is in a position today to play a positive role in furthering processes of practical rationalization."[25] If the integration of African nations into a world polity is understood in these terms, then it is as an example of "practical rationalization," and Bono has performed the role of rationalized religious broker in this process, by transforming religion into spiritual and moral terms compatible with neoliberal transactions.

Bono's prescription for spiritual and economic salvation is the rational political and economic order of a world polity. Such a rational global polity offers to the Western consumer of African need, and to an Africa in need, a secular answer to the soteriological question "what must I do to be saved?" As far as Bono is concerned, religion does not offer salvation to the modern consumer. Salvation can only come from the spiritual journey of individual desire to do something for the needy other in order to feel connected to that distant person. This affective connection offers moral transcendence to neoliberal consumer communities, which are imagined as culturally distant from those they help, but proximate to them by way of good intentions. Bono's promotion of the Product Red campaign, which I discuss in chapter 5, illustrates the personal practice of this consumer religion. The vitality of a society based on consumption is of the utmost importance to Western nation-states, whose people are no longer defined as citizens but as consumers. Multinational corporations need the protection of Western nation-states to guarantee their ability to extract resources around the world and convert them into usable goods to sell to consumers. Western nations thus represent consumption-driven societies and the corporations that need protected markets in which to sell their products. Aid to and investment in Africa expands global markets for these corporations, and entrepreneurial capitalism is the most recent medium for promoting that expansion. All of this I address in more detail in the following two chapters. Here, I want to emphasize how this self-interested model is promoted by the use of images of Africans in need of this-worldly salvation, Africans who need to be physically saved from death and economically rescued from debt. This humanitarian rationale for Western intervention is the religion of neo-liberalism, a public prescription for spiritual and economic salvation unbounded by religious institutions, beliefs, or traditions.

Christian theologians use the term *soteriology* to describe the study of religious doctrines of salvation. The third-century theologian Origen of Alexandria, for example, promoted a more universalist soteriology than sixteenth-century theologian John Calvin's doctrine of predestination. Sociologists of religion like Max Weber use the term a bit differently. Weber used the term as a way to compare salvation-oriented religions, juxtaposing "Asiatic and Occidental religions" to show how one group of people might be more "other-worldly," while another might be more "this-worldly" in the way it defines what one must do to be saved.[26] Such classifications now appear highly Euro-centric and normatively Protestant, as Weber saw Western Christianity, and in particular the Protestant Reformation, as the basis for all comparisons with other religions. I am not interested here in whether Weber got it right but in his focus on a particular theological expression of soteriology, the evolution of which he traces in relation to broader cultural forces, especially industrialization and the rise of capitalism. Weber's approach can be usefully applied to the study of popular culture in a fashion similar to what one might find in exegetical theology. This is the goal of adding the term *secularized* to the study of soteriology, for doctrines of salvation, in Bono's performative thought, have left church confines for the more expansive realm of popular culture.

As I argued in chapter 1, this diffusion of religious doctrine occurs over time. To understand the theological mechanics of that process, it is helpful to outline three aspects of Weber's theoretical description of soteriology. Weber argued that a social agent could not conceive of salvation or redemption without a coherent "image of the world," which is provided by the dominant society. But he also believed that the "germ" of this theodicy, or rationalized conception of a totalizing moral world, was found in "the myth of the redeemer." And, finally, Weber maintained that "almost always . . . some kind of theodicy of suffering has originated from the hope for salvation."[27]

Following Weber's three-part structure, used here to help understand religion around Bono, America is the dominant manufacturer of a soteriological "image of the world" (of democracy and free markets within a world polity), and Bono seizes upon these ideals and strives to remake them in his own interests. For Bono, the "idea of America," like the "idea of religion," is that which must be overcome. Bono's soteriological promotions are one "germ" of world polity, and are comparable, in terms of techniques of conversion, to those of evangelical revivalists. Bono's soteriological aspirations for Africa provide one form of theodicy for the idea of a world polity. In other words, Bono has explained the spread of democracy and the expansion of capitalist markets in Africa in terms of their salvific political and economic potential for those suffering across that continent.

In terms of his vision of the idea of America, Bono has juxtaposed biblical images of human struggle with God with global examples of human struggle with America. For example, "Bullet the Blue Sky," one of Bono's earliest sermons to America, moves across national boundaries (from El Salvador to the United States), across historical markers (from Jacob to John Coltrane), and across geographic location (from rural hills to city streets). This is an image of Bono lyrically tangled up with America.[28]

Bono is also tangled up politically with America, with its legislators, economists, theologians, and religious leaders.[29] His political buddies have ranged from Jesse Helms to Bill Clinton.[30] In 2002, he toured Africa with U.S. Treasury Secretary Paul O'Neill.[31] He has met frequently with Harvard economist Jeffrey Sachs.[32] He has pleaded his causes on the

Oprah Winfrey Show and in front of an evangelical audience at Wheaton College.[33] Pat Robertson has voiced his support for debt relief, Franklin Graham has helped Bono deliver Christmas gifts to African children, and Melinda and Bill Gates have helped fund DATA, the organization for debt relief and health funding in Africa that grew out of the Jubilee 2000 campaign.[34] Bono has engaged public figures outside the United States as well, from Pope John Paul II, to Desmond Tutu, to United Nations councils, but his primary allies are American. And for Bono, in terms of consumer culture, America equals the global anyway. "I live in America," he says. "Everyone lives in America."[35]

Bono draws on the American symbols of the U.S. Constitution, the American "idea," and the rhetoric of universal freedom, human rights, and participatory democracy in envisioning a global civil society, or world polity, built on these values. He imagines social change as flowing from the integration of social agents, from individuals to nation-states, into this polity. In his Harvard commencement address in 2001, Bono discussed America's responsibility to Africa and told the graduating class, "Isn't 'Love thy neighbour' in the global village so inconvenient? GOD writes us these lines but we have to sing them . . . take them to the top of the charts, but it's not what the radio is playing—is it? I know."[36] Referring to a transcendent moral authority, Bono makes a plea for global communal compassion on behalf of Africa. Invoking a type of prophetic discourse familiar to historians of American religion, Bono calls America to embrace an equality that, according to him, is yet unsung.

Bono preaches what he hears in Martin Luther King Jr., who proclaimed to his opponents, "We shall match your capacity to inflict suffering by our capacity to endure suffering. We shall meet your physical force with soul force."[37] Speaking in the name of Dr. King, Bono emphasizes a spiritual freedom inside each individual that is impossible to regulate externally. Bono's message to his audience: you can regulate bodies, but you can't regulate souls. Referring to the incarceration of Nelson Mandela in South Africa, he sings, "outside are the prisoners, inside the free." Bono sees Mandela as a modern-day Apostle Paul in his Roman cell, free in spirit and mind. It is the jailers outside, those representing apartheid, who are prisoners of their own injustice. Bono's prophetic call is to "set the prisoners free," to give them freedom to sell, to buy, to experience the commerce that binds the world together. Moving toward an imagined horizon of economic possibility, where the world's poor can release their spiritual colors on a global stage, Bono promotes a moral rendering of world polity and the transparent expansion of capitalist markets.[38]

Bono promotes an emerging U.S.-led world polity that bears his spiritual brand. This polity is marked by an incomplete international civil society that emphasizes certain shared values expressed in human rights discourses. Further, it is an extended imagining of U.S. civil society and exhibits all of its internal contradictions of promise and discontent. As spiritual performer, Bono sees himself as the conscience of this polity, laboring for the realization of globalization's great promise. Bono's faith in the promise of globalization is rooted in his belief that love can conquer all; this includes God, America, and capitalist markets. For Bono, only love can rattle the "iron cage" of late modern capitalism.[39] Bono invokes the name of Dr. King in the name of love, hoping for a future where the liberties of the few will become liberty for all. This message of transcendent love is both economically integrative and a prescriptive moral vision.

During a concert in Chicago in 2005, U2 finished the song "Running to Stand Still" with Bono singing "hallelujah" beneath a digital banner that read, "On December 10, 1948, the General Assembly of the United Nations adopted and proclaimed the Universal Declaration of Human Rights. Following the historic act the Assembly called upon all member countries to publicize the text of the declaration." As the banner faded away, the band transitioned to the next anthem, "Pride (In the Name of Love)," with video and audio clips of the articles of the Universal Declaration of Human Rights shown overhead. At the end of "Pride," Bono called on the audience to "sing for Dr. King, for Dr. King's dream, for a dream big enough to fit the whole world, a dream where everyone is created equal under the eyes of God. Everyone!" Bono then extended his homily from America to Africa, announcing that Dr. King's dream is "not just an American dream, or an Asian dream, or a European Dream; it is also an African dream!" Digital flags of African nations descended from above the stage as the band segued into "Where the Streets Have No Name." As the intro gradually ascended, Bono shouted rhythmically, "From the bridge at Selma over the Mississippi to the mouth of the river Nile. From the swamplands of Louisiana to the high peaks of Kilimanjaro. From Dr. King's America to Nelson Mandela's Africa, the journey of equality moves on."[40]

This is Bono's neoliberal promise. He will remind America of its higher moral calling. In the biblical narrative of Genesis, Jacob wrestles a messenger of God during the night. Struggling at daybreak, the messenger asks Jacob to release him. But Jacob replies, "I will not let you go unless you bless me." The man asks him, "What is your name?" "Jacob," he answers. Then the man says, "Your name will no longer be Jacob, but Israel, because you have struggled with God and with men and have overcome."[41] Performing Jacob, Bono struggles with America as a messenger of God. Like the messenger in the story, America has the power to name: it has the power to grant or depose a nation-state, and it has the power to save lives. Bono, through DATA, recognizes this power and calls on it on behalf of God's people. Wrestling with America at the dawn of a new century, Bono demands grace. With biblical authority, he demands a new covenant of fairness at the edge of economic possibility, referencing in lyrics and speeches the Technicolor future promised to Noah.

Jubilee 2000 and the Drop the Debt Campaign were part of Bono's vision of a new day after the flood. According to the DATA website, "DATA is a new organization which aims to raise awareness about the crisis swamping Africa: (DATA stands for) unpayable DEBTS, uncontrolled spread of AIDS, and unfair TRADE rules which keep AFRICANS poor." Bono, via DATA, was asking "the governments of the world's wealthy nations—the United States, Europe, Canada and Japan—to respond quickly and generously to this emergency." In order for African nations to receive this funding (and this is key), African leaders are required to adhere to the other meaning of the DATA acronym. They are asked to practice "DEMOCRACY, ACCOUNTABILITY and TRANSPARENCY—to make sure that help for African people goes where it's intended and makes a real difference."[42] In order to receive foreign monetary aid, African nations must reshape themselves in the image of the West.

Western nations use foreign aid and debt relief to control economic outcomes in Africa, and Bono has positioned himself as a spiritual broker in those financial relationships. U.S. foreign spending on world poverty reached its apex during the Cold War, when the United States saw fighting poverty as a means of preventing communism. Foreign aid fell sharply in the 1990s, after the Cold War, but picked up again after September 11, 2001. Economists Lael Brainard and Robert Litan argue, "The campaign against terrorism has provided a potentially powerful political rationale for foreign assistance—namely, that by strengthening foreign economies, aid may help weaken incentives for their residents to turn to terrorism. . . . September 11 reinforced the direct interest of the wealthier nations in strengthening the trading system by rectifying the perceived inequities that prevent millions of the world's poor from reaping the potential benefits of globalization." U.S. foreign spending in the form of developmental aid is one mechanism for expanding global markets and is justified by the rhetoric of a war on terrorism. As President George W. Bush vowed at the time, "The terrorists attacked the World Trade Center, and we will defeat them by expanding and encouraging world trade."[43]

Bono uses similar antiterrorist rhetoric to gain support for DATA. He claims that there are "potentially another 10 Afghanistans in Africa," and that the United States should "prevent the fires rather than putting them out."[44] He likens the United States to a brand that has lost its shine and links this image to the war on terror:

> If the United States is a brand—and all countries in a certain way are brands—when was the brand of the USA the most sparkling? The answer is, of course, after the Second World War. My father looked to America like Ireland was a part of it; he was so proud. Europeans were. That was after the Marshall Plan, which was not just about liberating Europe, of course, but about rebuilding Europe. Again, not just out of mercy, but as a bulwark against the Soviets in the Cold War. Well, this is a bulwark against Islamic extremism in the hot war. They are analogous.[45]

Bono's reference to the Marshall Plan is telling because it reveals the political model of the religion around him: the model for DATA is the

U.S. Marshall Plan. Bono's formula for social change draws on a tradition that envisions America as a beacon of peace and democracy to the world. Though America may stray at times, it is still called to protect the world from all threats to freedom, democracy, and the market, whatever form these threats may take, whether communist, atheist, or Islamic extremist.

This is Bono's economic response to the moral problem of Africa. What we need, he says, is a "Marshall Plan for Africa." As in Europe after World War II, it is in the interest of democracy, he says, to invest in Africa in order to economically jump-start the continent and integrate it into the global economy. As part of this plan, Western nations engineer markets in Africa that they regulate. The "unencumbered" free market, Bono says, "is not the solution either. All successful economies have protected their seed industries until they were strong enough to compete. We cannot deny for others what we demand for ourselves."[46] The "we" here includes the governing democracies of the West. And it is through those economic and political investments that Bono offers the solution to the moral problem of Africa.[47]

More than half a century before Bono preached his message of "love thy neighbour in the global village," U.S. Secretary of State George Marshall outlined his own American errand to the Harvard class of 1947. In his commencement address, Marshall famously advocated for U.S. political and economic involvement in the postwar reconstruction of Europe. Justifying involvement with reference to the economic benefits to America and the world, Marshall told his audience that

> the consequences to the economy of the United States should be apparent to all. It is logical that the United States should do whatever it is able to do to assist in the return of normal economic health in the world, without which there can be no political stability and no assured peace. Our policy is directed not against any country or doctrine but against hunger, poverty, desperation, and chaos. Its purpose should be the revival of a working economy in the world so as to permit the emergence of political and social conditions in which free institutions can exist.[48]

Marshall's strategy for creating global stability by expanding American economic markets and forging political consensus after World War II were promoted by President Harry Truman as part of his plan to fight communism. Like Bono, Truman had a fraught relationship with evangelicalism. He also did not personally like organized religion, focusing instead on its ethical content. Raised in mainline Presbyterian and Baptist churches, he looked down on revivalists. Yet, despite his personal differences with popular evangelicalism, he cast the American fight for freedom against the terror of communism in dualistic moral terms familiar to a broad range of Americans, including evangelicals, who saw the world in the black-and-white binary terms of good versus evil.

By promoting a Marshall Plan for Africa, Bono continues this American tradition of depicting the United States and its allies as redeemers or saviors on the world stage. In doing so, Bono preaches what Weber referred to as the "myth of the redeemer." Western nations have promoted this myth about Africa to justify the integration of nation-states into imagined international political spheres and expanding economic markets across the continent. According to Saskia Sassen, the nation-state is still an important actor in the global market economy, even if transnational networks and capital flows, which have produced shifting coalitions of interested social actors in globalized systems, have reconfigured it. Sassen defines sovereignty as the ability to regulate a defined region of power in accordance with an agent's will or self-interest. The nation-state historically illustrates this type of sovereignty. A national government can exercise its will (whether self-defined or representative of the will of "the people") upon its citizens who live within a geographical and/or ideological territory. Using coercion, states levy taxes, enforce legal codes, and regulate economic exchanges, among other things. Sassen observes that globalization disrupts national sovereignty, fracturing political identities and dislocating both coercive and consensual will. Globalization restructures the role of nation-states. Governments no longer have absolute control, if they ever did, within the spheres of power they occupy. Instead, they share these spheres with a number of political and financial actors.[49] In his advocacy work for Africa and with DATA, Bono promotes the idea that these disruptions provide spaces for change, and that an emerging world polity, or global civil society, organized around a universal rights regime, will triumph over the most powerful of nation-states.

Africa stands at the heart of Bono's political imagination; it is the place where human rights discourses can integrate individuals and nation-states into his imagined world polity, the shiny side of neoliberalism. This ideal world polity is based on corporate multiculturalism and liberal good intentions. Within this global community, those who have are asked to give, not as charity but as an investment, not as a handout but as a hand up. They are asked to give the gift of the market, to bring everyone into it, to get Third World countries like those in Africa healthy enough to trade their labor, their goods, and their ideas. The gift from the developed world is the opportunity to remake themselves in the image of success, as entrepreneurs, investors, creative capitalists. Bono's model of the good gift in a time of crisis is his response to the moral problem of life and death in Africa; it is his version of the Marshall Plan.

In the 1950s, American evangelicals supported President Truman's anticommunist foreign policy goals in the Marshall Plan, even as many opposed his domestic agenda, worrying that Truman's plan for America was "Communist-conceived" and just an extension of the New Deal.[50] Evangelicals, particularly those in the American South, had supported New Deal policies in the 1930s, but they later turned against federal intervention, in part out of fear that they were losing religious authority, but also because many of the white evangelicals who had gained economic mobility through federal aid wanted to shut the door on those moving up behind them, especially African Americans.[51] The postwar American landscape was marked by political polarization at home but near political consensus on anticommunist policies abroad. Despite the domestic rifts, the ethical moralism of Marshall and Truman resonated with evangelicals.[52] And it was Billy Graham who emerged as the popular spokesman of that evangelical moralism. In 1949, Graham preached an anticommunist message at a revival in Los Angeles and was thrust onto the American scene by the media efforts of William Randolph Hearst, who told his newspaper and magazine staffers, "Puff Graham!" That year, Graham appeared on the cover of *Life*, *Time*, and *Newsweek* magazines.[53]

As free labor was to Charles Finney and the threat of communism to Billy Graham, so are the challenges of debt, AIDS, and terrorism in Africa to Bono. The economist Jeffrey Sachs, who served as an advisor for Jubilee 2000, has joined Bono in advocating that Africa be integrated into the world economy as part of a "global Marshall Plan." Both Bono and Sachs believe that the same model of political and economic integration applied to Europe in the mid-twentieth century should be applied to Africa in the new millennium. Gesturing to their predecessor, Bono and Sachs have argued that the best way to assure stability at home and abroad for the United States is to fight global poverty with aid and ideology, not to police other nations with military force.[54]

As a component of the global Marshall Plan, Bono envisions DATA as a vehicle of democratization through the expansion of capitalist markets. In his promotion of this plan, Bono employs a religious rhetoric of universal human rights and economic responsibility. In Bono's global Marshall Plan, however, there are problems of missionary endeavor, problems of political and economic occupation, problems of bureaucratic overlay, and problems of totalizing eschatology. And all of these problems are tied to the history of European and American colonization of Africa. Elevating Africa in the early twenty-first century is not comparable to reconstructing Europe after World War II. The redeemer myth of economic transparency ignores the legacy of wealth extraction and theft; it ignores the long history of white, Western kidnapping and enslavement of Africans and the exploitation of African labor. Bono does not object to this memory loss, this sweeping of history under the rug. In fact, he promotes it. He hopes that the political and economic integration of Africa into "transparent" global markets will not only eliminate poverty but, in effect, erase history. He has preached a policy of forgive and forget in order to move forward. In other words, Bono believes in spiritual and economic rebirth for black Africans as well as white Irishmen. He believes that the ugly parts of our history can be erased by grace and gift. This is his neoliberal dream, that after the flood all the colors come out.

But what happens when they don't? The election of Donald Trump to the U.S. presidency in 2016 disrupted the neoliberal narrative of political progress and humanitarian grace. Within the scheme of neoliberalism, does the current political moment amount to a dream delayed? Or is there something within the neoliberal system itself, something religious, that makes possible the political ascension of both Trump and Bono as competing consumer brands?

To put this battle of brands in perspective, consider a moment from a U2 concert during the U.S. presidential campaign of 2016. That fall, U2 performed a few shows in the United States, and, as always, they incorporated political theater into the performance.[55] At a show in the San Francisco Bay Area, at the end of "Bullet the Blue Sky," Bono revised the lyrics to attack and humiliate Trump. "I can see those fighter planes" became "I can see those golden towers, I can see those shopping malls . . . and the candidate looks over all his creation. And the candidate sees that it is good." Bono then began a scripted argument with media clips of Trump projected on the big screen behind him:

> Bono: And the candidate says.
> Trump: I'm really rich. Turned out I'm much richer than anybody ever knew. Billions and billions and billions of dollars.
> Bono: And your point is?
> Trump: I'm really rich. Turned out I'm much richer than anybody ever knew. Billions and billions and billions of dollars.
> Bono: Well, look, we're very glad for you, candidate. Sincerely, we are. Only real question we have for you this evening: "What is your vision for this great nation?"
> Trump: I will build a great, great wall on our southern border. And I will have Mexico pay for that wall.
> Bono: A wall? Like the Berlin Wall? Like the Great Wall of China? [Bono pronounced this "Gina" to mock Trump's pronunciation.]
> Trump: I will build a great, great wall on our southern border. And I will have Mexico pay for that wall.
> Bono: Now, candidate, you understand it's not just Mexican people who are going to have a problem with

this wall of yours. It's everyone who loves the idea of America. Like the Irish, for example. Or the French. Or the Brazilians. Everyone who loves the idea of America, everyone who believes what they read at the foot of the bottom of the Statue of Liberty. [Bono then rapped the words of the Emma Lazarus poem: "Give me your tired, your poor, your huddled masses yearning to breathe free . . ."]

Trump: If I win, they're going back.

Bono: All of them? I mean, all of us?

Trump: If I win, they're going back.

Bono: Now, candidate. You're going to make a lot of people very upset around here. Because, candidate, good people are not gonna stay silent while you run off with the American dream. All right, candidate? You hear me, candidate? Smart girls from the Bay Area: not going to stay silent. Even the nerdy guys around here are gettin' revved up: not gonna be silent. And these people here, they know a little bit about the business of America. And these guys have a message for you, candidate. You're fired!

Trump: I love the old days. You know what they used to do to guys like that? They'd be carried out on a stretcher, folks.

Bono: What? Guys like the Edge?

Trump: I'd like to punch him in the face.

Bono: Like Adam Clayton?

Trump: I'd like to punch him in the face.

Bono: Like Larry Mullen Jr.?

Trump: I'd like to punch him in the face.

Bono: Anyone who stands up to you? Anyone who speaks up? You want to punch 'em in the face?

Trump: Build that wall! Build that wall! Build that wall!

Bono: Inside, it's America. Inside, it's America . . . Fortress Americaaaaa![56]

Closing the scene, Bono grabs a bullhorn painted like the America flag. Edge plays and Bono shouts, "You wanna make America great again, or you wanna make America hate again?" Bono repeats the question and then goes into a *Hamilton*-style musical rap about the greatness and diversity of America, beginning with the founding fathers and building to Martin Luther King and his dream.

This staged spectacle of Bono challenging Trump embodies the political tensions of neoliberalism: nationalism versus globalization, fortress America versus immigrant America, a conservative moral ethic of family, private property, and racial hierarchy versus a liberal ethic of universal individual freedoms, private property, and human rights. In the battle of Bono versus Trump, Bono represents the normative claim that the global expansion of free-market capitalism is the best—indeed, the only—way to advance democratic governance and human rights. This is his neoliberal political promise, his map for the "journey to equality."

To U2 fans, Bono's neoliberal postulates may appear paradoxical, given his political opposition to Reagan and Thatcher in the 1980s. Onstage, Bono delivers a political counterpunch to politicians and other authority figures associated with unjust policies. As with all things neoliberal, though, cultural dissent is not just a conflict between ideas and ideals but a battle over the presentation and representation of ideas and ideals. Bono tells Charlie Rose, "America is like the best idea the world ever came up with. But Donald Trump is potentially the worst idea that ever happened to America, potentially."[57] Bono offers the neoliberal promise of what he calls the big idea, which is the idea of wealth making democracy, rather than wealth only for oneself. He sees the promise of religious liberty in the slaveholder Thomas Jefferson. He sees the political promise of individual freedom in the American founding fathers. He sees the dream of Martin Luther King as a demand to make good on those promises. Bono sees himself and his approach to politics, economics, and spiritual integrity as what could be. And he sees Trump as what was. Bono promotes the image of the cosmopolitan sophisticate, depicting Trump as a philistine: crass, self-interested, and insincere. Bono is what could be, but is not yet. Trump is what it is. Bono represents the normative claim of neoliberalism. Trump represents the political reaction to the cultural performance of unfulfilled promises. He is the revelatory realism of ethical failure.

In a descriptive sense, neoliberalism is defined by this moral tension. Bono and Trump both offer righteous dissent as a political product, to be circulated, broadcast, analyzed, bought, sold, and consumed. The difference between the two is signaled in their respective degrees of moralism. Bono claims the material realm in the name of spiritual transcendence, of divinely guaranteed universal human rights. Trump claims the material realm in the name of manifest social rank, of a divinely ordained class order. Bono versus Trump is a battle of brands. And within the moral framework of neoliberalism, branding is everything. The brand is what marks the product, and "the product," writes Kathryn Lofton, "is a material way to access something ineffable."[58] Bono's brand saves lives. Trump's brand terminates them. Bono promotes Product Red, which licenses consumer goods for corporations that agree to donate a portion of the profits from the sale of those goods to the ONE Campaign, the NGO that fights poverty and disease and works to eliminate HIV/AIDS in African nations. Trump promotes all things embossed with the name Trump, including his reality TV show *The Apprentice*, where he is the boss who gets to fire losing contestants. For both Bono and Trump, the brand is the shorthand that closes the conversational circle and walls out discourse. You can't talk about the issue, whatever the issue, without talking about how you feel about the brand rep, the celebrity. If you criticize Bono, then you must not want to save people from deadly disease, because he does. If you criticize Trump, then you must not understand the reality of business, because he does; just look at his wealth. The celebrity brands of Bono and Trump reflect their political differences, of morally righteous capitalism versus gilded ambition, of Moses with the tablets versus Aaron with the golden calf.

In the political atmosphere of Trumpism, Bono presents himself onstage and in conversation as if such differences are self-evident. Trump stands for white nationalism; Bono stands for racial justice. But if you dig a bit deeper, you can see that Bono shares with Trump an essentialist view of race and racial difference, just as he does a belief in the social benefits of class difference and an evolutionary view of human society. Bono claims an outsider racial status rooted in his Irish history. He expresses eternal love for African and African American musical and religious creativity. Bono also acknowledges that he is not black. All of this I address in more detail in chapter 5. Here, I focus on the performance of the brand, on how Bono speaks for you. On the stage in northern California, he stood in for the mistreated other, ready to take it on the chin for those pummeled by a candidate who gives voice to what others know better than to say out loud, that the accumulation of capital is violent and brutal, and that those who suffer its most direct punches are those it considers not white.

Brand Bono performs the cultural difference of love versus hate. Beyond the representation of that idea of difference, though, Bono shares Trump's views on capital accumulation and business practice. Trump refuses to release his tax returns. Bono, as part of the corporation called U2, refuses to pay taxes in Ireland. As Harry Browne explains in *The Frontman*, when the Irish government decreased its tax exemption for artists in 2006, capping it at 250,000 euros annually, U2 moved its publishing business to Amsterdam, where its royalty earnings were taxed at a 5 percent rate.[59] That's the kind of move Trump would approve of. Smart business. It's a move the Rolling Stones also made more than three decades ago. But only Bono avoids, when he can, paying taxes to his government and also asks that government to give aid to Africa. In terms of business practices, there is less difference between Bono and Trump than meets the eye. Both men are businessmen who seek to maximize their profits and avoid paying taxes as much as possible. But only Bono claims the moral high ground by saying he is uncomfortable with tax cuts for the rich. Reflecting on his relationship with President George W. Bush, for example, he said, "You put other stuff out of your mind: tax cuts for the rich and an up-and-coming war in Iraq."[60] The image of himself that Bono likes to project is that of a rock star who cares for the poor, is against tax cuts for the rich, and opposes U.S. military intervention abroad. Yet Bono the businessman benefits from tax cuts for the rich, and some of his wealth comes from investments in video war games. What, then, is the economic difference between Bono and Trump, beyond the cultural performance of an oppositional political disposition? Bono mocks Trump for his gilded towers, but Bono was part of his own development projects of architectural excess, including an attempt to build a U2 Tower with an "egg-shaped recording-studio on top."[61] Bono, like Trump, avoids taxes, builds towers, and has his own product line. The only difference is the brand, the feeling that the product offers the consumer.

In making this comparison, I am not trying to reveal hypocrisy but rather to show continuity. A discernable feature of neoliberalism is its clear boundaries between different brands. It is easy to get caught up in media comparisons of the relative material excess of various celebrities. It is easy to call Bono a hypocrite. But the gilded towers are beside the point. It is not excess in itself that is the sin for Bono. Given what Bono preaches about the business practices of entrepreneurial capitalism, he is not hypocritical. He sees no contradiction between capitalism and justice, the accumulation of wealth and the betterment of society. To see what Bono considers the ideological difference between him and his rival, let us return to the part of the concert sermon in which Bono congratulates Trump for being so rich, saying, "we're very glad for you, candidate. *Sincerely*, we are." If you watch and listen to video from the audience, you can hear the laughter of the fans, who assume that Bono is being ironic and means the opposite of what he says, just as other critics and comedians, from Stephen Colbert to Alec Baldwin, do. But here is where fans may miss the neoliberal religion around Bono. For within the context of his economic views, Bono really *is* sincerely glad for Trump, as he is for anyone who is wealthy. Trump's transgression is not his wealth but his lack of good ideas. Like Oprah, Bono sees nothing wrong in having money, lots of money. And not just nothing wrong, not just a double negative; no, Bono sees wealth accumulation as the reflection of natural virtue. The problem with Trump is simply his provincial thinking, his drive to protect the wealth of his clan, of those who are loyal to *him*. He cares only about himself and his tribe, narrowly defined, rather than loyalty to a transcendent cause.

This is the difference in brand between Bono and Trump. The Trump brand is a prestige product: high-rise condos to make the rich resident feel richer than his neighbor, or a border wall that symbolizes the racial superiority of whiteness. The Bono brand is marketed as the morally superior product that connects the consumer to someone in need. The Bono brand helps the nerdy tech guy at the U2 show feel connected to the civil rights movement, even if he never took part in a protest march. Trump is the guy who punches those nerds in the face. He's the lying bully who calls out the insecure fibbers. The Trump brand confers license to be amoral, to punch people in the face, or shoot people in the street; it doesn't matter. It only matters whether you win or lose. The Bono brand says that it does matter. Sincerity is the ultimate goal. To love your neighbors, to care for them, and to show you care through purchasing the moral product: that is what's important.

Bono's problem with Trump is not that he is wealthy but that he does not use the grand idea of capitalism, of free-market enterprise, to solve the great moral problems of global poverty and disease, and in that pursuit to make the idea of individual wealth globally available to any and all entrepreneurs. For Bono, Bill Gates is a great leader because he has used his wealth to foster the idea of American democracy. Bono places Gates in the lineage of the founding fathers in U.S. history, whom Bono describes as "the most powerful people in the Americas." "If you think of George Washington as the greatest landowner," he says, "that's like Bill Gates, in terms of wealth."[62] In his vision of creative entrepreneurial capitalism, Bono moves beyond the older Rockefeller model of philanthropic capitalism, or noblesse oblige. The goal is not just to give back but to create the market conditions for a neoliberal vision of social justice, which inheres in freedom of commerce, freedom to consume the curated products of cultural difference no matter your race, ethnicity, creed, or political persuasion.

Bono's version of entrepreneurial capitalism differs from philanthropic capitalism. In his view, commerce itself is the creative enterprise, not to be thought of as the nine-to-five drudgery that most people endure, and that is separate from the communal feeling of spiritual connection. Bono sees commerce as a spiritual vocation. "The engines of commerce" are "the creative engines," to be used to solve big problems. "The creative departments of Coca-Cola, they're great advertisers," he says. "Can we use their advertising?" he asks.[63] Yes! We can use their advertising, and we can use their refrigerated trucks to deliver lifesaving medicines to Africans in need. In the liberal model of philanthropic capitalism, a rich individual or corporation accumulates wealth through commerce and then gives some of that wealth back to organizations to help solve social problems. In the neoliberal model, the commercial transaction itself generates the problem-solving agents of change.

To see this difference between liberal and neoliberal models of social change, take an excerpt from Bono's interview with Charlie Rose on *CBS This Morning* in September 2016. As Bono explained his work with the ONE Campaign and its relationship to the Bill and Melinda Gates Foundation, Rose commented that the work of that foundation went "beyond profit." Bono softly corrected Rose, saying, "But using profit." Rose interjected, "Profit gives you the freedom to do it." Bono shifted in his chair and said, "Using, I suppose, yeah, it's entrepreneurial capitalism is part of the program now. And by the way, I started out as an activist who had no understanding or even regard for commerce. Now I understand that commerce is essential, and the most essential component for taking people out of extreme poverty." For Rose, who thinks in the context of the older liberal philanthropic model, profit, in the moral calculus, is something to be overcome. He looks at Bill Gates as someone who spent the first part of his life making money with Microsoft, and the second part giving a lot of it away to good causes like education and disease prevention in places like Africa. For Bono, by contrast, making money and helping others are two sides of the same coin, two parts of the same harmonious whole—in the same way that melodies and ideas, he says, are "the same thing." "Even little businesses, start-ups, they're like melody lines to me." In Bono's vision of entrepreneurial capitalism, melody and ideas are, or should be, for sale, written into the consumption of commodities.

In this neoliberal pursuit, making lots of money entails no burden of personal responsibility. Wealthy individuals are not required to give back. They can, but they don't have to, which is another difference between liberal philanthropy and neoliberal commerce. Rather, wealthy persons and corporations use their brand, their class status and cultural celebrity, to work with others of their class to create the ideas that will change the world. They are supposed to be the institutional architects of global society. Wealth, for Bono, should be invested in for-profit enterprises, not given to charities. Those with wealth should make more wealth, not divest themselves of it or redistribute it. Governments may give aid to other governments, but only by investing in institutions that are in line with the neoliberal principles of free-market capitalism.

To put it another way, consider this brand difference in religious terms. Bono is the monotheist who calls Trump a pagan. For historians of religion, a monotheist belongs to a moral community with a collective belief in a single deity that is outside human history. This deity is credited with creating the cosmos and also with having the power to destroy it, thus giving human history a beginning that happened in the past and an end that will happen in the future. Premillennial dispensationalism, a theological view of the end times in which Christian believers are raptured, a tribulation occurs, and then Jesus returns to earth to usher in a millennial reign (a view shared by many evangelicals), is one example of a monotheistic view of linear human history. In the history of religions, monotheism evolved as various theological systems tried to purify preceding religious beliefs by rejecting the idea that the divine could appear in multiple forms within human history, and by denying that time was cyclical, that the cosmos was eternal, and that divine beings existed within those cosmic limits. Monotheists historically condemned such beliefs—the religions they set themselves against—as pagan. Monotheists believed that pagans worshipped false gods that were mere reflections of human desires or social motives. Monotheists contrasted pagan gods with one true God that transcended human history.

Such theological distinctions are complicated and tedious, and fraught with comparisons and rankings of ideas and beliefs as better or worse, true or false. I make this religious comparison not so as to rank monotheism above other religions, but by way of suggesting that monotheists cannot operate without such ranking and classification, since they believe in the moral superiority of their belief system, a superiority that cannot be claimed without the competitive threat of other gods. Monotheism not only creates the possibility of transgression—as false belief and insincere conviction—but demands that the transgression be expressed in a person or practice that can be readily contrasted with true belief and pure intention. The price of monotheism, argues Jan Assman, is the purification and expulsion of paganism and heresy. Monotheists, he contends, are "marked in their self understanding by an 'antagonistic acculturation,' and they have strong ideas about what is incompatible with the truth (or orthodoxy) they proclaim."[64] Monotheism does not make sense without an ongoing relationship with what it deems false beliefs and practices, contrasted with its own sincere belief and true practice.

Bono calls Trump a pagan threat to his monotheism. Trump is the sovereign king who seeks the favor of powerful divines, including the king of kings, only when he needs something. Why else would Trump visit the fundamentalist evangelical Liberty University, if not to get votes? And why else would evangelical pastors lay hands on him, if not to elect him president? He asked their blessing, and they gave it with their conditions. Bono is upset because he wanted to offer the blessing, on his own, higher terms. He lost out to the religious authorities. And so he considers them, like Trump, false. Bono speaks on behalf of the moral community that is his secular church. And then he contrasts his higher calling with Trump's self-interested moral relativism. Bono speaks in the name of love. Trump speaks in the name of Trump.

In the comparison between Bono and Trump, I am interested in the monotheist's claim to difference. Bono can only make this claim of promoting universal justice and equality in terms of antagonism to a competing brand. And the claim to wanting justice for all is his litmus test for global cosmopolitanism and political civility, which Trump, the discredited pagan, disregards. In the battle of brands between himself and Trump, Bono stands at the limit of neoliberal religion, unable to move forward. There is no shared political prayer on the horizon of this presidential term. There is no civility, conciliation, or consensus, no common cause. And so, onstage in concert, Bono and the band invoked the evangelical revival tradition. They looked back, in 2017, and relived the Joshua Tree Tour, playing the songs of their sacred past to stadium crowds, taking refuge in the spiritual landscape of the 1980s, framing the current issues of the day in the moral context of a continent in flames.[65]

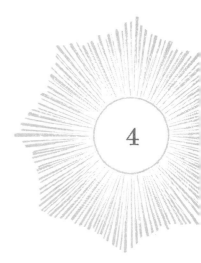

AROUND AFRICA

Bono says that Africa needs more globalization, not less. "One of Africa's big problems," he tells us, "is trying to foster an entrepreneurial culture. . . . Globalization has become a pejorative term, but it's meaningless. Globalization is like saying communication. Globalization has happened formally since deregulating international flow of money, going back to the eighties. . . . Africa needs more globalization now [in the early 2000s] than less. 'I think it's really funny! Globalization! What's it doing to Africa?' And Africans are saying: 'What do you mean? We can't get any!' What critics mean is the abuse of globalization."[1]

This chapter looks at critical complaints about globalization and economic intervention in Africa, examines humanitarian responses to that criticism by capitalists invested in the continent, and argues that humanitarian capitalist responses derive their meaning from a cultural system of neoliberal religion around Africa, a cultural system with which evangelicalism is entangled and which is a site of contestation between global corporate control and local communal autonomy. As multinational corporations seek greater access to African markets, evangelicalism continues to spread, rather rapidly, across the continent, particularly in sub-Saharan Africa, the locus of reform for Bono, Jeffrey Sachs, Bill Gates, and others. It is unclear how the spread of evangelicalism and overlapping charismatic movements will affect the economic development of the region. But it is clear that global elites are promoting the development of African Christianity in the image of American evangelicalism.

Not all evangelicals in Africa support neoliberal policies or Western intervention. But if the religious history of the United States suggests a pattern, the spread of evangelicalism may favor the economic interests of wealthy elites, in that it can create a religious environment of radical individualism and foster suspicion of public institutions, while bolstering faith in private companies that model evangelical business principles, all of which cultivates cultural conditions that allow neoliberal policies to persist, despite opposition. There has never been an enduring evangelical Left in the United States.[2] Whether there can be a sustained evangelical Left in Africa remains to be seen.[3] Historically, collective social activism and alternative community formations that signal an evangelical Left have emerged within frontier spaces but have been subsumed by the dominant economy once the frontier closed. The question whether modern evangelicalism can resist the pressure of consumer capitalism in Africa, as it has not done in America, is beyond the scope of this book to address. Nor does this chapter address the varieties of Christianity and economic models in Africa. Rather, it examines the ways in which elites who promote the neoliberal religion around Bono absorb economic critiques, and how they incorporate those critiques into their moral vision of paternalistic intervention.

External control is the operatic echo of philanthropic performance. Under the older top-down model of foreign aid, Western nations used the promise that they would give financial aid to African nations to help them feed their poor and hungry, in order to extend globalization on the continent, not merely as the internal deregulation of financial flows but as a system in which they control the global conditions of local economic development. The power to control is in the promise itself, manifest in the potential for financial exchange, and in the actual monetary amount of aid, which often was less than what Western nations promised to give. Take the example of Live 8, another iteration of Live Aid and another promotional display of global solidarity on behalf of the African poor. On July 2, 2005, crowds gathered at venues in the United Kingdom, France, Germany, Italy, the United States, Canada, Japan, South Africa, and Russia for benefit concerts, the goal of which was to "make poverty history" by influencing world politicians. To this end, the estimated three billion viewers were asked to give their names and not their money for the cause. The global display culminated in a concert finale, which the organizers called the "Final Push," in Edinburgh, Scotland, on July 4, the first day of the G8 summit meetings at the nearby Gleneagles Hotel.[4] By some accounts, the concert series did sway political opinion. For example, DATA reported that the G8 promised to "increase aid to Africa by US $25 billion by 2010."[5] Buoyed by this success, Bono described Live 8 as a "movement of church people and trade unionists, soccer moms and student activists" that gave "the poorest of the poor real political muscle for the first time."[6]

But that political muscle was not strong enough to hold politicians to their promises. A year after the summit, Oliver Buston, European director of DATA, reported that the G8 had followed through on only half of the commitments made at Gleneagles.[7] Some critics have argued that such lack of follow-through was intentional, or at least that the G8 promises were intentionally misleading. Stuart Hodkinson described the reality of the G8:

> More than half of the promised $50 billion in aid—which wouldn't kick in until 2010—wasn't really new money at all, but a dishonest amalgam of old pledges, future aid budgets and debt relief. And despite [the G8's statement] that "poor countries should be free to determine their own economic policies," only Britain had announced it would no longer tie overseas aid to free market reforms—a promise it would instantly break in the G8 debt deal. The US, in contrast, had made it immediately clear at Gleneagles that aid increases would require "reciprocal liberalisation" by developing countries. Worse, as Yifat Susskind, associate director of US-based women's human rights organization,

Madre, explains, Bush's "millennium challenge account," specifically praised by Bono and Geldof, "explicitly ties aid to cooperation in the US's "war on terror.""[8]

Western nations not only used aid but also the promise of aid to demand that African nations consent to free-market reforms, the type of reforms that gave companies like Monsanto a foothold in local economic development, and also that they agree to support U.S. foreign policy. Western nations withdrew aid that was intended to help relieve African debts and then offered it again, this time with more conditions. The net result was that African nations remained in debt to multilateral creditors, such as the IMF, the World Bank, and the African Development Bank. Eric Toussaint, of the Belgium-based Committee for the Abolition of Illegitimate Debt (formerly the Committee for the Cancellation of Third World Debt), surmised, "This precious funding will only be returned if countries meet 'specific policy criteria'—more long years of privatisation and liberalisation that increases school fees, health-care costs and VAT [value-added tax], removes subsidies for basic products and creates unfair competition between local producers and transnational corporations, all of which hurts the poor."[9]

Corporations that benefited from the extraction of African resources and the privatization of public services in African nations sponsored the G8 summit.[10] Hodkinson reported that "the corporate sponsors assembled by the organisers included: Nestlé, accused of exploiting the HIV/AIDS epidemic in Africa to sell more milk substitute products to infected mothers; Rio Tinto, the world's largest mining corporation, widely condemned for its longstanding record of human rights and environmental abuses across the global South; and Britain's biggest arms manufacturer, BAE Systems, whose export-led agenda, according [to] Mike Lewis of the UK's Campaign Against Arms Trade (CAAT), is 'fuelling conflicts across Africa, with catastrophic impacts on development, and diverting spending away from health and education.'"[11]

When asked what he thought about the G8 summit at Gleneagles and the promise to "beef up the development aid for Africa," Kenyan economist James Shikwati told the German news magazine *Der Spiegel*,

"For God's sake, please just stop." The *Spiegel* interviewer, though, didn't understand the response:

> *Der Spiegel*: Stop? The industrialized nations of the West want to eliminate hunger and poverty.
>
> Shikwati: Such intentions have been damaging our continent for the past 40 years. If the industrial nations really want to help the Africans, they should finally terminate this awful aid. The countries that have collected the most development aid are also the ones that are in the worst shape. Despite the billions that have poured in to Africa, the continent remains poor.

Still, the interviewer needed an explanation, so Shikwati explained how foreign aid encourages bureaucratic corruption, weakens local markets, hinders entrepreneurship, and creates more problems than it solves.[12]

Note two things about this exchange. First, the German interviewer meets Shikwati's resistance to foreign aid to Africa with well-intentioned surprise; the West just wants to feed the hungry and help the poor prosper. What's wrong with that? Second, Shikwati's opposition to outside intervention and foreign aid is based on the principal economic assumptions of neoliberalism and globalization—namely, that deregulating markets and encouraging business entrepreneurship and free trade, not handouts, is the path to prosperity. Given that Western neoliberals share similar principles and promote them in their own societies, you might think they would welcome such a position. But they don't. "Shockingly misguided" and "amazingly wrong"—this is how Jeffrey Sachs described Shikwati's position. For Sachs, Shikwati's libertarian policies threaten humanitarian goals. Like the *Spiegel* interviewer, Sachs made an implicit moral judgment about Shikwati's view, saying, "This happens to be a matter of life and death for millions of people, so getting it wrong has huge consequences."[13]

The *Spiegel* interview and Sachs's reaction illustrate how the moral defense of neoliberal intervention in Africa is not always a matter of one religious view against another. Nor is it simply a matter of capitalism versus communism.[14] Shikwati shares with Sachs an unyielding faith in the doctrinal truth of free-market capitalism. Sachs's dismissal of Shikwati is not like his resistance to communism. Rather, the two men are engaged in a sectarian squabble over interpretive authority from within the same overarching belief system. Shikwati is a self-trained libertarian economist who bases his views on the work of conservative free-market economist Larry Reed, who has served as president of the Foundation for Economic Education in Manhattan and the Mackinac Center for Public Policy in Michigan. In a 2006 article, the *New York Times* described how "Mr. Shikwati was a young teacher in western Kenya when he came across an article by Mr. Reed on the genius of capitalism." Shikwati wrote to Reed in Michigan, and "over the next four years, Mr. Reed sent books, reports, magazines, tracts—even occasional sums of money—as Mr. Shikwati embraced capitalist theory with a passion. Then he started a one-man think tank of his own." Nine months later, the *Times* noted, he was invited to a Heritage Foundation dinner in the United States and was celebrated by Reed as a "passionate advocate for liberty in an unlikely place."[15]

The Heritage Foundation has promoted, since the late 1970s, what is best described as a fundamentalist evangelical view of free-market capitalism. The mission of the Washington, D.C.–based think tank is "to formulate and promote conservative public policies based on the principles of free enterprise, limited government, individual freedom, traditional American values, and a strong national defense."[16] The Heritage Foundation was influential in the Reagan revolution of the early 1980s, and has since been a powerful force in shaping conservative policy, offering staff and advice to Republican administrations in the United States. Historians of American religion have observed that the kind of economic mission the Heritage Foundation promotes runs deep in evangelical Christianity. According to historian Sarah Hammond, "groups such as the Christian Business Men's Committee International, the Business Men's Evangelistic Clubs, and the Gideons . . . believed that businessmen were God's instruments to Christianize the world." From the 1930s on, evangelical businessmen saw industrialization and consumer goods as material means to Christian conversion. They fought against organized labor and modeled the factory after their vision of Christian community. They used industrial profits to fund evangelical outreach, including worship services, revivals, and Bible studies. And they believed that "if they could convince the masses to buy their products," writes Hammond, "then they must try to bend them to God's will."[17]

Shikwati's criticism of Western aid is expressed as a kind of layman's dissent that aims to correct what he sees as the misguided ways of the institutional elites who govern the world. The economic philosophy of Shikwati's libertarianism shares an elective affinity with American evangelicalism, or a mutual attraction of political and religious ideals for how to use private wealth and support entrepreneurial innovation. Both libertarianism and evangelicalism are cultural carriers of a radically disruptive antiestablishment impulse. Bono has promoted the institutionalization of this dissent in organizations like DATA and the ONE Campaign, despite his disavowal of organized religion. These organizations, and others like them, create a desire to help others in need, and then control the proper release of that desire, funneling that help only through the institutional channels that they promote. This is a pattern familiar to historians of American evangelicalism. Donald G. Mathews describes the essence of evangelicalism as "preaching liberty to the captives." And he shows how, over the course of the nineteenth century, white evangelicals hijacked a social movement with the potential to overturn the established racial and class order. They turned the promise of justice for all to narrower ends, in order to achieve economic upward mobility and social and political influence for themselves alone. By "creating their own institutions and networks of communication," Mathews argues, "white Evangelicals finally achieved—in their own minds at least—the pinnacle of refinement and respectability."[18]

The history of American evangelicalism and business shows that preaching liberty to the captives almost always results in economic terms favorable to free-market capitalism. Socialism is rarely if ever an option. And when socialism has been attempted, whether in religious communes or labor organizations, it has been short-lived, quickly suppressed and turned to the familiar end of economic profit for the few. The radical edge of evangelicalism is its economic individualism, not its labor collectivity. The evangelical emphasis on individual sovereignty and local autonomy is potentially disruptive to the social consolidation of political control in any institutional system. What Shikwati professes is exactly that, an attempt to regain individual sovereignty for business entrepreneurs and local autonomy for small business owners. In the United States, evangelicalism has promoted such efforts. And in Africa, evangelicalism will probably continue to play a similar role. In the *Times* article, for example, there is a telling moment when Shikwati visits a home in Bukura to show how his libertarian model of malaria control works. Wilberforce Mutokaa tells how he is glad to have his mud hut sprayed for mosquitos to prevent malaria, the service paid for by Shikwati in the hope that Mutokaa will pay for future treatments, once he realizes the benefits. On the wall of the hut is "a poster of the evangelist T. D. Jakes," an African American minister and proponent of the prosperity gospel.[19]

Evangelicals have a missionary interest in Africa, while multinational corporations have an economic interest. But these interests are mutually reinforcing. In their attempt to gain converts, missionaries translate local histories into modern futures, depicting their would-be Christians not as blank slates, exactly, but as native people in need of civilizing, personhood, technology, and, most important, their help. Christian missionaries promote a process of denial that erases the existing religion of the people. Describing this process in South Africa, historian of religion David Chidester argues that, in the nineteenth century, "total denial was a comparative strategy particularly suited for the conditions of a contested frontier. On the battlefield, the enemy had no religion. At the front lines of a contest of religions, Christian missionaries adopted this strategy of denial."[20] Though missionary efforts have evolved over the course of centuries, with some missionary epistemologies shifting recently to a more postmodern approach that seeks to "contextualize the gospel in the local culture," the common cause of Christian missions, from the nineteenth century to the present, is to offer Christian conversion to native people in need of good news.[21] And this is where the religion around Bono, which serves the interests of multinational corporations, takes the stage to deliver the neoliberal gospel of millennial commerce.

Conversion, however, does not always mean consent. The political outcome of conversion is not always a given. Conversion to the religion of empire does not guarantee acquiescence to authorities who do not impose the same set of economic rules on all citizens and subjects. What it does guarantee, historians and anthropologists tell us, is a structuring convergence toward common communication that does not necessarily demand shared meaning but compels the speaker to use its medium, so that professions of belief and proclamations of dissent share the same narrative genre, of autobiography and testimony, of personhood, of a modern self with personal agency, a new self that makes its own future and is held accountable for that self-making.[22] To ensure submission to new world freedom, outside influence is necessary, in order to maintain the given advantages in the system that predispose outcomes that favor those in power. Foreign aid provides this kind of outside influence, as a religious source of political control, to be used for certain ends and particular purposes. It is crucial that those who benefit from the system as it is address, contain, and redirect dissent. And this is what Bono and other capitalist humanitarians do: they offer assurance that they hear, support, and speak for righteous dissenters, but they do so in a way that ultimately reframes the dissent as support of the economic agenda of the political establishment.

Corporate economic intervention can adapt to criticism, but it maintains a humanitarian moralism that is a secular expression of evangelical mission, replete with the affective power of spiritual goodness. Bono is one celebrity manifestation of this neoliberal religious power. He offers an "affective investment" for corporations, politicians, and charitable organizations to use for their purposes.[23] This investment carries with it a politically expressive form of cultural evangelicalism that limits economic alternatives as it absorbs African dissent in a way that perpetuates outsider intervention and regulates internal access to self-sustaining resources. The result is continued African economic dependence on the humanitarian gifts of Western nations, corporations, and consumers.

To see how Bono absorbs critique without changing his thinking, consider his reaction to the Ghanaian economist George B. N. Ayittey. In 2005, Ayittey published *Africa Unchained: The Blueprint for Africa's*

Future, in which he argues that African problems should be solved by Africans, adding skeptically, "Africans have no future because their leaders don't use their heads and the Western donors who give them money don't use theirs either."[24] Rather than use traditional institutional channels of Western aid funneled through governmental bureaucracies, Ayittey advocated grassroots entrepreneurial capitalism. Bono found this approach compelling and was directly influenced by Ayittey, whom he later met at a 2007 TED conference. What convinced Bono in Ayittey's work was the concern with institutional corruption and the emphasis on entrepreneurship. Both of these concerns resonated with his evangelical suspicion of public institutions. And it is fair to say that Bono has listened to most everything in the critiques of Ayittey and others like him except the part about Africans solving African problems. Consonant with the history of white evangelicals in the United States, he is unwilling, or unable, to stop trying to control dissenting voices and social movements. In Ayittey's and Shikwati's criticism of corrupt bureaucracies, Bono finds another justification for foreign intervention, through aid that comes with conditions. Michka Assayas once asked him, "Have you ever said to yourself, these people may be right, I may be wrong?" Bono replied, "Oh yeah . . . I realized that a lot of aid for instance had been incredibly badly mishandled over the years, creating worse situations. It's not enough just to ask for money. I learnt that the skeptics and the cynics had a real point, and that without strict conditionalities, there was no point in giving. You're actually propping up sometimes the most evil despots by aid."[25] Here again, Bono invokes a moral imperative. No one with goodness in his heart wants to fund evil despots. So foreign aid needs strict "conditionalities."

This type of humanitarian intervention, then, claims to take criticism seriously by demanding that foreign aid come with conditions. One of those conditions is that recipients agree to a kind of agricultural reform in which multinational corporations are the principal reforming institutions. Consider two examples. In 2006, the same year that Bono delivered his speech at the National Prayer Breakfast, the Bill and Melinda Gates Foundation joined the Rockefeller Foundation in establishing the Alliance for Green Revolution in Africa (AGRA).[26] Bono and the ONE Campaign fully embraced AGRA's "sustainable agriculture agenda," which featured agreements with biotech seed producer Monsanto to introduce and distribute genetically modified seeds in Africa.[27] And in 2008, Warren Buffett and Bill Gates gave a $47 million grant to the Water Efficient Maize for Africa (WEMA) project. The goal of the program, sponsored by the Bill and Melinda Gates Foundation, was to offer drought-resistant corn varieties to African farmers in order to increase yield. The program also partnered with Monsanto, a company from which the Gates Foundation in 2010 bought half a million shares of stock for $27 million, to develop and offer the seeds free to farmers in at least five nations in sub-Saharan Africa, with royalty payments arranged through the organizations that distributed the seeds.[28] At the 2012 G8 summit, Monsanto announced its commitment to invest $50 million in African agricultural development, focusing specifically on Tanzania.[29] These types of interventions are significant because they illustrate the neoliberal strategy of using a life-and-death moral crisis, in this case malnutrition and starvation, to justify economic intervention and the political expansion of corporate control and property rights in a frontier market.

On the issue of agricultural reform, the interventionist approaches supported by the Gates Foundation ultimately serve the economic interests of global corporations, not the actual needs of local communities. According to Phil Bereano, professor emeritus in the field of technology and public policy at the University of Washington, "Gates's grants do not support locally defined priorities, they do not fit within the holistic approach urged by many development experts and they do not investigate the long-term effectiveness and risks of genetic modification."[30] Much of the debate over agricultural reform is centered on technology, on whether genetically modified organisms are safe, and on whether they can be effective in drought conditions. While these are important questions, for the purpose of understanding religion around Bono, I am interested in Bereano's point that the key issue in this case is not technology but control. "Food sovereignty," he argues, "is about ownership and power." "The difference," he says, "is not a difference between people who are pro-technology and Luddites. No one wants to see starving people in Africa. People understand climate change is a major threat, but the justification of these kinds of technologies changes. They used to say GM food was required to feed the world; now they say it's required to feed the world and deal with climate change."[31] How proponents of agricultural reform adapt to critique is significant, for it reveals the underlying TINA doctrine of neoliberalism, that there is no alternative. Any evidence that suggests that there are other ways to feed the world is dismissed, suppressed, or, when acknowledged, shelved by a new crisis that demands an immediate response.[32]

AGRA, for example, responded to criticism of the top-down institutional model of its green revolution, which allows multinational corporations, NGOs, and government officials to make decisions that affect local farmers, by reforming its approach. It did so by promoting a farmer-led model that encouraged dialogue between institutional officials and African farm leaders. But according to Eric Holt-Giménez, director of the Institute for Food and Development Policy, and Raj Patel, a research professor at the LBJ School of Public Affairs at the University of Texas, this dialogue happened after decisions had already been made. And even when biotech companies supported the input of local farmers, they did so only as long as that input supported their vision and yielded to their control. Biotech companies, for example, supported the International Assessment of Agricultural Knowledge, Science and Technology for Development (IAASTD) in 2008, but one of the conclusions of that assessment was that biotech ownership and GM seeds were not the best way forward, and that "achieving food security and sustainable livelihoods for people now in chronic poverty requires ensuring access to and control of resources by small-scale farmers." As Holt-Giménez and Patel explain, "even though the idea of a worldwide agricultural assessment originally came from the biotechnology industry, when it became clear that genetically modified seeds were not to be hailed as the solution to the food crisis, both Syngenta and Monsanto abandoned the IAASTD process, and refused to endorse the final report."[33]

Against that backdrop, Bono's policy mentor, the economist Jeffrey Sachs, while director of Columbia University's Earth Institute, argued that Monsanto's drought-resistant seeds, used in Malawi, for example, could only help. He dismissed "human safety concerns" as insignificant. And he felt that concerns about the property rights of farmers had been addressed. Such rights were controversial, as Monsanto owned the technology in the seed, and if the seed spread to another farmer's crop, then Monsanto owned that farmer's crop, and if a farmer saved seed purchased from Monsanto to grow in another season, then Monsanto filed suit against him. But Sachs believed that none of this would be a problem in Africa. On the pattern of Monsanto's suing farmers over patent rights, Sachs said, "I frankly don't believe they're going to fool around on this. I'm quite convinced they want to find a way to do this—but not as their moneymaker. They need to be aware of handling this with a lot of sensitivity." To demonstrate that sensitivity, Monsanto announced that it would not charge farmers royalties for their patented seeds, but would instead issue the license to organizations that distributed aid. Those organizations would pay for the license and then issue a sublicense to the farmers free of charge. The net outcome of this arrangement is that Monsanto still owns the seeds and receives payment for that ownership. Describing this arrangement, Sachs expressed faith in the corporation's good intentions, saying, "in general there is an issue with intellectual property vis-à-vis the very poor. It came up with the AIDS medicines. And I think the analogy is very real here, as well. . . . When I spoke to Monsanto, I stressed that they're going to have to take lessons from what was initially a debacle—where medicines were not available to the very poor. . . . There are ways to use the patent system but apply it to high income markets. Make it available to the poor essentially at production cost. If it is done this way it answers some of the concerns—not all of them but many."[34] In Sachs's professed faith in Monsanto we see another glimmer of religion in the system. Belief in the good intentions of those in power signals a political belief in progressive civility, of good will from those who don't have to give but give anyway.

Bobby Shriver introduced Bono to Jeffrey Sachs, in order to prep him for his lobbying efforts with U.S. politicians in the lead-up to the Jubilee 2000 campaign. Bono was his self-described "rock star student," fully convinced by Sachs's "operatic" passion, the "wildness" of his rhetoric juxtaposed with the "rigor" of his logic.[35] Sachs studied with the economist Abram Bergson at Harvard, an authority on the Soviet economy. Bergson introduced Sachs to economists associated with the

Mont Pelerin Society, which promotes neoliberal economic policies and whose members "see danger in the expansion of government, not least in state welfare, in the power of trade unions and business monopoly, and in the continuing threat and reality of inflation."[36] Sachs became associated with "shock therapy" (a term that Sachs does not like), which removed market regulations and imposed what Japhy Wilson describes as "neoliberal reforms, including privatization, trade liberalization, macroeconomic stabilization, and the abolition of subsidies and price controls." Shock therapy was marked by its suddenness and rapid pace. Such suddenness was, Wilson explains, Sachs's attempt to return to a "natural order" of things, rather than toward a socially constructed future "utopian reality."[37] Belief in this "natural order," though, demands a religious anthropology, or an economic view of the world based on a "just so" story about the origins and inevitability of capitalism. Other economists have argued that there is no such once-upon-a-time, no divine hand that writes the story. Instead, we write our own history. In the mid-twentieth century, Karl Polanyi observed that a self-regulating market is not "natural."[38] "*Laissez faire*," he wrote, "was enforced by the state."[39] Highlighting Polanyi's point, Ronaldo Munck has noted that "since [the 1990s] the notion of economic 'reform' has become synonymous with 'opening up' the market and driving back the state."[40]

When applied in various parts of the world, Sachs's economic model failed dramatically. Sachs's approach was first applied in Bolivia, where it ended hyperinflation and transformed the country into a free-market economy but also "increased poverty and political repression."[41] Sachs's economic program was then applied to eastern Europe and Russia after the fall of communism at the end of the 1980s. One commentator declared that Sachs's shock therapy in Russia produced "the longest and deepest recession in recorded human history."[42] Sachs concluded that the Russian effort had been corrupted by the misguided communist attempt to impose an imagined state as economic reality. After the failure in Russia, Sachs focused on cleansing capitalism of its social diseases, in order to restore it to its "natural" state. Determined to avoid another failure, he tried with even greater force to engineer the natural state within which a self-regulating market could flourish. Unlike Russia, with its flawed economic history, sub-Saharan Africa, to Sachs, had no economic history; lacking a capitalist past, it was the perfect, pristine proving ground for his theory. He felt certain that his model would work in the region which he viewed as unspoiled by faulty versions of economic development.

So Africa became the petri dish for Sachs's revised "clinical economics." Using a medical metaphor, Sachs imagined the African economy as an important limb of the sick body of capitalism, which needed to be returned to its natural state of health. Drawing on his forebear Adam Smith, Sachs assumed that capital accumulation is "natural and inevitable."[43] Africa was a site where Sachs could imagine the origins of capitalism in "a single farm household."[44] He thus advocated external state intervention and international aid as necessary steps to restore capitalism to its natural state of health and order.

For Sachs, what hindered the natural entrepreneurs of Africa was the lack of economic infrastructure. One of his key initiatives, the Millennium Villages Project, invests public-sector funds in rural areas of Africa to improve quality of life through economic interventions that aim simultaneously to end poverty while increasing private-sector saving and investments. The goal of this project is to provide the roads, transportation, clinics, electricity, clean drinking water, and education that poor villagers need in order to realize their entrepreneurial essence.[45] For Sachs, "Almost all of Africa is the private sector. Farmers, that's the private sector . . . but they can't get started because they're so impoverished. So we should help a private sector-led development by helping these farmers use inputs, boost their productivity. . . . Bring in microfinance and let them rip. And that's basically the model."[46]

The capital inputs that Sachs promoted were supposed to connect local African farmers to the global market of large-scale agribusiness, a development that invariably reduces the overall number of farmers in favor of large-scale industrial production. In U.S. history, the rise of industrial agriculture significantly reduced the number of African American farmers and put those who remained in debt to multinational companies like Monsanto. It is difficult to imagine a different result, using the same model of agricultural reform, in Africa.

Integrating private farmers into the global economy, without protections, rather than supporting local agricultural systems, creates greater dependency on multinational corporations that are protected by Western governments. Small African farmers, for example, are encouraged to give up farming and find other types of work considered entrepreneurial and not subsistence-based. The history of farming in Africa has always been one of tension between local farmers trying to feed their communities and multinational corporations that grow cash crops on fertile land, pushing local farmers onto marginal land. "Aid and debt forgiveness also stifled state-led industrialization and development," notes historian Alan McPherson, "because they required 'structural adjustments including dismantling national food schemes and systems of credit, import quotas, price controls, and reserve stocks. . . . National governments pushed farmers to shift prime irrigated lands to production for export.'"[47] One result of increased agricultural globalization, in Africa as elsewhere, has been food insecurity. But Sachs does not advocate that corporate ownership of land, which has grown over time, be ended or dismantled. Nor does he advocate that land owned by large multinational corporations be repurposed to grow native crops that could be used to feed the world, crops that are less profitable, crops that have local value but not market value.[48]

The story of agricultural reform in Africa illustrates how economic models that promote the neoliberal practices of privatization, free markets, and corporate intervention deflect criticism while ultimately limiting small farmers' access to resources they need to ensure that local communities are self-sustaining. Evangelicalism is entangled in these issues of development and aid in ways that are not yet understood or easy to predict.[49] It is unclear whether the spread of evangelicalism in Africa will foster support for or suspicion of biotechnology. In the United States, there is no single evangelical view on genetically modified crops. Fundamentalist evangelical farmers actively resist the use of GM crops and corporate-driven industrial agriculture, while a presumed majority of evangelical consumers accept (or are unaware of) the use of biotechnology in food production.[50] Research in Africa on attitudes toward the use of GM crops suggests that religious organizations, along with NGOs, are key players in resisting institutions that promote their use, which in South Africa, for example, include "academia, government, producer and consumer organizations, and industry."[51]

Further, those who promote biotech interventions in Africa tend to see the religious rejection of GM crops as influenced by a misguided cultural resistance to the agricultural science of the United States and Europe.[52] Parsing the details of this debate is beyond the scope of this book, but I mention it in order to signal the significance of evangelicalism as a potential obstacle to multinational corporations that seek to expand markets throughout the continent. This book is concerned with the religion around Bono, a religion that diffuses evangelicalism into broader spheres of everyday life while spreading a neoliberal religion that is focused on Africa. As promoters of neoliberalism seek inroads into Africa, evangelical missionaries continue to foster various sectarian affiliations. Whether those missionary ventures will affect the future profits of multinational corporations positively or negatively is uncertain, which means that corporations need Bono, or, more precisely, the religion around Bono, to help control that outcome.

To get a sense of the global impact of evangelical Protestantism on Africa, take these statistics, cited by Asteris Huliaras: "In 1900 only 7% of the world's evangelicals lived in the Third World. By 1985 this share had shifted to 66%." In 2002, evangelical churches had nearly 800 million adherents worldwide, of whom some 500 million resided in the global South. And evangelicalism (especially its Pentecostal and charismatic varieties) is growing most spectacularly in Africa.[53] Consider also that as of 2011, according to the Pew Forum on Religion and Public Life, sub-Saharan Africa was home to 38 percent of the world's evangelical population, 44 percent of the world's Pentecostal population, and 17 percent of the world's charismatic population. Based on Pew projections, 40 percent of the world's Christian population will reside in sub-Saharan Africa by 2060. That number includes Catholics as well as Protestants, but the breakdown in 2011 put Protestants at 57 percent, Catholics at 34 percent, and members of the Eastern Orthodox (Catholic) Church at 8 percent. So Protestantism already has a numerical head start and is projected to increase its lead among Christians, with evangelicals having the most to gain. According to Pew, "Sub-Saharan Africa [in 2011] has both the greatest concentration of evangelical Christians and the largest share of the world's evangelicals." To put that in perspective, there are more evangelicals in sub-Saharan

Africa than there are in the Americas, according to Pew. Still, within sub-Saharan Africa, evangelicalism is a relatively small percentage of the overall population, which means that there is room to grow. In 2011, evangelicals made up only 13 percent, Pentecostals only 15 percent, and charismatics only 7 percent of the region's total Protestant population.[54]

Pew's figures notwithstanding, such self-identifying labels are difficult to quantify. What is clear is that sub-Saharan Africa is in the midst of a bull market for evangelical—including Pentecostal and charismatic—forms of Christianity, which all overlap with one another. These groups gain both new converts from outside Christianity and defectors from other Christian denominations. Against this backdrop, sub-Saharan Africa is the focus of Bono's and Sachs's advocacy efforts as well as the investment focus of multinational corporations. And while the future appears promising for Western missionaries, corporations, and financiers, it is not guaranteed. There are competitors in the region. Pew projects that Islam, another monotheistic missionary religion, will grow significantly in the coming decades, increasing from 16 to 27 percent of the global Muslim population.[55] In fact, Islam in sub-Saharan Africa is projected to grow at a faster rate than Christianity, though Christians would still outnumber Muslims. In 2010, Christians made up 63 percent and Muslims 30 percent of the regional totals. By 2050, Christians are projected to be at 59 percent and Muslims at 35 percent of the total population.

As noted in chapter 3, Bono uses the threat of Islamic extremism in Africa to help justify his vision of a Marshall Plan for the continent. Onstage, though, Bono promotes peace among all of Abraham's children. He promises equality for all who practice good religion. The sectarian name of that religion is less important to him than the political and economic positions it promotes. Bono never says that he fears the spread of good Islam in Africa. He just tells the politicians of the West that they should fear the spread of Islamic extremism there. He is concerned less about whether a person is Muslim or Christian than whether a given national government and economic system are favorable to the free-market principle that private corporations should be the primary building blocks of nation-states. Historically, evangelical religion has fostered cultural conditions favorable to neoliberal economic principles. In the United States, it has promoted these principles since the Reagan era of the 1980s, and it prepared the ground for economic neoliberalism even before that.[56] It is a good bet that where evangelicalism is a strong political actor, market conditions will favor multinational corporations that benefit from the governmental rules, regulations, protections, and military backing of the United States. This is not to say that other religions can't or don't help promote such market conditions. It is only to say that in the modern history of capitalism, evangelical Protestantism has been the most politically powerful religion in this respect.

The evangelicalism that Bono promotes with regard to Africa uses the idea of the common good (expressed in efforts to save people from deadly diseases or feed the hungry) to promote the economic interests of multinational corporations. It is the premise of this book that those economic interests are not in fact aligned with the overall common good, even though they champion it. But on AIDS relief and debt relief in Africa, two of the major issues that Bono, along with other evangelicals, has addressed, is there anything wrong with Bono's using his celebrity platform to support U.S.-led programs, including those proposed and enacted by George W. Bush, that saved hundreds of thousands of lives, and urged debt forgiveness for struggling African nations? Isn't there a serious argument to be made that aid in the form of development is better than direct, top-down aid distributed by corrupt or tyrannical governments? Is it important that Bono has changed his view on aid in Africa, shifting from the top-down model of government aid to a more diffuse development model of microlending that encourages entrepreneurship? When people are starving and dying, what are we supposed to do?

I don't claim to have the answers to these questions. I honestly don't know what to do, other than listen, question, and learn. I am not an economist, or a policy expert, or a scholar of Africa. In short, I'm not qualified to tell you what to do. What I am is a scholar of the study of religion. And what I know from the study of religion is that gift giving is a practice of power, and political empires conquer frontiers in the name of the good.[57] I am not saying that you, or we, shouldn't help other

people. But I am suspicious of demands that we help others by under-
taking economic interventions that benefit the wealthiest and most
powerful individuals and corporations in the world. On the issue of
AIDS relief, does it matter that DATA agreed to pay full prices to pharmaceutical companies for antiretroviral drugs, when Nelson Mandela
and others wanted to challenge their medical patents?[58] Does it matter
that when it comes to a life-and-death issue, a corporation is allowed
to own—and to charge a high price for—the very thing that can save your
life? Does it matter that as the criticism of pharmaceutical companies
grew louder, Bono joined the chorus—not to challenge property rights
but only to bargain for lower prices?[59]

Ananya Roy, professor of urban planning and social welfare at the
Luskin School of Public Affairs at UCLA, argues that one of the key
themes of the "millennial" generation is "poverty capital." Roy says
that "the study of poverty is marked by an ethics of distance" that allows
researchers to produce knowledge, "truth," about why people are poor
and what should be done about it. With the production of this knowledge, brokers emerge to "manage poverty." These brokers advertise,
buy, and sell, openly trading poverty capital as they develop new markets for producers and consumers through microfinance and philanthropic consumption.[60] The Gates Foundation, for example, considers
the world's poor "a fast-growing consumer market," according to critic
Phil Bereano.[61] I hope that it is clear by now that in the religion around
Bono, accumulating wealth and alleviating poverty are not considered
contradictory goals. The challenge to those, like myself, who reject this
belief is that neoliberal policies do help some people, and their proponents use any evidence of success to suggest that extending those
policies will only help more people. Studies of microfinance suggest
that, yes, democratizing capital does help some poor people succeed
in business. But those studies also suggest that entrepreneurs are most
likely to succeed only in stable economic conditions.[62] If the up-and-
coming businessperson suffers a personal crisis—of health or housing,
for example—and she can't afford the medical bills or the rent or the
mortgage, then she doesn't make it. To guarantee that everyone has a
fair chance to succeed would require public support for a bulwark of
social services, especially health care, housing, and education. And the

neoliberal practices of privatization and financialization destabilize and undercut public services, thus contributing to the social crises that elites use to justify even more market solutions.

To see how corporations trade in poverty capital, consider how proceeds from the Product Red campaign are used to subsidize corporate responsibility to workers, thus increasing corporate profits while reducing wages and benefits. The Red campaign, which I address in more detail in chapter 5, illustrates Ananya Roy's observation that "millennial development relies greatly on the modern, Western self who is not only aware of poverty's devastation but is also empowered to act upon it in responsible ways."[63] Corporations trade in poverty capital by using millennials' desire for ethical consumption to pay for social services, like health care for their workers, that they should pay for through corporate taxes that support public services. Social responsibility in this relationship is effectively privatized, and corporations benefit from this privatization. To see how this works, consider two examples of how the Global Fund to Fight AIDS, Tuberculosis, and Malaria, to which Product Red proceeds contribute, supports "private-sector enterprises" that offer targeted health-care services. Patricia Daley, professor of the human geography of Africa at the University of Oxford, details how in one project the Global Fund gave $154 million to "extend Anglo-Gold Ashanti's (the goldmining multinational corporation) malaria control programme in Obuasi district, Ghana, to 40 other districts countrywide. The corporation's programme was designed to reduce employees' absenteeism due to sick leave and involved spraying pesticides in all public and private structures in the area." She also describes how "a similar strategy in Liberia is used by the Liberia Agricultural Company (rubber plantations) and Firestone Mining to provide antiretroviral treatments to its workers and their families." Daley concludes that "even though these interventions may have provided much needed relief for residents, they, nevertheless are presented by these multinationals as fulfilling corporate social responsibility (CSR) through direct action against poverty." And, most significantly for understanding the function of neoliberal religion in Africa, the influx of capital was "derived partly from RED's ethical consumers," rather than entirely from corporate profits.[64]

The Product Red campaign uses the health crises of malaria and HIV in Africa to persuade consumers to buy one product rather than another, with the promise that their purchase with help alleviate those crises. The companies that sell Red products benefit from an increased brand value. And the funds generated by the Product Red campaign also benefit corporations like Firestone Mining by paying for social services that the company should cover, or that should be covered by a more public and collective plan. The net outcome is that Western consumers are effectively taxed by the Product Red campaign, by paying a higher price for the branded product, which in turn supports the health care of those companies' workers. The social costs of free-market capitalism are privatized and passed along to worker-consumers, who continue to accrue more debt while losing wages. The net effect in these cases is that consumers of Red products subsidize corporate profits by reducing the financial responsibility of those companies to their workers, enabling them to withhold employee benefits like health care while at the same time marketing their company name and their product brand as signaling humanitarian concern for the well-being of all people.

As I describe in more detail in chapter 5, the Product Red campaign illustrates a process of cultural representation of African need that increases the profitability of corporations while also increasing the consumer debt of those who purchase Red products. In the globalization of Africa, there is a distinctive class difference between moral consumers who want to help and moralized Africans who need that help, and corporations are the cultural mediators of this class difference. Cultural representation, argues Kate Nash, professor of sociology at the University of London, is used to limit global citizenship, and Bono plays a key role in producing those limits by promoting the cultural conditions of class distinction. "Cultural politics provide the conditions of citizenship," Nash writes, "of its weakening and displacement on the one hand, or of its re-creation, its transformation beyond the usual boundaries of the nation, on the other. It is in culture, as much as in law and structures of global governance, that global citizenship must be created if it is to become a reality rather than a normative ideal." Nash further argues that the cultural identity of the global citizen is created within the cosmopolitan state, which Bono promotes. That cultural identity is built on the idea of social equality. But we see this relationship only through one side of cultural production, from the West. If that relationship is to be more equitable, Nash contends, we need a "genuinely popular transnational media, in which material commonalities and differences are debated from divergent socio-economic perspectives as well as creating and sustaining emotionally charged campaigns."[65]

What Nash describes is a process of cultural representation, a process, I argue, that neoliberal religion mediates, a process in which Bono connects to African "culture" but does not allow Africans to connect to the same global consumer culture. This is illustrated most clearly in the fact that Red products are marketed for Africa but not in Africa.[66]

Discussing the one-sided cultural production of a globalized Africa, observers have criticized celebrity activism, contrasting celebrities' philanthropic fundraising efforts with the facts of corporate control. Samar Al-Bulushi, in a 2011 letter to George Clooney concerning Sudan, noted that "nearly 10 per cent of the land in the brand new nation of South Sudan has already been sold or leased to corporations, many of them foreign corporations. Foreign investors have signed agriculture, biofuel and forestry deals that cover 2.64 million hectares of land (approximately the size of Rwanda). These deals took place in the context of a global rush for African farmland in the wake of the food, fuel and financial crises of 2007–08. Two of the largest deals have been negotiated with American companies: Jarch Capital and Nile Trading and Development." Al-Bulushi concludes that "in this era of 'global solidarity,' it appears that so-called 'humanitarians' and capitalists employ the same language of partnership and empowerment."[67]

In this chapter, I have argued that the language that humanitarians and capitalists share with Bono is the language of neoliberal religion, which presents Africans in life-and-death moral crises that demand economic interventions led by multinational corporations, with the promise that those interventions will spiritually connect Western consumers to African producers and end extreme poverty through more, not less, globalization. The power of neoliberal religion lies in the premise of Bono's message: that if *we* don't act, then *they* will suffer or die. In the previous chapters, I tried to show how that premise is a secularized version of an evangelical soteriology that if *you* don't act, by accepting Jesus, then *you* will suffer a spiritual death. Bono rejects the confessional limits of that soteriology, and offers instead a broader vision not just of what *I* must do, but what *we* must do to be saved, and what we must do is help Africans in need. Neoliberal religion around Africa is a religion of love for sale, love for the poor, love that forgives you for your purchase as it forgives its African debtors. But that is not all there is to neoliberal religion. For there is always more love to buy, in the name of love for others, and that kind of love keeps us in its debt.

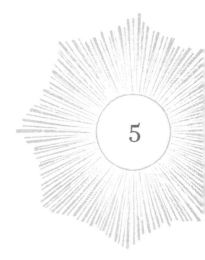

5

LOVE AND DEBT

"What country has ever gotten rich from aid?" Ugandan journalist Andrew Mwenda asked at the 2007 TEDGlobal conference in Tanzania, an event that Bono helped organize, and he wasn't expecting an answer. From the audience, though, a voice rang out. Jennifer Brea described the scene:

> Near the front of the darkened auditorium a white man with orange sunglasses stood to object. It was Bono! The audience (myself included), exuberant in the presence of celebrity, craned their necks to catch a glimpse. Aid saved Ireland from the potato famine, Bono declared. . . .
>
> After his impassioned defense of aid, an African man in the audience asked Bono, "Where do you place the African person as a thinker, a creator of wealth?" . . .
>
> Visibly wounded by the question, confused how anyone could misinterpret his good intentions, Bono, like the proverbial white man with black friends, set out to prove how down he is with the black man.

Africans are the "most regal people on earth" and music is in their DNA, he told the room of mostly doctors, engineers, and businessmen. He then began singing a traditional Irish dirge to show us how Celtic music has Coptic roots, and so is fundamentally African. I wasn't the only one giggling in the back row.[1]

Brea's account captures a disconnected celebrity from a distance. No one questions his sincerity. No one doubts that Bono believes what he says. No one says his love is false. What they are angry about, or laughing at, is his inability to listen to what others say to him, and to hear what he says to them—to recognize the cartoonish absurdity of his essentialist comparisons, which take a historical probability, like a Coptic connection to Celtic music, and render it as racial idealism, of the genetically musical African. What this encounter illustrates is that Bono is a rock star with the soul of a nineteenth-century romantic.[2] He is in love with an idea. He is in love with the idea of the noble African who, he believes, gave music to the world . . . back then, but not now.

Bono is the lead singer in one of the most successful stadium rock bands of all time. He is one of the most visible and vocal celebrities for African causes. And he believes with unrelenting sincerity that there is an African essence to music performed by Africans. Yet, with the exception of the Soweto Gospel Choir, which made an appearance in the promotional video for the 2010 World Cup in South Africa, Bono has rarely tried to bring African music or musicians onto his global stage. Unlike Paul Simon, who creatively engaged the genre of world music and collaborated with musicians in South Africa, defying the UN-approved cultural boycott of the apartheid government in the 1980s, Bono has not mixed his music with what he considers African beats.[3] Michka Assayas once said to him, "Knowing the extent of your passion for Africa, I am surprised that it has never spilled over into U2's music. I mean your music has always been—" Bono interjected, finishing the sentence: "fairly white." "Actually, yes," Assayas replied. Bono continued:

Let's go further. The Irish aren't white. We're more rosy pink. . . . I like African music . . . but the concept of World

Music didn't really do it for me. . . . It turns out that the groove-based music isn't our strength. My voice doesn't sound great singing over a groove. My voice seems to prefer chord changes in the more Western sense. It's finally that. I remember that we were coming up with some pretty good grooves, but the songs weren't very good. With Brian Eno at the helm, we were experimenting with a lot of grooves, but I remember saying to Edge: "I think my voice might need a few chord changes." I am not black. I am white. Might as well accept it.[4]

Bono claims that he likes African music but says he can't sing it, because he is "not black" and because he is "white," even as he jokes that the Irish "aren't white" but "rosy pink." The joke only works, of course, if the Irish are white, now, in the moment when the laugh is offered, if they are taken for granted as white, at least in comparison to Africans, which is Bono's claim. If we join that statement of self-proclaimed whiteness together with his response at the TED conference, we see that Bono can sing Irish music and claim that it is African. But he won't sing African music and claim that it is white. Because, he tells the world, he is *not* black, even as he claims that we all are genetic Africans.

In July 2007, Bono served as guest editor for the Africa issue of *Vanity Fair*. One story in the issue included a text box that described how scientists have tracked minor genetic mutations over tens of thousands of years back to Africa. "With no claim to culture or place, genetic Africans are everywhere," is how international studies scholars Lisa Ann Richey and Stefano Ponte described the message of that story. The *Vanity Fair* issue positioned Africa as spatially distant, as a "place from which everyone has moved."[5] Africa is a placeholder for the human past, and as such it possesses a primitive naturalness. Africa tells a human origin story, and the rest of the world, particularly Europeans and Americans, are its modern descendants, rootless and detached, in search of home, hoping to return and feel connected. The *Vanity Fair* story uses cutting-edge DNA research to argue, as Spencer Wells did in his article "Out of Africa" in the same issue, that Africa is the source of all humanity.

But, as Zine Magubane observes, this science-based narrative connects a present West to a past Africa—now dead—that depicts Africans as "atavistic throwbacks."[6] The same issue of *Vanity Fair* contains advertisements for Product Red products in general. One of them is part of the 2006 Product Red American Express ad campaign featuring Brazilian model Gisele Bündchen with Maasai model Keseme Ole Parsapaet. Richey and Ponte describe how the ad "markets the difference between 'my card' [personified by the Western model] and 'my life' [personified by the African model Parsapaet, who is in physical contact with Bündchen but still set apart, at a distance] . . . and does so in ways that make this difference safe, manageable, and not politically challenging."[7] Such racial maneuvering is not new. It is part of a political narrative with a religious history.

If you read through Bono's interviews over the years, you will consistently find the expressive pattern of a blackface minstrel. "Yeah, it's the Irish, we're the white niggers," he says. "White music is so much more uptight spiritually. Most black artists came from the Church anyway." "Prince is Duke Ellington to me!" Tom Jones is a "white guy with a black voice, and the sexual charge of it."[8] Over and over again, Bono uses his Irish history to claim outsider racial status. He expresses eternal love for African and African American musical creativity, which he identifies by its groove, its sexuality, and its religious origins. But he always offers his love from a distance, for he claims in the present moment, now and forever, that he is not like them; he is not black.

In colonial terms, the Irish were racial outsiders. Into the 1950s and 1960s, boarding houses in England still displayed signs reading, "No Blacks, No Irish, No Dogs." And when Irish immigrants arrived in the United States in the eighteenth and nineteenth centuries, self-identified "native" Anglo-Americans considered them not as white but as on the social level of freed African slaves. Historically, the Irish often have drawn on their experience with discrimination and identified with other outsiders, advocating their freedom. Bono claims this dissident tradition, pushing back against racial injustice and colonial imperialism, as did the "Liberator" Daniel O'Connell, who sent an appeal from Ireland in 1841 to the Irish in America to join the abolitionist cause, and as did John Riley, the Irish-American soldier who defected to the Mexican side in the Mexican-American War.[9] Bono speaks as if he is part of their lineage.

But Bono is connected to another Irish American tradition, that of performing blackness in order to overcome outsider status and achieve economic success. In the United States, ethnic immigrants, the Irish among them, used the dramatic convention of blackening the skin with burnt cork and exaggerating their facial features so as to move beyond their outsider status and become "white." The Irish entered a nation where race was defined in terms of a black/white binary, and they were forced into this binary.[10] The white power structure considered Irish ethnic markers a sign of racial inferiority. To overcome those ethnic markers, which were used to discriminate against them, and to claim the same racial category as the WASPs, in order to secure jobs and feed their families, Irish Americans in the nineteenth century performed in blackface to demonstrate publicly, through the use of contrasting phenotypes and controlled stereotypes, that they were not black.[11]

Through blackface minstrelsy, nineteenth-century Irish immigrants in northern U.S. cities sought to secure their racial standing by positioning themselves in relation to the racial "blackness" upon which southern whites had built the social hierarchy of the antebellum planation and its divinely sanctioned moral order.[12] "Performed primarily in northern, urban venues to white male audiences," according to historian Annemarie Bean, "early minstrelsy situated itself in the South, giving a symbolic significance to a contained universe located on the plantation which also allowed a permissible attitude of 'anything goes.'" In these performances, Bean writes, "the plantation culture of the South existed as a performed cultural imaginary of the urban displaced white man."[13] The institution of slavery in the South was the cultural source of American whiteness. To perform in blackface was to locate oneself within a cultural production of African blackness that worked for whites so long as Africans were enslaved. And that cultural production was performed at a distance. Southerners who lived in close proximity to enslaved Africans did not need to perform blackface with the same urgency as northern immigrants, because they could measure racial difference in the physical division between those who were held against their will and those who were not. The racial freedom of the displaced urban white man was not as self-evident. Performing in blackface was his attempt to make it so. To further illustrate the contingency of this process, consider that southerners did not widely perform in blackface until after the Civil War and Reconstruction, when the election of black politicians and the rise of a black middle class threatened their racially guaranteed social status, which could no longer be guaranteed. At the turn of the century, those southerners, like the displaced urban white man, had to prove themselves white.

The antebellum rules of blackface minstrelsy persisted in American popular culture through the twentieth century. D. W. Griffith's *Birth of a Nation* (1915), for example, the first film ever screened at the White House, used actors in blackface as part of its religious justification for white political control of black bodies. Warner Brothers featured Al Jolson in blackface in *The Jazz Singer* (1927), the story of a second-generation Jewish immigrant who struggles to overcome the religious severity of his Old World father in order to pursue a career as a Broadway performer. In that film, blackface is the spiritual medium through which Jakie Rabinowitz reconciles his American identity, as Jack Robin, with his father's past and his mother's future. *The Jazz Singer* could have told its secularizing immigrant story without the use of blackface. But the fact that the film did use blackface signals that it is difficult, if not impossible, for immigrants to the United States to become American without going through the racial binary of black or white. Blackface provided a ritual tool within popular culture for ethnic immigrants to perform that racial difference and attempt to control which side they were placed on, not just as self-identification but as a social location that wasn't solely dependent on phenotype. Blackface promoted the idea that racial difference was religiously recognizable in the performance of primitive blackness associated with southern plantation life, and by trying to control that religiosity, ethnic immigrants claimed a secular distance, showing themselves as American, as not of the Old World, where the image of the old was conflated with an immigrant's religious place of origin, in this case Judaism in Europe, with a racial site of origin, here the Africanness of black musical expression. This is why the scene in the film where Jack Robin looks in the mirror and sees himself in blackface, and then sees his father in the synagogue, is so significant—because it captures the religious-racial duality of American identity, and offers an opportunity to reconcile that dualism through the seamlessness of popular culture, which, in the idea of America, the idea that Bono believes in, is a secular tradition of black music that carries forth new spiritual futures.

In its popular expression, blackface is the historical medium of Bono's spiritual sincerity. It is a musical tradition that moved from the Old World to the New, eventually providing the cultural basis for American consumer identity. It is a racialized tradition that returned to Europe in the nineteenth century by way of American musicians, who exported its claims to racial authenticity as they sought a broader audience. It is a tradition that white supremacists used to control the presentation of authentic black music, presenting it as recognizable in excessive expressions of physical features, bodily movements, and revivalist rhythms of sexual desire and spiritual happiness.[14]

More recently, blackface has been used in American culture with ironic intent, as critical commentary on the colonizers, as it was in Ben Stiller's *Tropic Thunder* (2008). Why else, you might ask, would Robert Downey Jr. have agreed to play that role? Bono, though, could never be cast as one of Stiller's characters. Irony is not his thing. In 1993, publicist Neil Storey said of Bono, "He's very serious about what he does, but he's always portrayed as this serious person. Like with the current thing they have going (Zoo TV), they have to explain that it's a joke. It's either not a very good joke or something has been lost. It is inconceivable you should have to explain a parody to anyone."[15] Bono has to explain his jokes because he refuses to let his ironic commentary stand alone. For him, irony must always be coupled with a message of hope and optimism, good news. That is his self-image: a spiritually sincere rock star. That is the image his fans expect.

Describing the popular music of the 1990s, Bono says that it was "not ironic . . . it was wrapped in irony . . . even then it was ironic in a very idealistic way." Brian Eno described the U2 of that era by saying, "They are much more ironic now and I don't mean that they are therefore not sincere because I think irony and sincerity aren't exclusive. But when I first met them they were entirely in the sincere mode . . . but now they are capable of being in the middle of it but also standing outside it and realizing that they are playing with form and they can twist forms around."[16] Zoo TV was Bono's attempt to play with form, to stand outside the sincere mode that defined his spiritual quest for authenticity. But despite his best effort to act aloof, he could never let go of the search. And most fans and commentators saw it that way, as something "seemingly detached, ironic," but really just as a cover for something meaningful underneath, an alternative cultural form of social resistance, or an apparent embrace of postmodern ideas that actually wasn't.[17] Bono could never present himself as a musical artist in any way that was not recognized as based on authentic soul searching. Even as he played with the consumer forms of popular culture, he defined himself in relation to spiritual blackness. In the wake of the experiments with packaged irony in the 1990s, U2's revived moral concern for Africa and the Product Red campaign was a return to brand form, discarding shiny wrappings in order to make the brand appear a more transparent medium that consumers could use in order to morally connect with African blackness.

This tension between sincerity and irony is a hallmark of blackface minstrelsy, which has a complex global history.[18] Bono is connected to the particular strand of that history that runs through the American cultural context. He engages the cultural tropes of African blackness produced in blackface performances in the United States, without recognizing the historical context of those performances. Bono has never, as far as I know, performed in actual blackface. He has not blackened his face or worn the minstrel mask in the same way that Al Jolson did in *The Jazz Singer*. He has, however, been connected to marketing promotions for Product Red that feature white models in blackface, such as Kate Moss on the cover of an issue of *(Red) Independent* magazine.[19] Bono is a man of ideas who prefers to speak indirectly, but he will let others say what he means in more literal terms. Without blackening his own skin, but comfortable with others who blacken theirs, Bono follows the cultural pattern of the displaced urban white male who finds his identity in his proximate embrace of racial alterity.

Bono speaks of himself as emerging from the "suburban blank" of Dublin. He feels that he came from a place without a past. His early years were marked by emptiness and anger, by a feeling of not having a tradition of his own, and by a sense that he and the band came out of nowhere. U2 was a modern religious arrival that traveled to America to find success. And after they found it in the spiritual landscape that was the *Joshua Tree* album, Bono and U2 ventured further into the heartland of America to tether the floating feeling and ground their spiritual transcendence in the racial authenticity of performative blackness. The result was *Rattle and Hum*, a journey through America to Africa. "I had a kind of epiphany," Bono told Assayas,

> . . . just sitting outside the Sunset Sound Studios in Los Angeles, when we were working on *Rattle and Hum*. The studio was way down east on Sunset Strip. And on a Saturday night, I would watch the parade of Mexican hot wheels, jumping trucks, muscle cars, and people cruising by, listening to rap breaking in America. Nineteen eighty-eight was incredible: incredible sound systems, deep sub-low bass, a cacophony of rhythm, chanting, disconnected voices, hip-hop coming from all directions. Amazingly sophisticated pop music. [*suddenly imitates human beat box and syncopated rhythms*] And I'm thinking: "I know this music. It's African music."

In his multicultural experience with America, Bono found the singularity of African music, a genealogical source that survives the technological age:

> The epiphany was realizing that technology had brought African music to the descendants of Africa in America. People who had no memory of their continent of origin, and no direct experience of the call-and-response music that is Africa. Yet through technology, through digital samplers, scratching old vinyl, their music was swimming back up the river through swing, rock 'n' roll, soul, electronica, to its birthplace, which sounds to my ears so like hip-hop. How did that happen? Pure African music arriving through the DNA, through the genes of those people. That blew my

mind. It still blows my mind because of what it suggests of a kind of folk memory, of what we all might carry with us from our ancestors. And not just music, gifts, maybe even prejudices.[20]

Nearly twenty years before Bono sang a Celtic tune in Tanzania, he had his epiphany in L.A., that African Americans carried with them, in their genes, "pure African music."

Bono is not the first person to think in terms of African survivals. The question of how much African culture and religion survived the slave trade and persisted in the Americas has generated much writing among historians and anthropologists. In 1941, the anthropologist Melville Herskovits published *The Myth of the Negro Past*, in which he argued that "the descendants of Africans brought to the New World have retained Africanisms in their cultural behavior."[21] By recognizing the survival of these "Africanisms," Herskovits hoped scholars might overcome what he saw as the racist view that Africans lacked their own culture. Bono also claims to confront a "sneaky racism" when he speaks of the African origins of Irish music, tracing, for example, the melodies of the Shanos singer to northwestern Africa, or the Coptic roots of *The Book of Kells*. For him, racism is expressed as the willful ignorance of such Africanisms. It's the kind of racism he saw in his father, his "old man Bob Hewson," who, he says, would have given you "a clip on the ear" if you told him such things.[22] But the comparison ends there, because Herskovits considered race a sociological and cultural construct, not a biological essence. More specifically, Herskovits rejected any argument, such as that offered by the German ethnomusicologist Erich von Hornbostel, that music was genetic rather than cultural, inherent rather than learned.[23] Bono speaks as if he, like Herskovits, is combatting racism by recognizing a present continuity with an African past. But his view of this continuity is closer to the essentialism of von Hornbostel, who wrote in the early twentieth century.

Bono speaks as an advocate of racial justice and equality, but his views on race are best classified as "romantic racialism," the term historians have used to describe the well-intentioned racism of the abolitionist Harriet Beecher Stowe, who campaigned against slavery and affirmed the humanity of blacks, but believed them spiritually superior and naturally inferior to whites and therefore ill-suited for self-governance.[24] Bono's views of Africans are quite similar, in that he considers them fully human and spiritually noble, but unable, without the economic intervention and institutional oversight of Western nations and multinational corporations, to govern themselves. In this way, his ideas are much like those of the nineteenth-century anthropologist E. B. Tylor, who espoused the idea, radical for his day, that all humans were connected, and that Africans were just as human as Europeans, but then placed Africans at the primitive end of a cultural evolutionary continuum, with modern Europeans as contrasting moderns. Bono claims a radical distance from the sneaky racism of his parents (as many of his fans do), but still places Africans at the undeveloped end of an economic evolutionary continuum that strings a line to the free-market West as its aspirational model. For Bono, we're all genetically connected, but we're not all political and economic equals . . . yet.

Bono locates his prophetic power—his political authority to paint an economic horizon for the world's poor—in his racial presentation of a dissident history that he claims to share with colonized others, notably Africans and African Americans. Like Al Jolson's character in *The Jazz Singer*, he reconciles his historical self of ethnic subjugation with his eternal self of musical success through his emotional presentation of racial difference. In 1988 he wrote an essay, under his given name, Paul Hewson, titled "Bono: The White Nigger," for the volume *Across the Frontiers: Ireland in the 1990s*, edited by Richard Kearney. What is striking about that essay is the way its author takes a racial slur historically connected to Irish subjects and renders it a positive performative trait. "I was called a 'White Nigger' once by a black musician," Hewson writes, "and I took it as he meant it, as a compliment." But at what moment did the racial slur become a compliment, and what kind of compliment was it, if it was one at all? For the "I" in that sentence is Bono, not Paul. The "I" is a persona, not a person. Paul Hewson is the Irish subject who descended from an ethnic group of people who were colonized as the racial outsiders of Europe. The British considered his people to be like blacks, not white. But Bono is the prophetic performer who is racially recognized by himself, and by his fans, as the rock star who draws his authentic power from the black likeness of past Irishness, only to claim the present whiteness of the celebrity brand of his spiritual sincerity.

Bono presents this sincerity as a spiritual love for Africans. And he expresses his love for Africa using the cultural traditions of American minstrelsy, which Eric Lott describes in terms of white love for black bodies and white theft of black soul. Lott writes that the black-face minstrel show was a "simultaneous drawing up and crossing of racial boundaries" and a "mixed erotic economy of celebration and exploitation."[25] This lovers' row of the minstrel show persisted well after white musicians took off the mask. Bono is just one of many white performers who searched for authenticity in their relationship with American black music. Bob Dylan, who stole Lott's book title for his *Love and Theft* album, is the most famous among them, and it is Dylan whom Bono credits, in part, with sparking his search for musical roots.

In his essay for the *Across the Frontiers* volume, Hewson reflected on how meeting Dylan challenged him to rethink U2's origins—to reconsider his belief that "U2 came out of a void, a black hole; [that] we seemed completely rootless." He describes this meeting with Dylan, now well documented by U2 biographers, critics, commentators, and theologians—cyclically cited in the collective print of U2 studies—in 1985 at Slane Castle:

> [Bob was sitting] there talking about the McPeeke Family . . . this Irish group I'd never even heard of . . . and how he used to hang around backstage at Makem & Clancy concerts—yeah, I said, I remember they used to be on the Late Late Show! . . . And then I began to listen more carefully to the bold and bald sound of Irish Folk singers. . . . I told Dylan and Van Morrison, who was there at the time, that I felt we didn't belong to any tradition, it was like we were lost in space, floating over many traditions but not belonging to any one of them. It then struck us that there was a journey to be undertaken. There was something to be discovered.

Hewson's journey took Bono and U2 to America to discover black music, and through black music to find their Irishness: "We started looking back into American music, Gospel, Blues, the likes of Robert Johnson . . . John Lee Hooker. Old songs of fear and faith . . . [and] we found the 'Irish Thing' through the American: Gospel, Blues, Robert Johnson, Bob Dylan, these became passports home." But what exactly was the "Irish Thing" that Hewson discovered through old American songs of fear and faith? For Hewson, it was the emotion, the passion, the antithesis of UK *cool* that the Irish had in common with African Americans. "Though this passion to me is an Irish characteristic," he wrote, "in American blacks it's called *soul*."[26]

U2 was not the first European band to find its identity in the racial-ized tropes of American popular music. A long list of British blues bands, with the Stones at the top, did the same thing. But Hewson as Bono was attempting something different from Mick Jagger as minstrel. His persona, Bono, was a sincere sexual being, a born-again self, with an evangelical soul. Noel McLaughlin and Martin McLoone concluded that in *Rattle and Hum*, "U2's sound . . . was at some distance from the 'bump and grind' and libidinal racial authenticity appropriated most famously by the Rolling Stones. The U2 fascination with African America was more to do with furthering their brand of 'caring rock,' drawing on a mix of African-American political struggles (most notably the Civil Rights movement) and a respect for musical traditions, than with reproducing any racialized sexual essentialism. In this sense . . . sexuality in U2 was sublimated into 'lofty,' spiritual or political concerns."[27] In other words, Bono's "Irish Thing" was not Jagger's Little Red Rooster. Bono claimed a higher, more spiritual sexuality. But both Bono and Jagger imagined black musicality in essentialist terms; they just differed in their modes of expression. Bono differed from Jagger as the transcendent differs from the immanent, as writing a love poem differs from a back-door rendezvous. But both committed the same cultural transgression of love for black bodies and theft of black soul.

For Hewson, the implied difference between U2 and the British bands was that, against the backdrop of the English scene, "The Irish, like the blacks, feel like outsiders." To Hewson, this outsider status was both musical and political: for U2, the two were inseparable. To sing was a political act. And to sing from below looking up signified the class dif-ference between the oppressed and the oppressor, the activist and the aggressor. Implied in Hewson's narrative was the notion that the Irish were to England what blacks were to America: beating hearts of colonial empire, musical souls trapped in colonized bodies.[28] This journey to America for Bono and U2, the musical voyage of Irish discovery, took a cultural route similar to that of their migrant forebears, who claimed whiteness in America through blackface minstrel performances.

Nowhere in the U2 catalog are the cultural workings of minstrel love and theft as obvious as in the *Rattle and Hum* album and documentary film, released in 1988, the same year Hewson wrote about his American journey from blackness to Irishness. McLaughlin and McLoone describe *Rattle and Hum* as "a problematic and flawed attempt by the band to 'un-whiten' its sound and to intertwine the two authenticities of blackness and Irishness."[29] *Rattle and Hum* was U2's coming-to-Elvis moment, with visits to Graceland and Sun Records. It was their attempt to place themselves within American gospel and blues musical traditions, to invoke the king of rock 'n' roll in order to politically mine his musical mimicry, and shout love sincere in the name of Martin Luther King Jr. to make you see the racial connection and experience the messianic moment.

When Bono later spoke about forgiving African debts, he demanded that we "feel like we're making history." *Rattle and Hum*, the film, was musically saturated with that engineered feeling. Shot in timeless black and white, the documentary portrays the band arriving on the American music scene as distant enough to be self-important, but close enough to be accessible and engaging. The viewer gets the feeling. The band has made it. And now that they have your attention, they would like to let you know that the band members are Irish and possess the emotional musical quality that marks the black essence of American music. Lauren Onkey writes that in *Rattle and Hum*, "blackness is evoked to access primal expressions of authentic emotion, to legitimize the Irish as Celtic soul brothers. This forges a purportedly unproblematic link with African-Americans: the Irish have been oppressed, and therefore soul and rhythm and blues are appropriate vehicles for Irish musicians."[30] *Rattle and Hum* self-consciously captures Bono performing several interracial musical unions, with awkward earnestness that elides ironic conceit. He offers no attempt to hide it. You better believe he believes it. Between the documentary and the record, Bono sweats with B. B. King, performs with the Harlem Gospel Choir, and gives a political speech about South African apartheid, with references to Little Steven, Desmond Tutu, and a man in a shantytown just outside Johannesburg.

After 1988, the interracial juxtapositions of *Rattle and Hum* that defined U2 were superseded by secular Europop, which eventually gave way to a revivalist return to the spiritual transparency of the earlier U2 years, where musical transcendence was once again positioned as a Western sound carrying a prophetic message of hope for an Africa in need. Transcendence was made in the journey between musical styles and vast continents that maintained the distance in order to cross it. Other white musicians, like Jagger and Richards, wanted to collapse the distance, as they tried to fit themselves into the performative idea of an authentic African American blues tradition. U2 always stood outside, in relation to but not within, even when they tried. McLaughlin and McLoone contend that, "critically, it was not . . . the album's flawed attempt at authenticity that was the problem; rather, it was its hybridity that made [*Rattle and Hum*] fit uncomfortably in the authenticity paradigm." On the song "Silver and Gold," they note, "Bono talks about apartheid, then tells Edge to play the blues, but then he just does his usual echo, sonic, space, that isn't the blues."[31] In other words, Bono and U2 were unable to remake themselves in the image of their beloved convincingly. They were neither Dylan nor the Stones. They were not trickster minstrels. So they dropped the American blues and tried a more European aesthetic, only to find again the moral mask of Africa in need.

Bono, though, remembers it differently. "Listening to black music helped us get the groove ready for Achtung Baby," he maintains.[32] Critics and fans considered that album a different kind of project, something more Euro and less concerned with racial authenticity. But it is important that Bono believes in the connection, because in later concerts, videos, and albums, he returned to what got him there: his love for black bodies and theft of black soul. If the message was sublimated in *Achtung Baby*, and wrapped in irony in the later *Zooropa* and *Pop* albums and their supporting tours, it resurfaced under the bright house lights of the Elevation Tour in support of *All That You Can't Leave Behind*, and that transparent sincerity shaped the albums and tours that followed. Bono's mantra in those later performances: "The goal is soul." His political vision: an "African dream." What began as U2's journey to America to discover black soul in the late twentieth century would continue into the twenty-first with Bono bridging "Dr. King's America" and "Nelson Mandela's Africa." In American gospel and blues, U2 tried to claim its musical authenticity. But unlike other minstrel acts, they were unable to perform musical authenticity from within, as if they were black. Bono's brand of spiritual sincerity needed an even more distant blackness to stand in relation to; it needed what was on the other side of American blackface, a romanticized image of Africa as a place of racial purity and primitive religion, a place that connects us as a human race, a place that represents our shared genetic past: Africa, a place, a person, our mother, to whom we owe our love.

In the story of religion around Bono, when did love and theft become love and debt? In 2002, Bono appeared on *The Oprah Winfrey Show* to promote DATA, the NGO that worked to eradicate the debt of African countries and end the AIDS crisis on the continent. Four years later, he returned to Harpo Studios to launch Product Red in the United States. This time, he came not to ask for money on behalf of African nations but to promote products in the name of love for Africans. While DATA lobbied for direct aid from governmental authorities and conscientious citizens, Product Red persuaded corporations to brand some of their products as Red, and to give up to 50 percent of the profits from the sale of those products to programs and services in Africa. On the day of the launch, Oprah and Bono showed the audience how Product Red would work. In the middle of the show, they left the studio and headed to Michigan Avenue in Chicago for a shopping spree at the downtown Gap store. There, the two perused the Product Red apparel: Red Gap jeans, Red Gap T-shirts, Red Converse shoes. Oprah declared, "I want the whole world to go Red."

Product Red is but one example of a consumer religion that infuses brand products with moral value and transforms the purchase of products into a spiritual practice. Its moralism is revivalist, as it confronts the consumer with the salvific consequences of personal choice. Bono promotes Product Red by saying that the immediate need to save African lives is more important than longer-term labor issues—that is, the material conditions of workers in factories that make Red products. He has said, for example, "We are for labour issues. Labour issues are very serious but six and a half thousand Africans dying is more serious."[33] Religious urgency supersedes social critique. And this urgency is pitched to corporations as potentially profitable. Ponte and his co-authors note that "RED improves a company's brand without challenging any of its actual operations and practices, and increases its value and perception." With Red, "money making and giving are the same."[34] Bono does not invoke the term *religion* to describe such strategic marketing of moral urgency. Rather, he uses the language of spirit and spirituality. I hope it is clear by now that such an evasion is a political strategy used by the powerful to invoke their secular privilege to stand against religion, even as they participate in the formation of ever more powerful systems of religious demands. In the practice of Christianity, for example, believers may be confronted with the eternal consequences of spiritual life and death, in a face-to-face or material sense, when they attend church, make a confession, or hear a sermon on what one must do to be saved. After they leave those religious spaces, believers may be asked to contemplate such eternal questions as they move through their mundane routines at home and work, or they can, if they choose, ignore those questions until the next Sunday. But regardless of what or whether you believe, every time you see an advertisement for a Red product, or come face to face with your Le Creuset (Red) teapot with infuser, you are confronted with life and death. The brand says that only you can save someone else from dying. And in saving their physical life, you may find your own spiritual salvation. This religion through material consumption demonstrates the religious difference that defines millennial capitalism, the difference between mere personal consumption and salvific social purchase.

To get a sense of how this works, take the last lines of the Red Manifesto: "(RED) is not a charity. It is simply a business model. You buy (RED) stuff. We get the money. Buy the pills and distribute them. . . . If they don't get the pills, they die. We don't want them to die. We want to give them the pills. And we can. And you can. And it's easy. All you have to do is upgrade your choice." When Product Red first launched, marketers made it easy to calculate the moral value of brand purchases by including on the website an "impact calculator" that consumers could use to measure how much their purchases would affect lives in Africa. The purchase of one Armani watch, for example, would save seven African lives. Red no longer lets the consumer use the actual calculator, but it still offers a calculated moral value for its products. If you are considering Red Beats by Dre for a holiday gift, you should know that not only are these wireless headphones "more comfortable than ever," but that for $199.95 you also provide a seventeen-day supply of life-saving pills.

Here, I am interested in the moral sincerity that Bono promotes in Product Red and its link to his prophetic desire for musical authenticity in U2. Bono's sincere mode is revealed as a singular expression of a religious heart: a spiritual call for redemptive love through his musical performances and political advocacy for Africa. Connecting spiritual sincerity with the religious idea of an Africa in need creates the possibility of a reformed American pop-culture game in which the minstrel rules feel different, almost reversed, as the admirer finds in the object of affection an opportunity not to steal but to give out of a sense of obligation, so as to resolve a moral debt. But as the giver gives to the one she sees in need, that very gift she gives on credit, and thus she takes upon herself, as Christ did for the sinner, the debt that she forgives. The spiritual practice embodied in the purchase and consumption of Product Red commodities offers the consumer class the opportunity to be like Jesus and help your economic neighbor. This is the defining feature of millennial capitalism. For it is the missionary obligation—to spend in order to give, in order to save someone else from neglect, poverty, illness, or death—that transforms the individual consumer into a religious actor. Buying Product Red items allows you to be a good Samaritan—and not *just* a good Samaritan but a good-*looking* Samaritan. Remember the class distinction. For Lott, blackface signified white working-class desire for transracial union, but because this desire was expressed solely in racial terms, without dissolving class distinctions, the love remained distant. Sobered by class ambition, whites stole what they considered the soul of blackness, while maintaining racial boundaries that marked communal distance, appropriating staged enchantments of intoxicating enthusiasm and charisma for psychological privilege and economic gain. If you want to be good, it is not good enough simply to love your neighbor. You can't simply be a good Samaritan; you must also be a good-looking good Samaritan. When you offer your hand, make sure there's an Armani on your wrist. And you can. Wherever Red products are sold, you will find the way through your purchase. This is the good news for consumers who want to be morally good *and* be part of the good-looking class.

Consider again how class difference is maintained by the fact that Product Red commodities are marketed for the cause *of* Africans but never marketed *to* Africans. Critics of Bono and his promotion of Product Red often remark on this irony. He, the band, the corporations—they all make money from a white consumer class by selling its members the feeling of social justice and financial aid to blacks in America and Africa. How is this all that different, in musical terms, from how the Stones, or Led Zeppelin, or Elvis imagined black gospel and blues, appropriated it, and made money and a career with it?

As noted earlier, Bono was dogged by criticism when U2 moved part of its business operations to Amsterdam in 2006 to take advantage of lower tax rates. But the Stones had already moved their operations there in 1972. Why do we hold Bono to a higher standard? Because only Bono claims a moral cause as his own and asks you to save African lives by buying his brand. Mick Jagger and Keith Richards never said they were doing anything other than making music and making money. Bono, though, says that by making music and making money, he is changing the world. And you can too. This is the difference between Bono and the others, the religious difference of millennial capitalism.

By virtue of the political seriousness of his religious sincerity, Bono *appears* to reverse the pop-culture game of minstrelsy at a historical moment when developed, industrial nation-states, the colonizers, are trying to reintegrate former colonial territories, now independent nation-states themselves, into the global economy in order to expand consumer markets. To convert the colonized subject into a neoliberal consumer requires prophetic persuasion. Bono provides the political services of a religious broker, bringing his spiritual capital to the table. Lobbying European and American political and economic leaders for debt relief for African nations, Bono helps integrate those nations into global free markets. Bono has worked with Jeffrey Sachs to reimagine the place of Africa in his imagined world polity. He has converted numerous politicians, from Bill Clinton to Jesse Helms, to his African cause. As noted earlier, he famously moved Helms to tears, owing in no small part to what Eunice Shriver remembered as Bono's ability to connect with Helms "in a spiritual way" and persuade him through his "sincerity and evident knowledge."[35] Bono delivers the good news of love replacing theft, of forgiveness replacing debt.

So when did love and theft become love and debt? In 1988, the year the album *Rattle and Hum* was released, the U.S. national debt stood at $2.6 trillion. By comparison, the collective debt of African nations was roughly $270 billion in the late 1980s, or one tenth of the U.S. debt. But the African debt was deemed a crisis because its debt-to-GDP ratio was vastly higher than that of the United States or European nations. In terms of actual dollars—forgetting for a moment the economic rules of the game, which involve class distinctions, resource extraction, and mortgage-rating agencies—the United States obviously had (and has) the higher debt by far. And consider that while debt relief to sub-Saharan African nations since 2000 has helped decrease those nations' overall debt to official lenders like governments, the World Bank, and the IMF, the region's debt to private lenders has steadily increased, such that it now surpasses its debt to official lenders. In 2015, that private debt was slightly higher than the roughly $150 billion owed to official lenders.[36] Consider also that in 2000, U.S. national debt stood at $6 trillion and is now more than $18 trillion (or sixty times greater than sub-Saharan African official and private debt combined). Since 2000, U.S. household debt has outpaced household disposable income.[37] Whether in Africa or in America, rising debt is a common trend, but to see one and not the other as a crisis requires a certain economic perspective on religious difference. It requires that one be classified as in need and the other as obligated to meet that need. And it rests on the belief that the financial obligation to give is a moral duty in the missionary terms of evangelical Christianity, a prophetic intervention in the spiritual balance of life and death.

In the nineteenth century, European and American colonists and missionaries in Africa were horrified by the religious and spiritual practices of their primitive subjects, whether fetishism or animism or spirit possession. Then as now, religion provided a system that distinguished good from bad. It hid the irony that in the colonial taxonomy of good religion and bad superstition (in today's terms, good debt and bad debt) the modern citizen of the West had, to rephrase Lott, simultaneously drawn up and crossed categorical boundaries. In the Product Red campaign, the gift of debt relief to Africa via DATA is derived from the credit card debt of the American consumer. Americans purchase Red products, from Converse kicks to Starbucks coffee, on credit. In 2006, one of the first Red campaign products was an American Express credit card. What Red sells is love for Africa, love for black bodies. This love is cast not as a theft but as a gift, bought on credit. There is, of course, still theft in the system, but it is hidden within it, as market derivative. For the consumer of popular culture, the minstrel game that Bono plays is now about debt, in the form of a gift given on credit, rather than about theft, just as its racial logic is no longer expressed as colonial racism but instead as neoliberal multiculturalism.

Bono reverses the minstrel game of American popular culture, replacing the racial irony of love and theft with the religious sincerity of love and debt. He does this through U2's music and through his political advocacy for economic and health reform in Africa, including his work with the Drop the Debt and Product Red campaigns. These campaigns expand credit markets in the United States through the moral consumption of African debt and health reform. In *Ritual and Its Consequences*, Adam Seligman and his coauthors argue that "reform is the key link between the pervasiveness of the sincere trope and modern consciousness and politics. Modern civilizations are, to a great extent, civilizations of permanent reform."[38] Connecting the trope of sincerity to modern consciousness and politics in turn makes it possible for consumers not only to buy love in the symbolic terms of material gifts, of flowers and chocolates, but to buy love in order to gift it as an economic commodity with life-saving potential. And they do all this on credit, taking on their own consumer debt in the name of debt relief for African others. To practice the very thing you seek to correct in others is the spiritual discipline of neoliberal religion around Bono.

When do love and theft become love and debt? When, as anthropologist Webb Keane argues, the concept of sincerity is connected to the language of moral questions (how many lives saved for a Starbucks Red stainless steel tumbler?), when we "take the concept of sincerity to be inseparable from some kind of judgment." For in being sincere, Keane writes, "I am not only producing words that reveal my interior state but am producing them for you; I am making myself (as an inner self) available for you in the form of external publicly available expressions." Sincerity demands transparency. (Hear Bono speak of love. Hear Bono speak of free markets.) Sincerity clarifies the connection between the seen and unseen, and between speech and silence. For Keane, sincerity is "a kind of public accountability to others for one's words with reference to one's self."[39] Sincerity is what removes the Hallmark quotation marks from the sentiment "I love you" and gives the consumer the ability to judge between this card and that one, and to buy the card with religious value, not as love for sale but love for real.

Bono, through both U2 and the Red campaign, sells an ability to remove the quotation marks, to make it real. This is how he transacts business in the currency of love, connecting his own desire for "one love" to those who speak in "the name of love," from Martin Luther King Jr., to Desmond Tutu, to Nelson Mandela. In an attempt to create critical distance, to gain musical authenticity, to speak with spiritual sincerity on behalf of the authentically religious, Bono has imagined modern America in terms of an African dream. He has performed that vision onstage, throwing love from his heart to his fans. His musical performance conveys his prophetic vision of an artistic neoliberal spirit for sale. His moral self is his corporate gift, a love that returns to sender with a profit. His evangelical earnestness for the benefit of others in need is the religious sincerity of millennial capitalism.

NOTES

INTRODUCTION

1. "2010 FIFA World Cup: ESPN FIFA World Cup Commercial—U2 Magnificent," April 22, 2010, https://www.youtube.com/watch?v=n1OvZt_gps.
2. Comaroff and Comaroff, *Millennial Capitalism*, 2.
3. Molosankwe, "Power Cut Leaves Paralysed Boy Immobile."
4. On the SECC's role in reconnecting electricity for Soweto residents, see the 2006 documentary film *The Big Sell Out*, directed by Florian Opitz.
5. Egan and Wafer, "Soweto Electricity Crisis Committee," 1. See also Fiil-Flynn, "Electricity Crisis in Soweto."
6. Greenberg, "Market Liberalisation and Continental Expansion," 73–75.
7. Bond, *Elite Transition*, 124, 213, 220.
8. Eskom, Annual Report 2009, "Powering the 2010 FIFA World Cup South Africa," http://www.financialresults.co.za/eskom_ar2009/ar_2009/info _sheets/2010.htm.
9. Umraw, "How Much Trouble Is Eskom In?"
10. Consider also how at the 2010 FIFA World Cup, only authorized vendors, which included Coca-Cola and Adidas among other major corporations, were allowed to sell products near World Cup stadiums; informal traders, who are among the working poor in South Africa, were not allowed. See Rodrigues, "South Africa's World Cup." Amnesty International reported human rights concerns around such practices; see Amnesty International, "Human Rights Concerns." And there were protests against these exclusionary zones, but the policy remained in place. See Gorman, "Protests Gather." The Creative Workers Union of South Africa was a bit more successful; it protested to get more local artists to perform as part of the festivities, lobbying to increase the number of acts from three to seven, though they were still overshadowed by performers like Bono, Shakira, and the Black Eyed Peas. See Jeffries, "World Cup Is About Politics." Moreover, infrastructure construction, as often is the case with these kinds of events, was not the catalyst it was claimed to be for overall urban development or for alleviating poverty. See Pillay and Bass, "Mega-Events as a Response." These were the economic facts of a neoliberal dream, a dream of equality for everyone but a reality for few.
11. See Seales, *Secular Spectacle*; and Seales, "Race and Religion."

12. On blackface performances' expressing an "ideology of love," see Roberts, *Blackface Nation*, 261–62.

13. "Scott Calhoun," https://www.atu2.com/about/bio/scottcalhoun.html. See also http://u2conference.com/aboutthedirector.

14. On consumer religion, see Lofton, *Consuming Religion*. For a discussion of how affect has been used to define the limits of individual religious experience, see Bender, *New Metaphysicals*, 8.

15. Noll, *American Evangelical Christianity*, 9.

16. Smith, *Christian America*, 16.

17. Certain versions of classical secularization theory imagine that the disestablishment of religion (its separation from the state) makes possible the diffusion of religious values into secular institutions and popular culture. This kind of argument was made by Talcott Parsons, who saw the outcome of secularization differently from other sociologists, like Peter Berger, who believed that disestablishment would lead to the privatization (and later the deprivatization) of religion. Parsons predicted in 1974 that traditional religious values associated with church traditions (such as those identified with a Protestant ethic, for example) would become less doctrinally specific and more conceptually abstract in postindustrial America, resulting in a "new religion of love" that would have a "strong individualistic emphasis," and that individuals would "form attachments of love to other objects also with a high valence attached to the individuality of the object." It would be interesting to speculate about what Parsons might think of Bono, who sings in the name of love and who brands objects in his Product Red campaign (which seeks to engage the private sector in raising money to help eliminate HIV/AIDS in Africa, discussed later in the book) as expressing a love for others that is for sale to individuals who want to buy those objects to help others they have never met. See Parsons, "Religion in Postindustrial America"; Berger, *Sacred Canopy*; Berger, *Desecularization of the World*.

18. I am arguing here that capitalism favors certain religious expressions over others. Sixteenth-century Calvinism was one of those religious expressions, but not the only one. That a more recent popular cultural practice promotes a religious ascetic discipline does not necessarily mean that the cultural practice is another name for Calvinism, as many have argued. For a persuasive example of this argument, see Logan, "Lean Closet." Countering that historical argument, I consider Calvinism just another name for capitalist practice in a particular place and at a particular time. Thinking more globally and more comparatively, there are a variety of religious expressions beyond Calvinism that promote capitalist discipline—for example, the religious expressions of capitalism in the Hindu allegories used to train service employees at a mall in Kolkata, India. See Maitra, "Laboring to Create Magic," 129–30, 142–43.

19. This is Durkheim's thesis in *Elementary Forms of Religious Life*.

20. It is my contention here that the history of evangelicalism has been too restricted by standard preachers and pastors and needs to repopulate itself

for greater salience in the study of American religious history as the social, cultural, and economic history of global empire. Works that shift the focus away from the standard figures include O'Neill, *Secure the Soul*; Stephens, *Devil's Music*; Hammond, *God's Businessmen*; and Grem, *Blessings of Business*.

21. For a consideration of how religion and economics have blended in American scholarship, see Lofton, "Considering the Neoliberal," 270–71.

22. See Mathews, "Southern Rite of Human Sacrifice."

23. Bono, "The Good News on Poverty (Yes, There's Good News)," TED talk, February 2013, https://www.ted.com/talks/bono_the_good_news_on_poverty _yes_there_s_good_news.

CHAPTER 1

1. On the distinction between prophetic and priestly, or "office," charisma, see Weber, "Religious Rejections of the World and Their Directions," in *From Max Weber*, 328.

2. "U2: Joshua Tree 30th Anniversary," U2 interview by Zane Lowe, July 21, 2017, https://www.youtube.com/watch?v=vsKZ3YrF_3Q.

3. See Gunn, *English People at War*; Marshall, *Heretics and Believers*.

4. Paseta, *Modern Ireland*; BBC Newsbeat, "Northern Ireland's Violent History," January 8, 2013, http://www.bbc.co.uk/newsbeat/article/20930976/northern irelandsviolenthistoryexplained; "The Northern Ireland Assembly," http:// www.nidirect.gov.uk/articles/northernirelandassembly. See also McKittrick and McVea, *Making Sense of the Troubles*.

5. Quoted in McGee, *U2: A Diary*, 6.

6. "What Is It Like to Be an Evangelical Christian in Ireland?," *Journal.ie*, August 24, 2014, http://www.thejournal.ie/evangelicalchristiansinireland 1633238Aug2014; Pew-Templeton Global Religious Futures Project, "Ireland," http://www.globalreligiousfutures.org/countries/ireland#/ ?affiliations_religion_id=0&affiliations_year=2010&region_name=All %20Countries&restrictions_year=2016.

7. Pew Research Center, "Religious Landscape Study."

8. Noble, "Changing Face of Irish Christianity."

9. Rothman, "Church of U2"; Kristy Etheridge, "Poem from U2's Bono to Billy Graham," Billy Graham Evangelistic Association, September 1, 2014, http:// www.billygraham.org/story/apoemfromu2sbonotobillygraham; "Pope 'Hangs Out' with Popstars, Wears Shades," September 23, 1999, http://www.atu2 .com/news/popehangsoutwithpopstarswearsshades.html; "The Spiritual and the Religious: Is the Territory Changing?," Dr. Rowan Williams: 14th Archbishop of Canterbury, April 17, 2008, http://aoc2013.brix.fatbeehive .com/articles.php?/1208/thespiritualandthereligiousistheterritorychanging.

10. Stockman, *Walk On*, 15.

11. Taylor and Israelson, *Political World of Bob Dylan*, 188.

12. Hurtgen, "Boy, Baby, and Bomb," 219; Assayas, *Bono in Conversation*, 133.

13. Assayas, *Bono in Conversation*, 166.

14. Huston, *U2: Changing the World*, 10.

15. Waters, *Race of Angels*, 151.

16. Browne, *Frontman*, 14 (Browne refers to the Shalom Christian Fellowship simply as "Shalom"). See also Stockman, *Walk On*, 25–27.

17. Stockman, *Walk On*, 16–17.

18. Taylor and Israelson, *Political World of Bob Dylan*, 188; McPherson, *World and U2*, 9.

19. Quoted in Cogan, *U2: An Irish Phenomenon*, 22.

20. Block, "Bono Bites Back."

21. Taylor and Israelson, *Political World of Bob Dylan*, 190.

22. Block, "Bono Bites Back."

23. Graham, *U2: The Early Years*, 24, quoted in Browne, *Frontman*, 15.

24. Garrett, *Gospel According to U2*, 26.

25. Worthen, *Apostles of Reason*, 3–5.

26. McLoughlin, "Awakenings as Revitalizations"; Mathews, "Second Great Awakening."

27. See Hatch, *Democratization of American Christianity*.

28. Kidd, *George Whitefield*.

29. Johnson, *Shopkeeper's Millennium*, 3.

30. Finney, "Revival of Religion," 322.

31. See the entry "Charles Grandison Finney," in Queen, Prothero, and Shattuck, *Encyclopedia of American Religious History*, 236.

32. Mathews, "Second Great Awakening," 25, 39.

33. Hatch, *Democratization of American Christianity*, 9.

34. In "Sign of the Armageddon," Kathryn Lofton argues that muscular revivalists were "more mediums for a message than mentors for the struggling people who listened." They were speakers, not pastors.

35. "Online blog," October 26, 2005, accessed January 22, 2006, personal.umich.edu/~gzmyslow/blogoctober2005.

36. See the U2 concert video, *Vertigo 2005: Live from Chicago* (DVD, 2005, produced by Hamish Hamilton and Ned O'Hanlon).

37. Hatch, *Democratization of American Christianity*, 9.

38. Lofton, "Preacher Paradigm."

39. "Transcript of Bono's Speech at Labour Party Conference," September 29, 2004, http://www.atu2.com/news/transcriptofbonosspeechatlabourparty conference.

40. Bono regularly uses U2 concerts as a political venue. See Barro, "Why Would a Rock Star?"

41. I attended this concert on June 22, 2001; these are my personal observations.

42. Finney, "Revival of Religion," 324.

43. Fox News, "Helms Pow Wows with Celebrity Set."

44. Finney, "Revival of Religion," 324.

45. See the concert video *U2 Go Home: Live from Slane Castle Ireland* (DVD, 2003, directed by Hamish Hamilton and Maurice Linnane).

46. Johnson, *Shopkeeper's Millennium*, 140.

47. Quoted in Moody, "Revivalism," in Gaustad and Noll, *Documentary History of Religion*, 279.
48. Lawton, "Bono Unplugged."
49. Ellis, *"Billy Sunday,"* 149.
50. Weber, *Sociology of Religion*, 46–47.
51. Bordowitz, *U2 Reader*, 173, 176.
52. Bebbington, *Evangelicalism in Modern Britain*, 2–3.
53. See, for example, Chidester, *Authentic Fakes*; Forbes and Mahan, *Religion and Popular Culture*.
54. For a sociological study of how those in the counterculture movement changed later in their lives, see Tipton, *Getting Saved from the Sixties*.
55. Harding, *Book of Jerry Falwell*, 16–25.
56. Smith, *Christian America*, 197–228.
57. The history of the Southern Baptist Convention is one example of how theological approaches within an evangelical denomination were much more varied in the United States before the fundamentalist political takeover of the 1980s. See Leonard, *Baptists in America*.
58. For more on the religious Right, both before and during the 1980s, see Sutton, *American Apocalypse*; Hammond, *God's Businessmen*; Burnidge, *Peaceful Conquest*; and Greene, *No Depression in Heaven*.
59. Eskridge, *God's Forever Family*, 173.
60. Taylor and Israelson, *Political World of Bob Dylan*, 189; Thompson, "Remembering Larry Norman."
61. Block, "Bono Bites Back."
62. Galbraith, "Meeting God in the Sound," 122.
63. Assayas, *Bono in Conversation*, 126.
64. Galbraith, "Meeting God in the Sound," 120, 123.
65. Assayas, *Bono in Conversation*, 125.
66. "U2: Joshua Tree 30th Anniversary," U2 interview by Zane Lowe, July 21, 2017, https://www.youtube.com/watch?v=vsKZ3YrF_3Q. For an interpretation of Dylan's elusiveness, see Lofton, "Don't Want to Fake You Out."
67. Quoted in Taylor and Israelson, *Political World of Bob Dylan*, 189–90.
68. Quoted in Urbanski, *Man Comes Around*, xviii.
69. Jay Cocks, "Band on the Run: U2 Soars with a Top Album, a Hot Tour, and Songs of Spirit and Conscience," in Bordowitz, *U2 Reader*, 51.
70. Block, "Bono Bites Back."
71. Quoted in Sounes, *Down the Highway*, 323.
72. Taylor and Israelson see the U2 albums *War* and *October* as expressing "a Christian spirituality and anarchism." And *War*, they state, "addresses sociopolitical issues, but it does so from a Christian anarcho-pacifist point of view." *Political World of Bob Dylan*, 187, 190.
73. Quoted in Stockman, *Walk On*, 40.
74. Bono, interview by Charlie Rose, *CBS This Morning*, September 20, 2016.
75. Assayas, *Bono in Conversation*, 320.
76. Weber, *Sociology of Religion*, xliii–xliv.
77. Brennan, "Davos 2019."

78. Assayas, *Bono in Conversation*, 284.
79. Jackson, *From Civil Rights to Human Rights*, 331; Roy, *Capitalism: A Ghost Story*, 38. For an account of the negative impact of neoliberalism on African Americans after the civil rights movement of the 1960s, see Johnson, *Race, Religion, and Resilience*.
80. Assayas, *Bono in Conversation*, 124.
81. Bono, interview by Rose.
82. Block, "Bono Bites Back."
83. Assayas, *Bono in Conversation*, 255, 200.

CHAPTER 2

1. That fans recognize Bono as a prophet is one of the things that distinguish him from the other members of the band. His claim to prophetic status extends beyond his influence as a musician to his work for social causes. While fans may describe the Edge's chord progressions in religious terms, they don't refer to the Edge—or any other band member—in the same way. Bono's prophetic status sets him apart from U2 even as the band defines him.
2. Hochman, "Celebration," 77.
3. Bellah et al., *Good Society*, 60.
4. King, "New Internationalists," 922.
5. Brothers, "Time to Heal," 263.
6. On the formation of a U2 community as a shared cultural identity, see Williams, "'One but Not the Same.'"
7. The approach I take in this chapter, which focuses on written and published accounts by U2 fans, differs from the broader focus on fandom seen in typical fan studies. For a survey of fan studies, see Booth, *Companion to Media Fandom*.
8. For an account of this process, see Wuthnow, *Restructuring of American Religions*.
9. For a historical survey of how Americans have sought spirituality outside church institutions, see Fuller, *Spiritual, but Not Religious*.
10. See, for example, Schmidt, *Restless Souls*.
11. Bellah et al., *Habits of the Heart*, 221, 235.
12. Lofton makes this point in *Consuming Religion*, 2–5, 84.
13. McPherson, *World and U2*, xxiii.
14. Welch, "We Get to Carry Each Other," 1, 8.
15. Catanzarite, *U2's Achtung Baby*, 105.
16. Trost, "Transgressive Theology," 100.
17. Garrett, *Gospel According to U2*, 94, 112.
18. Bono, "Ten for the Next Ten."
19. Browne, *Frontman*, 118–22.
20. Rothman, "Church of U2."
21. Galbraith, "Meeting God in the Sound."
22. McPherson, *World and U2*, xxiv.

23. Atchley, *Encountering the Secular*, 28–29.

24. Quoted in Beard, "Gospel of Heaven and Hell," 249.

25. Galbraith, "Drawing Our Fish in the Sand," 181.

26. Ibid., 221.

27. Snow, *U2: Revolution*, 2.

28. Quoted in Stokes, *U2: In the Name of Love*, 73.

29. I use the term *evangelical humanism* to describe a normative impulse to promote Christianity as embedded in all aspects of human experience and personal perception, including art, poetry, literature, music, dance, and philosophy. Historians of Christianity have used the term to distinguish, as Nicholas Wolterstorff puts it, "the evangelical wing of the Renaissance humanist movement from the movement in general." According to Wolterstorff, evangelical humanists were more committed to reforming the church and gave "higher priority to the Bible than most other humanists." See Wolterstorff, "Christian Humanism of John Calvin," 80–81. Constructing an intellectual history that connects Bono to this Renaissance legacy is beyond the scope of this book. I do, however, think he shares overlapping traits with the evangelical humanists that Wolterstorff and William Bouwsma identify; see also Bouwsma, *John Calvin*. This isn't to say that Bono is another John Calvin. He's more poetic performer than systematic theologian. But that also serves the point, as he grounds his poetry in scripture, as evidenced in his support of Eugene Peterson's idiomatic translation of the Bible. If we are to compare him to professional theologians, his closest contemporary peer is probably Rob Bell, who argues for the reform of evangelicalism within its humanistic limits, using a universalist vibe well suited to the spiritual markets that Bono promotes, much more so than to the more Calvinist expressions of American evangelicalism. See, e.g., Bell, *Love Wins*.

30. Vagacs, *Religious Nuts, Political Fanatics*, 80–81.

31. *Christianity Today*, "Bono's Thin Ecclesiology."

32. For an ethnographic account of the emerging church movement, see Bielo, *Emerging Evangelicals*.

33. Holm-Hudson, "Et Tu, U2," par. 3.

34. Eugene Peterson, "Foreword," in Whiteley and Maynard, *Get Up Off Your Knees*, xiv.

35. "Bono and Eugene Peterson: The Psalms," April 26, 2016, https://www.youtube.com/watch?v=l4oS5e9oKY.

36. Dyer, "Politics of Evangelicals," 1020.

37. Scharen, *One Step Closer*, 9–10.

38. Quoted in Garrett, *Gospel According to U2*, x.

39. Ibid., 5, 13, 21, 57.

40. Stokes, *U2: In the Name of Love*, 50.

41. Michelle Perez, "Foreword," in Beeaff, *Grand Madness*, xi.

42. Beeaff, *Grand Madness*, 254.

43. McPherson, *World and U2*, xiii, xiv, 102.

44. Garrett, *Gospel According to U2*, 59.

45. Moritz, "Beyond Strategy, Towards the Kingdom," 27.

46. Gleddiesmith, "Bono and the Band."

47. Niequist, "Too Much Bono in the Church," 42, 45.

48. Breuer, "Was the U2charist Plagiarized?"

49. Garrett, *Gospel According to U2*, 15.

50. "Bono Church," *U2charist/U2 Eucharist: News, Comments, and Information about the U2 Eucharist*, blog, March 9, 2011, http://www.u2charist.com/28/bonochurch.

51. Marsh and Roberts, "Soundtracks of Acrobatic Selves," 430.

52. Assayas, *Bono in Conversation*, 145.

53. Reid, *History of Modern Africa*, 129.

54. Lofton, *Oprah*, 5.

55. See Sassen, *Losing Control?*

56. Sassen, *Globalization and Its Discontents*.

57. Associated Press, "Bono Among Figures Named in Leak."

58. Hardt and Negri, *Empire*, xiv.

59. Lewis, *Boomerang*, 83–89.

60. U2 360° Tour, FNB Stadium, Johannesburg, February 13, 2011, http://www.u2.com/tour/date/id/4539.

61. Quoted in David Cole, "Bono on Africa," February 21, 2011, http://www.one.org/international/blog/bonoonafrica.

62. JamBase, "Live Nation Names U2 360."

63. Finfacts Ireland, "Irish Economy 2011."

64. Mann, *From Empires to NGOs*; Over, *Human Rights*, 104.

65. Mills, *Power Elite*, 71.

66. Assayas, *Bono in Conversation*, 94–95.

67. Lofton, "Sign of the Armageddon."

68. Assayas, *Bono in Conversation*, 149.

69. Barker, "Geldof and the Aid Industry," 105.

70. Assayas, *Bono in Conversation*, 283, 98.

71. Quoted in Hicks, "Global Poverty and Bono's Celebrity Activism," 43.

72. Yrjölä, "Invisible Violence of Celebrity Humanitarianism," 3.

73. Andrews et al., "Cool Aid?"

74. Hicks, "Global Poverty and Bono's Celebrity Activism," 62.

75. Tyrangiel, "Constant Charmer," 48.

76. Ibid.

77. McPherson quotes Garrett, Traub, and Calhoun in *World and U2*, xv.

78. Smith, "Hugging Bono, Engaging Marsh."

79. Smith, *New Measures*, 1–6.

CHAPTER 3

1. Sharlet, *Family*, 24.

2. Wallis, "Bono's Best Sermon Yet."

3. A transcript of Bono's speech is available at https://www.worldhunger.org/bonosremarksatthenationalprayerbreakfast.

4. For the intellectual genealogy of neoliberalism, traced through the concept of consumer sovereignty, of which the emergence of neoliberal politics in the 1980s is only the latest manifestation, see Olsen, *Sovereign Consumer*.

5. Scott, *Omens of Adversity*, 4.

6. Harvey, *Brief History of Neoliberalism*, 2.

7. As noted in the introduction, I see the neoliberal religion around Bono as a cultural system that includes sectarian religious influences, such as those associated with evangelicalism, but it is more than just the sum of religious beliefs that influence economic practices. For a discussion of sectarian religious influences within neoliberalism, see Hackworth, *Faith Based*, chapter 2, "Religious Neoliberalism(s)."

8. For a discussion of TINA in relation to Latin America, see Munck, "Neoliberalism, Necessitarianism, and Alternatives."

9. TINA is an economic position associated with post-Keynesian capitalists; it became a favorite slogan of British Prime Minister Margaret Thatcher in the 1980s. Evans, *Thatcher and Thatcherism*, 9, 30, 46.

10. Bono, interview by Charlie Rose, *CBS This Morning*, September 20, 2016.

11. "About ONE," http://www.one.org/us/about.

12. Joseph, "Bono Apologizes."

13. Kaufman, "Live Aid: A Look Back."

14. "U2: Joshua Tree 30th Anniversary," U2 interview by Zane Lowe, July 21, 2017, https://www.youtube.com/watch?v=vsKZ3YrF_3Q; Assayas, *Bono in Conversation*, 211.

15. McPherson, *World and U2*, 81.

16. Browne, *Frontman*, 61.

17. Quoted in Bowler and Dray, *U2: A Conspiracy of Hope*, 182–83.

18. Assayas, *Bono in Conversation*, 218, 215.

19. There is also an Irish tradition of supporting dissidents. In the 1970s and 1980s, for example, the Irish anti-apartheid movement supported South African exile leader Kader Asmal, who taught at Trinity College Dublin. See Lodge, "An 'Boks Amach,'" cited in Browne, *Frontman*, 57.

20. Browne, *Frontman*, 62.

21. O'Neill, *Secure the Soul*, 131.

22. Grubbs, *Secular Missionaries*; Curtis, *Holy Humanitarians*; McAlister, *Kingdom of God*, 238–39.

23. Barker, "Celebrity Philanthropy," 148.

24. For a description of the limitations of "globalization from above," see Falk, "Making of Global Citizenship." For a statement of the inherent potential of "globalization from below," see Portes, "Globalization from Below."

25. Casanova, *Public Religions in the Modern World*, 233.

26. See Weber's classic *Sociology of Religion*.

27. Weber, *From Max Weber*, 273–74, 280.

28. For more examples of Bono's homiletics, listen to "The Hands That Built America" on the soundtrack of the movie *Gangs of New York* (Island/Interscope Records, 2002); see also U2's performance at the halftime show of the 2002 Super Bowl.

29. For examples of the theological tension between evangelical Christians and Bono, see, e.g., Falsani, "Bono's American Prayer"; LeBlanc, "Honest Prayer, Beautiful Grace."

30. Hertzberg, "Them Too"; Mclaughlin, "Bono and U2."

31. Reuters, "Bono, U.S. Treasury Secretary to Tour Africa."

32. Gewertz and Powell, "Rocker Bono to Grads."

33. Bono appeared on Oprah's show on September 20, 2002.

34. Wasike, "Largest Plane Brings Xmas Gifts."

35. Lealand, "American Popular Culture," 34.

36. For a transcript of Bono's Harvard commencement address of June 6, 2001, see https://news.harvard.edu/gazette/story/2001/06/classdayaddressjune 6th2001bono.

37. King, "Loving Your Enemies," in *Strength to Love*, 40.

38. These goals are shared by the United Nations. They include the eradication of extreme poverty and hunger, gender equality, universal primary education, and the eradication of HIV/AIDS. Brainard and Litan, "No Stepping Back," 32.

39. For the classic description of the "iron cage," see Weber, *Protestant Ethic*, 181.

40. This performance is captured on the concert video *Vertigo 2005: U2, Live from Chicago* (DVD, 2005, produced by Hamish Hamilton and Ned O'Hanlon).

41. Genesis 32:26–28 (NIV).

42. These statements were posted at http://www.data.org/aboutdata.htm. That website has since been redirected to one.org, which no longer posts them.

43. Brainard and Litan, "No Stepping Back," 32.

44. Quoted in Nudd et al., "Stuck in a Moment," 42.

45. Quoted in Wilson, "Bono: Appeal to America's Greatness."

46. Assayas, *Bono in Conversation*, 264.

47. Speaking at Georgetown University in 2012, Bono explained, "Commerce is real. That's what you're about here. It's real. Aid is just a stopgap. Commerce, entrepreneurial capitalism takes more people out of poverty than aid, of course, we know that. We need Africa to become an economic powerhouse. . . . It's not just in their interest . . . it's in OURS. . . . It's in our national interest, in our national security interest too, your national security interests in particular. We want to see the region fulfill its potential." For a transcript of Bono's speech, delivered on November 12, 2012, see Joe Jervis, "Bono Turns Up the Volume for Social Enterprise," *Guardian*, November 14, 2012, https://www.theguardian.com/socialenterprisenetwork/2012/nov/14 /socialenterpisebonogeorgetown.

48. A transcript of Marshall's Harvard commencement address of June 5, 1947, can be found at https://www.marshallfoundation.org/marshall/themarshall plan/marshallplanspeech.

49. See Sassen, *Globalization and Its Discontents*.

50. Sutton, *American Apocalypse*, 308.

51. For an account of how southern white Protestant support for New Deal policies during the 1930s was fractured by religious devotion to Jim Crow racial segregation, see Greene, *No Depression in Heaven*, 194–95.

52. Chafe, *Unfinished Journey*, 104.

53. See the entry "Billy Graham," in Queen, Prothero, and Shattuck, *Encyclopedia of American Religious History*, 263–65.

54. For a discussion of the Marshall Plan as an "expansion of American markets," see Cini, "From the Marshall Plan to EEC." For Bono's interpretation of the Marshall Plan as pragmatic rather than ideological, see Assayas, *Bono in Conversation*, 101. For Jeffrey Sachs's commentary on the Marshall Plan and its influence on DATA and the Jubilee 2000 movement, see Sachs, *End of Poverty*, 341–42. Former vice president Al Gore has also been a proponent of a "global Marshall Plan." See Gore, *Earth in the Balance*, 298.

55. On the political spectacle of U2 concerts, see Morely and Somdahl-Sands, "Music with a Message."

56. See https://www.youtube.com/watch?v=V7oIDeDM6ek.

57. Bono, interview by Rose.

58. Lofton, *Consuming Religion*, 9.

59. Browne, *Frontman*, 36–37. On Bono's response to criticism of his tax moves, see Shepherd, "U2: 'People Don't Hate Us Enough.'"

60. Assayas, *Bono in Conversation*, 94.

61. Browne, *Frontman*, 49.

62. Ibid., 142.

63. Bono, interview by Rose.

64. Assman, *Price of Monotheism*, 2. For an analysis of Jan Assman's account of justice, monotheism, and history, see Moin, "Cosmos and Power."

65. Greene, "U2 Resurrect 'The Joshua Tree.'"

CHAPTER 4

1. Assayas, *Bono in Conversation*, 284.

2. As American religious historian Brantley Gassaway describes them, evangelicals have at times been "left-leaning." Gassaway and other scholars see evangelicals like Jim Wallis and Tony Campolo as representing a political alternative to the religious Right in the United States; see Gassaway, *Progressive Evangelicals*; Schwartz, *Moral Minority*. It is my contention throughout this book, however, that the issue is not political ideology but rather whether the practice of evangelicalism offers any sustained practical critique of neoliberal policies, not just in terms of theological dissent but in the formation of economic communities and the promotion of consumer behavior.

3. For a discussion of this question, see Freston, *Evangelicals and Politics*, 188.

4. According to the BBC, "Organisers estimated that 85% of the world's population would have been able to tune into the event." See BBC, "Live 8 Attracts 9.6m UK Viewers."

5. DATA, "G8 Stall on Aid Promises."

6. See "One Year On," June 29, 2006, https://www.u2.com/news/article/1959.

7. DATA, "G8 Stall on Aid Promises."

8. Hodkinson, "G8—Africa Nil."

9. Quoted in ibid.

10. On the negative impact of liberalization and media privatization on public discourse in Africa, see Hacket, "Devil Bustin' Satellites."

11. Hodkinson, "G8—Africa Nil."

12. Thielke, "Spiegel Interview with African Economics Expert."

13. Quoted in DeParle, "Preaching Free-Market Gospel."

14. For examples of communism in Africa that would be dismissed by both Sachs and Shikwati, see Adi, *Pan-Africanism and Communism*; James, *History of Pan-African Revolt*.

15. DeParle, "Preaching Free-Market Gospel."

16. "Mission," https://www.heritage.org/aboutheritage/mission.

17. Hammond, *God's Businessmen*, 8.

18. Mathews, *Religion in the Old South*, xvii.

19. DeParle, "Preaching Free-Market Gospel."

20. Chidester, *Savage Systems*, 94.

21. For examples of a more contextual approach to missionary work, see Hiebert, *Missiological Implications*. For a discussion of how revised missionary approaches relate to the use of microfinance, see Fikkhert and Mask, *From Dependence to Dignity*.

22. Hindmarsh, *Evangelical Conversion Narrative*; Keane, *Christian Moderns*, 129.

23. Daley, "Rescuing African Bodies," 378.

24. Ayittey, *Africa Unchained*, 446.

25. Assayas, *Bono in Conversation*, 100.

26. Browne, *Frontman*, 151; see also Morvaridi, "Capitalist Philanthropy."

27. Browne, *Frontman*, 152; Gimenez, "Monsanto in Gates' Clothing?" At present, in 2019, AGRA continues to pursue its stated goal "to increase the incomes and improve food security for 30 million households in 11 African countries by 2021." See "Who We Are," http://www.agra.org.

28. Ludwig, "Monsanto and Gates Foundation Push GE Crops."

29. "Monsanto Announces $50 Million Commitment to African Agricultural Development at Symposium on Global Agriculture and Food Security," May 18, 2002, https://monsanto.com/news-releases/monsantoannounces50 millioncommitmenttoafricanagriculturaldevelopmentatsymposiumonglobal agricultureandfoodsecurity.

30. Bereano, "Gates's Excellent African Adventure," 92.

31. Heim, "Q&A with Phil Bereano."

32. Several studies suggest that organic farming, which does not use proprietary seeds or patented pesticides, is profitable, sustainable, and better for the environment than industrial agriculture. For one example, see Reganold, "Can We Feed 10 Billion People?" For a survey of the environmental destruction caused by industrial agriculture, see Kimbrell, *Fatal Harvest*.

33. Holt-Giménez and Patel, *Food Rebellions*, 128, 154–55.

34. Aston, "Jeff Sachs."

35. Sachs, *End of Poverty*, xiv.

36. "The Mont Pelerin Society," https://www.montpelerin.org.

37. Wilson, "Shock of the Real," 308.

38. On the social production of the "natural order" of neoliberal markets, see also Harrison, "Economic Faith," 1304.

39. Polanyi, *Great Transformation*, 139.

40. Munck, "Neoliberalism, Necessitarianism, and Alternatives," 497.

41. Wilson, "Shock of the Real," 308.

42. Clarke, "Globalization and the Subsumption," 187, quoted in ibid., 309.

43. Ibid., 310.

44. Ibid. See also, Sachs, *End of Poverty*, 51.

45. Wilson, "Shock of the Real," 313.

46. Sachs, *Millennium Villages Project*, quoted in ibid., 314.

47. McPherson, *World and U2*, 88.

48. Jenkins, *Food Fight*, 187.

49. Melanie McAlister, a scholar of global evangelicalism, argues that missionaries in Africa spread "ideas about economic and social development" through their everyday practices, like hanging laundry, and that this kind of on-the-ground religious influence needs to be studied if we are to gain a broader understanding of development beyond public policy debates. See McAlister, *Kingdom of God*, 39. On the hybridity of religious and development discourses, and the unintended consequences of those who use and mix those discourses, see DeTemple, *Cement, Earthworms, and Cheese Factories*.

50. See Walker, *Growing Good Things to Eat*, chapter 7, "Rehoboth Ranch and Windy Meadow"; Grem, "Marketplace Missions."

51. Aerni, "Stakeholder Attitudes," 464.

52. Paarlberg, *Starved for Science*.

53. Huliaras also notes that "although African evangelicals can be stubbornly independent and often align themselves with the African left, they generally hold a very positive view of the United States." Huliaras, "Evangelical Roots of U.S. Africa Policy," 162; see also 175.

54. Pew Research Center, "Global Christianity," 55, 68.

55. Ibid., 68. See also Pew Research Center, "Growing Share of Muslims Expected."

56. On the political involvement of evangelicals in the United States from 1925 to the 1980s, see Sutton, *American Apocalypse*. On the political antecedents of neoliberalism up to the 1930s, see Kiely and Saull, "Neoliberalism and the Far-Right."

57. See Mauss, *Gift*; Hardt and Negri, *Empire*, 43.

58. Browne, *Frontman*, 77.

59. Richey and Ponte, *Brand Aid*, 37–38.

60. Roy, *Poverty Capital*, ix–xi.

61. Bereano, "Gates's Excellent African Adventure," 92.

62. Ganle, Afriyie, and Segbefia, "Microcredit."

63. Roy, *Poverty Capital*, 12.

64. Daley, "Rescuing African Bodies," 381.

65. Nash, "Global Citizenship as Show Business," 168, 179.
66. Browne, *Frontman*, 100.
67. Al-Bulushi, "Mapping War Crimes in Sudan."

CHAPTER 5

1. Brea, "Africans to Bono."
2. For commentary on the "narcissistic idealism of Romantic love" in *Achtung Baby*, see Stein, *"Epipsychidion, Achtung Baby."*
3. Denselow, "Paul Simon's Graceland."
4. Assayas, *Bono in Conversation*, 216–17.
5. Richey and Ponte, *Brand Aid*, 71.
6. Magubane, "(Product) Red Man's Burden," 102.22.
7. Richey and Ponte, *Brand Aid*, 82.
8. Assayas, *Bono in Conversation*, 99, 247.
9. For a detailed account of how the Irish were treated in England and the United States, and how they responded, see Ignatiev, *How the Irish Became White*.
10. For a discussion of this process, see Gomez, *Exchanging Our Country Marks*.
11. Blackface minstrelsy was the "most popular entertainment form" in the United States in the nineteenth century, according to Eric Lott, and was principally performed in the urban North. Lott, *Love and Theft*, 3–6.
12. For example, Irish Catholics performed in blackface in Fourth of July parades and in other public places; see Ignatiev, *How the Irish Became White*, 42. James Barrett has argued that blackface performances in the mid-nineteenth century "allowed Irish Americans to separate their own collective persona from that of African Americans and, in the process, earn a more secure place in the racial hierarchy." Barrett, *Irish Way*, 159.
13. Bean, "Presenting the Prima Donna," 23.
14. Hornback, *Racism and Early Blackface*; Roberts, *Blackface Nation*, 262, 284.
15. Quoted in Bordowitz, *U2 Reader*, 259.
16. Quoted in Gittins, *U2: The Best of Propaganda*, 156.
17. See Ramer, "Century Apart," 456; Quinn, "U2 and the Performance"; McLaughlin, "Bono!"
18. For a wide-ranging survey of the cultural expressions of blackface minstrelsy, see Cockrell, *Demons of Disorder*. For the argument that blackface minstrelsy is potentially subversive, see Lhamon, *Raising Cain*. For a study of the musical performances of blackface minstrels in the mid-nineteenth century, see Mahar, *Behind the Burnt Cork Mask*.
19. Richey and Ponte, *Brand Aid*, 77–78.
20. Assayas, *Bono in Conversation*, 224–25.
21. Herskovits, *Myth of the Negro Past*, 16.
22. Assayas, *Bono in Conversation*, 225.
23. Mintz, "Introduction," xiv.

24. Evans, *Burden of Black Religion*, 11. For a discussion of the term *romantic racialism* in relation to *Uncle Tom's Cabin*, see Eiselein, *Literature and Humanitarian Reform*, 53–54.

25. Lott, *Love and Theft*, 6.

26. Hewson, "Bono: The White Nigger," 189–90.

27. Ibid. On U2 sexuality, see Reynolds and Press, *Sex Revolts*, 76–83.

28. As noted earlier, that comparison between Irish and Africans as colonized subjects was not without historical context, though Hewson offered none.

29. McLaughlin and McLoone, *Popular Music in Ireland*, 188.

30. Onkey, "Ray Charles on Hyndford Street," 162–63.

31. McLaughlin and McLoone, *Popular Music in Ireland*, 190.

32. Browne, *Frontman*, 66.

33. Quoted in Ponte, Richey, and Baab, "Bono's Product (RED) Initiative," 313.

34. Ibid., 314.

35. Quoted in Hertz, *Debt Threat*, 17.

36. Richard Walker, "The Coming African Debt Crisis," *Economist*, November 13, 2014, http://www.economist.com/news/21631955worryingbuildupborrowing comingafricandebtcrisis.

37. From 1988 to 2008, U.S. household debt increased from 80 to 130 percent of disposable income. See Gabriel Stain, "Chart of the Week: U.S. Household Debt Still Above Sustainable Area," Adam Smith Institute, June 11, 2013, http://www.adamsmith.org/blog/economics/chartoftheweekushousehold debtstillabovesustainablearea.

38. Seligman, Weller, and Simon, *Ritual and Its Consequences*, 132.

39. Keane, *Christian Moderns*, 211.

Adi, Hakim. *Pan-Africanism and Communism: The Communist International, Africa, and the Diaspora, 1919–1939.* Trenton: Africa World Press, 2013.

Aerni, Philipp. "Stakeholder Attitudes Towards the Risks and Benefits of Genetically Modified Crops in South Africa." *Environmental Science and Policy* 8, no. 5 (2005): 464–76.

Amnesty International. "Human Rights Concerns in South Africa During the World Cup." June 4, 2010. https://www.amnesty.org/en/pressreleases /2010/06/humanrightsconcernssouthafricaduringworldcup.

Andrews, Gavin, Robin A. Kearns, Paul Kingsbury, and Edward R. Carr. "Cool Aid? Health, Wellbeing, and Place in the Work of Bono and U2." *Health and Place* 17 (2011): 185–94.

Assayas, Michka. *Bono in Conversation with Michka Assayas.* New York: Penguin, 2005.

Assman, Jan. *The Price of Monotheism.* Translated by Robert Savage. Stanford: Stanford University Press, 2010.

Associated Press. "Bono Among Figures Named in Leak of Tax Haven Documents." *Bloomberg News*, November 6, 2017. https://www.bloomberg.com /news/articles/20171106/bonoamongfiguresnamedinleakoftaxhaven documents.

Aston, Adam. "Jeff Sachs: Why We Need GM Seeds to Help Fight Food Shortages." *Bloomberg News*, June 12, 2008. https://www.bloomberg.com/news /articles/20080611/jeffsachswhyweneedgmseedstoolhelpfightfood shortages.

Atchley, J. Heath. *Encountering the Secular: Philosophical Endeavors in Religion and Culture.* Charlottesville: University of Virginia Press, 2009.

Ayittey, George B. N. *Africa Unchained: The Blueprint for Africa's Future.* New York: Palgrave Macmillan, 2005.

Barker, Michael. "Bob Geldof and the Aid Industry: 'Do They Know It's Imperialism?'" *Capitalism Nature Socialism* 25, no. 1 (2014): 96–110.

———. "Celebrity Philanthropy: In the Service of Corporate Propaganda." In *Managing Democracy, Managing Dissent: Capitalism, Democracy, and the Organisation of Consents*, edited by Rebecca Fisher, 145–58. London: Corporate Watch & Freedom Press, 2013.

Barrett, James. *The Irish Way: Becoming American in the Multiethnic City*. New York: Penguin, 2012.

Barro, Robert J. "Why Would a Rock Star Want to Talk to Me?" *Business Week*, July 16, 2001, 24.

BBC News. "Live 8 Attracts 9.6m UK Viewers." July 4, 2005. http://news.bbc.co.uk /2/hi/entertainment/4648051.stm.

Bean, Annemarie. "Presenting the Prima Donna: Femininity and Performance in Nineteenth-Century American Blackface Minstrelsy." *Performance Research* 1, no. 3 (1996): 22–30.

Beard, Steve. "The Gospel of Heaven and Hell." In *Spiritual Journeys: How Faith Has Influenced Twelve Music Icons*, 237–64. Lake Mary, Fla.: Relevant Books, 2003.

Bebbington, David W. *Evangelicalism in Modern Britain: A History from the 1730s to the 1980s*. London: Routledge, 1989.

Beeaff, Dianne Ebertt. *A Grand Madness: Ten Years on the Road with U2*. Tucson: Hawkmoon, 2000.

Bell, Rob. *Love Wins: A Book About Heaven, Hell, and the Fate of Every Person Who Ever Lived*. New York: HarperCollins, 2011.

Bellah, Robert N., Richard Madsen, William M. Sullivan, Ann Swidler, and Steven M. Tipton. *The Good Society*. New York: Random House, 1991.

———. *Habits of the Heart: Individualism and Commitment in American Life*. Berkeley: University of California Press, 1985.

Bender, Courtney. *The New Metaphysicals: Spirituality and the American Religious Imagination*. Chicago: University of Chicago Press, 2010.

Bereano, Phil. "Bill Gates's Excellent African Adventure: A Tale of Technocratic AgroIndustrial Philanthrocapitalism." In *The GMO Deception: What You Need to Know About the Food, Corporations, and Government Agencies Putting Our Families and Our Environment at Risk*, edited by Sheldon Krimsky and Jeremy Gruber, 91–94. New York: Skyhorse, 2014.

Berger, Peter L., ed. *The Desecularization of the World: Resurgent Religion and World Politics*. Grand Rapids: William B. Eerdmans, 1999.

———. *The Sacred Canopy: Elements of a Sociological Theory of Religion*. New York: Anchor Books, 1967.

Bielo, James S. *Emerging Evangelicals: Faith, Modernity, and the Desire for Authenticity*. New York: New York University Press, 2011.

Block, Adam. "Bono Bites Back." *Mother Jones*, May 1, 1989. https://www .motherjones.com/media/1989/05/bonobitesback.

Bond, Patrick. *Elite Transition: From Apartheid to Neoliberalism in South Africa*. London: Pluto Press, 2014.

Bono. "Ten for the Next Ten." Op-ed. *New York Times*, January 2, 2010.

Booth, Paul. *A Companion to Media Fandom and Fan Studies*. Hoboken: John Wiley & Sons, 2018.

Bordowitz, Hank, ed. *The U2 Reader: A Quarter Century of Commentary, Criticism, and Reviews*. Milwaukee: Hal Leonard, 2003.

Bouwsma, William J. *John Calvin: A Sixteenth-Century Portrait*. New York: Oxford University Press, 1988.

Bowler, Dave, and Bryan Dray. *U2: A Conspiracy of Hope*. London: Pan Books, 1994.

Brainard, Lael, and Robert E. Litan. "No Stepping Back: America's International Economic Agenda for 2003–05." *Brookings Review* 21, no. 1 (2003): 32–37.

Brea, Jennifer. "Africans to Bono: 'For God's Sake Please Stop!'" American Enterprise Institute, July 3, 2007. https://www.aei.org/publication/africansto bonoforgodssakepleasestop.

Brennan, Joe. "Davos 2019: U2 Frontman Calls on Business Leaders to Fight Against Extreme Poverty." *Irish Times*, January 23, 2019.

Breuer, Sarah Dylan. "Was the U2charist Plagiarized?" *Sarah Laughed*, blog, May 4, 2008. http://www.sarahlaughed.net/u2charist/u2charist_faq.

Brothers, Robyn. "Time to Heal, 'Desire' Time: The Cyberprophesy of U2's 'Zoo World Order.'" In *Reading Rock and Roll: Authenticity, Appropriation, Aesthetics*, edited by Kevin J. H. Dettmar and William Richey, 237–67. New York: Columbia University Press, 1999.

Browne, Harry. *The Frontman: Bono (In the Name of Power)*. London: Verso, 2013.

Bulushi, Samar al-. "Mapping War Crimes in Sudan: An Open Letter to George Clooney." *Pambazuka News*, September 6, 2011. https://paanluelwel .com/2011/09/08/mappingwarcrimesinsudananopenlettertogeorge clooney.

Burity, Joanildo A. "Entrepreneurial Spirituality and Ecumenical Alterglobalism: Two Religious Responses to Global Neoliberalism." In *Religion in the Neoliberal Age: Political Economy and Modes of Governance*, edited by Tuomas Martikainen and François Gauthier, 21–36. New York: Routledge, 2016.

Burnidge, Cara Lea. *A Peaceful Conquest: Woodrow Wilson, Religion, and the New World Order*. Chicago: University of Chicago Press, 2016.

Calhoun, Scott, ed. *Exploring U2: Is This Rock 'n' Roll? Essays on the Music, Work, and Influence of U2*. Lanham, Md.: Scarecrow Press, 2012.

Casanova, José. *Public Religions in the Modern World*. Chicago: University of Chicago Press, 1994.

Catanzarite, Stephen. *U2's Achtung Baby: Meditations on Love in the Shadow of the Fall*. New York: Continuum, 2007.

Chafe, William Henry. *The Unfinished Journey: America Since World War II*. New York: Oxford University Press, 2003.

Chidester, David. *Authentic Fakes: Religion and American Popular Culture*. Berkeley: University of California Press, 2005.

———. *Savage Systems: Colonialism and Comparative Religion in Southern Africa*. Charlottesville: University Press of Virginia, 1996.

Christianity Today. "Bono's Thin Ecclesiology." Editorial. March 1, 2003. https:// www.christianitytoday.com/ct/2003/marchwebonly/29.37.html.

Cini, Michelle. "From the Marshall Plan to EEC: Direct and Indirect Influences." In *The Marshall Plan: Fifty Years After*, edited by Martin Shain, 13–37. New York: Palgrave, 2001.

Clarke, S. "Globalisation and the Subsumption of the Soviet Mode of Production Under Capital." In *Anti-Capitalism: A Marxist Introduction*, edited by A. Saad-Filho, 187–98. London: Pluto, 2004.

Cockrell, Dale. *Demons of Disorder: Early Blackface Minstrels and Their World*. Cambridge: Cambridge University Press, 1997.

Cogan, Višnja. *U2: An Irish Phenomenon*. West Link Park, Ireland: Collins Press, 2006.

Comaroff, Jean, and John L. Comaroff. *Millennial Capitalism and the Culture of Neoliberalism*. Durham: Duke University Press, 2001.

Curtis, Heather D. *Holy Humanitarians: American Evangelicals and Global Aid*. Cambridge: Harvard University Press, 2018.

Daley, Patricia. "Rescuing African Bodies: Celebrities, Consumerism, and Neoliberal Humanitarianism." *Review of African Political Economy* 40, no. 137 (2013): 375–93.

DATA (Debt AIDS Trade Africa). "G8 Stall on Aid Promises to Africa: Emergency Trade Talks Last Hope for St. Petersburg Summit." July 16, 2006. http://www.live8live.com/docs/ResponsetoOutcomes.doc.

De La Torre, Miguel. *Faith and Resistance in the Age of Trump*. New York: Orbis Books, 2017.

Denselow, Robin. "Paul Simon's Graceland: The Acclaim and the Outrage." *Guardian*, April 19, 2012.

DeParle, Jason. "Preaching Free-Market Gospel to Skeptical Africa." *New York Times*, November 18, 2006.

DeTemple, Jill. *Cement, Earthworms, and Cheese Factories: Religion and Community Development in Rural Ecuador*. Notre Dame: University of Notre Dame Press, 2012.

Durkheim, Emile. *The Elementary Forms of Religious Life*. Translated by Karen E. Fields. New York: Free Press, 1995.

Dyer, Jennifer. "The Politics of Evangelicals: How the Issues of HIV and AIDS in Africa Shaped a 'Centrist' Constituency in the United States." *Journal of the American Academy of Religion* 82, no. 4 (2014): 1010–32.

Egan, Anthony, and Alex Wafer. "The Soweto Electricity Crisis Committee: A Case Study for the UKZN Project Entitled Globalisation, Marginalisation and New Social Movements in Post-Apartheid South Africa." Research report prepared for the Centre for Civil Society and the School of Development Studies, University of KwaZulu-Natal, 2004.

Eiselein, Gregory. *Literature and Humanitarian Reform in the Civil War Era*. Bloomington: Indiana University Press, 1996.

Ellis, William T. *"Billy Sunday": The Man and His Message*. Swarthmore: L. T. Myers, 1914.

Eskridge, Larry. *God's Forever Family: The Jesus People Movement in America*. New York: Oxford University Press, 2013.

Evans, Curtis J. *The Burden of Black Religion*. Oxford: Oxford University Press, 2008.

Evans, Eric J. *Thatcher and Thatcherism*. 2nd ed. New York: Routledge, 2004.

Falk, Richard. "The Making of Global Citizenship." In *Global Visions: Beyond the New World Order*, edited by Jeremy Brecher, John Brown Childs, and Jill Cutler, 39–50. Boston: South End Press, 1993.

Falola, Toyin, and Matt Childs, eds. *The Yoruba Diaspora in the Atlantic World*. Bloomington: Indiana University Press, 2004.

Falsani, Cathleen. "Bono's American Prayer." *Christianity Today*, March 1, 2003. http://www.christianitytoday.com/ct/2003/003/2.38.html.

Fiil-Flynn, Maj. "The Electricity Crisis in Soweto." Municipal Services Project, Occasional Papers No. 4, August 2001. https://www .municipalservicesproject.org/publication/electricitycrisissoweto.

Fikkhert, Brian, and Russell Mask. *From Dependence to Dignity: How to Alleviate Poverty Through Church-Centered Microfinance*. Grand Rapids: Zondervan, 2015.

Finfacts Ireland. "Irish Economy 2011: Ireland May Seek to Restructure Its Sovereign Debt." May 31, 2011. http://www.finfacts.ie/irishfinancenews /article_1022435.shtml.

Finney, Charles G. "A Revival of Religion Is Not a Miracle." In Gaustad and Noll, *Documentary History of Religion*, 321–23.

Forbes, Bruce David, and Jeffrey H. Mahan. *Religion and Popular Culture*. Berkeley: University of California Press, 2017.

Fox News. "Helms Pow Wows with Celebrity Set over Africa AIDS Epidemic." March 14, 2002. http://www.foxnews.com/story/helmspowwowswith celebritysetoverafricasaidsepidemic.

Freston, Paul. *Evangelicals and Politics in Asia, Africa, and Latin America*. Cambridge: Cambridge University Press, 2001.

Fuller, Robert C. *Spiritual, but Not Religious: Understanding Unchurched America*. New York: Oxford University Press, 2001.

Galbraith, Deane. "Drawing Our Fish in the Sand: Secret Biblical Allusions in the Music of U2." *Biblical Interpretation* 19, no. 2 (2011): 181–222.

———. "Meeting God in the Sound: The Seductive Dimension of U2's Future Hymns." In *The Counter Narratives of Radical Theology and Popular Music: Songs of Fear and Trembling*, edited by Mike Grimshaw, 119–36. New York: Springer, 2014.

Ganle, John Kuumuori, Kwadwo Afriyie, and Alexander Yao Segbefia. "Microcredit: Empowerment and Disempowerment of Rural Women in Ghana." *World Development* 66 (2015): 335–45.

Garrett, Greg. *We Get to Carry Each Other: The Gospel According to U2*. Louisville: Westminster John Knox Press, 2009.

Gassaway, Brantley W. *Progressive Evangelicals and the Pursuit of Social Justice*. Chapel Hill: University of North Carolina Press, 2014.

Gaustad, Edwin S., and Mark A. Noll, eds. *A Documentary History of Religion in America to 1877*. 3rd ed. Grand Rapids: William B. Eerdmans, 2003.

Gewertz, Ken, and Alvin Powell. "Rocker Bono to Grads: Rebel Against Indifference." *Harvard University Gazette*, June 7, 2001. https://news .harvard.edu/gazette/story/2001/06/rockerbonotogradsrebelagainst indifference.

Gimenez, Eric Holt. "Monsanto in Gates' Clothing? The Emperor's New GMOs." *Huffington Post*, August 26, 2010. https://www.huffingtonpost.com/eric holtgimenez/monsantoingatesclothin_b_696182.html.

Gittins, Ian. *U2: The Best of Propaganda; 20 Years of the Official U2 Magazine*. Boston: Da Capo Press, 2003.

Gleddiesmith, Stacey. "Why Bono and the Band Are Some of the Best Worship
    Leaders of Our Time." *Thinking Worship: Moving Toward a Deeper Theology
    of Worship*, blog, June 22, 2011. http://www.thinkingworship.com/2011
    /06/22/whybonoandthebandaresomeofthebestworshipleadersofourtime.

Gomez, Michael A. *Exchanging Our Country Marks: The Transformation of African
    Identities in the Colonial and Antebellum South*. Chapel Hill: University of
    North Carolina Press, 1998.

Gore, Al. *Earth in the Balance: Ecology and the Human Spirit*. Boston: Houghton
    Mifflin, 1992.

Gorman, Elizabeth. "Protests Gather Against FIFA Exclusion Zones." Aljazeera, June
    15, 2014. https://www.aljazeera.com/indepth/features/2014/06/brazil
    worldcupprotestsgatheragainstfifaexclusion201461413550951917.html.

Graham, Bill. *U2: The Early Years; Another Time, Another Place*. London: Mandarin
    Paperbacks, 1989.

Greenberg, Stephen. "Market Liberalisation and Continental Expansion: The
    Repositioning of Eskom in Post-Apartheid South Africa." In *Electric
    Capitalism: Recolonising Africa on the Power Grid*, edited by David A.
    McDonald, 73–108. Cape Town: HSRC Press, 2009.

Greene, Alison Collis. *No Depression in Heaven: The Great Depression, the New Deal,
    and the Transformation of Religion in the Delta*. New York: Oxford Univer-
    sity Press, 2016.

Greene, Andy. "U2 Resurrect 'The Joshua Tree,' Preview New Album at U.S. Tour
    Opener." *Rolling Stone*, May 15, 2017. https://www.rollingstone.com
    /music/musiclivereviews/u2resurrectthejoshuatreepreviewnewalbumat
    ustouropener193350.

Grem, Darren. *The Blessings of Business: How Corporations Shaped Conservative Chris-
    tianity*. New York: Oxford University Press, 2016.

———. "The Marketplace Missions of S. Truett Cathy and Chick-fil-A." In *Sunbelt
    Rising: The Politics of Space, Place, and Region*, edited by Darren Dochuk
    and Michelle Nickerson, 293–315. Philadelphia: University of Pennsyl-
    vania Press, 2011.

Grubbs, Larry. *Secular Missionaries: Americans and African Development in the 1960s*.
    Amherst: University of Massachusetts Press, 2009.

Gunn, Steven. *The English People at War in the Age of Henry VIII*. New York: Oxford
    University Press, 2018.

Hacket, Rosalind. "'Devil Bustin' Satellites': How Media Liberalization in Africa
    Generates Religious Intolerance and Conflict." In *Displacing the State:
    Religion and Conflict in Neoliberal Africa*, edited by James Howard Smith
    and Rosalind I. J. Hackett, 163–208. Notre Dame: University of Notre
    Dame Press, 2012.

Hackworth, Jason. *Faith Based: Religious Neoliberalism and the Politics of Welfare in
    the United States*. Athens: University of Georgia Press, 2012.

Hammond, Sarah Ruth. *God's Businessmen: Entrepreneurial Evangelicals in Depres-
    sion and War*. Edited by Darren Dochuk. Chicago: University of Chicago
    Press, 2017.

Harding, Susan. *The Book of Jerry Falwell: Fundamentalist Language and Politics.* Princeton: Princeton University Press, 2000.

Hardt, Michael, and Antonio Negri. *Empire.* Cambridge: Harvard University Press, 2000.

Harrison, Graham. "Economic Faith, Social Project, and a Misreading of African Society: The Travails of Neoliberalism in Africa." *Third World Quarterly* 26, no. 8 (2005): 1303–20.

Harvey, David. *A Brief History of Neoliberalism.* New York: Oxford University Press, 2005.

Hatch, Nathan. *The Democratization of American Christianity.* New Haven: Yale University Press, 1989.

Heim, Kristi. "Q&A with Phil Bereano on Genetic Engineering in Agriculture." *Seattle Times*, December 8, 2010.

Herskovits, Melville J. *The Myth of the Negro Past.* Boston: Beacon Press, 1958.

Hertz, Noreena. *The Debt Threat: How Debt Is Destroying the Developing World.* New York: HarperCollins, 2004.

Hertzberg, Hendrik. "Them Too." *New Yorker*, June 10, 2002. https://www.newyorker.com/magazine/2002/06/10/themtoo.

Hewson, Paul. "Bono: The White Nigger." In *Across the Frontiers: Ireland in the 1990s*, edited by Richard Kearney, 188–91. Dublin: Wolfhound Press, 1988.

Hicks, Douglas A. "Global Poverty and Bono's Celebrity Activism: An Analysis of Moral Imagination and Motivation." In *Global Neighbors: Christian Faith and Moral Obligation in Today's Economy*, edited by Douglas A. Hicks and Mark Valeri, 43–62. Grand Rapids: William B. Eerdmans, 2008.

Hiebert, Paul. *The Missiological Implications of Epistemological Shifts: Affirming Truth in a Modern/Postmodern World.* Harrisburg, Pa.: Trinity Press International, 1999.

Hindmarsh, D. Bruce. *The Evangelical Conversion Narrative: Spiritual Autobiography in Early Modern England.* New York: Oxford University Press, 2005.

Hochman, Steve. "A Celebration: U2 Fans Join the Club." In *U2: The Ultimate Compendium of Interviews, Articles, Facts, and Opinions from the Files of Rolling Stone*, edited by the editors of *Rolling Stone*, 75–79. New York: Rolling Stone Press, 1994.

Hodkinson, Stuart. "G8–Africa Nil." *Red Pepper*, November 1, 2005. https://www.redpepper.org.uk/G8Africanil.

Holm-Hudson, Kevin. "Et Tu, U2? 'Wake Up Dead Man' and Bono's Perceived Betrayal of the Faith." *Journal of Religion and Popular Culture* 16, no. 1 (2007). https://doi.org/10.3138/jrpc.16.1.005.

Holt-Giménez, Eric, and Raj Patel. *Food Rebellions! Crisis and the Hunger for Justice.* Oakland, Calif.: Food First Books, 2009.

Hornback, Robert. *Racism and Early Blackface Comic Traditions: From the Old World to the New.* Cham, Switzerland: Palgrave Macmillan, 2018.

Huliaras, Asteris. "Evangelical Roots of U.S. Africa Policy." *Survival* 50 (2008–9): 161–82.

Hurtgen, John. "Boy, Baby, and Bomb: U2's Use of Antilanguage." In Calhoun, *Exploring U2*, 216–28.

Huston, Jennifer L. *U2: Changing the World Through Rock 'n' Roll*. North Mankato, Minn.: Capston Press, 2015.

Ignatiev, Noel. *How the Irish Became White*. New York: Routledge, 1995.

Jackson, Thomas F. *From Civil Rights to Human Rights: Martin Luther King, Jr., and the Struggle for Economic Justice*. Philadelphia, University of Pennsylvania Press, 2007.

JamBase. "Live Nation Names U2 360 Most Successful Tour Ever." April 11, 2011. https://www.jambase.com/article/livenationnamesu236omost successfultourever.

James, C. L. R. *A History of Pan-African Revolt*. Oakland, Calif.: PM Press, 2012.

Jeffries, Michael P. "Yes, the World Cup Is About Politics." *Guardian*, June 11, 2010.

Jenkins, McKay. *Food Fight: GMOs and the Future of the American Diet*. New York: Penguin Random House, 2017.

Johnson, Cedric. *Race, Religion, and Resilience in the Neoliberal Age*. New York: Palgrave Macmillan, 2016.

Johnson, Paul E. *A Shopkeeper's Millennium: Society and Revivals in Rochester, New York, 1815–1837*. New York: Hill and Wang, 1978.

Joseph, Yonette. "Bono Apologizes as Accusations of Bullying and Abuse Hit Charity He Co-Founded." *New York Times*, March 11, 2018.

Kaufman, Gil. "Live Aid: A Look Back at a Concert That Actually Changed the World." MTV News, June 29, 2005. http://www.mtv.com/news/1504968 /liveaidalookbackataconcertthatactuallychangedtheworld.

Keane, Webb. *Christian Moderns: Freedom and Fetish in the Mission Encounter*. Berkeley: University of California Press, 2007.

Kidd, Thomas S. *George Whitefield: America's Spiritual Founding Father*. New Haven: Yale University Press, 2014.

Kiely, Ray, and Richard Saull. "Neoliberalism and the Far-Right: An Introduction." *Critical Sociology* 43, no. 6 (2017): 821–29.

Kimbrell, Andrew. *Fatal Harvest: The Tragedy of Industrial Agriculture*. Sausalito: Foundation for Deep Ecology, 2002.

King, David. "The New Internationalists: World Vision and the Revival of American Evangelical Humanitarianism, 1950–2010." *Religions* 3, no. 4 (2012): 922–49.

King, Martin Luther, Jr. *Strength to Love*. New York: Harper and Row, 1963.

Knight, Arthur. "'The Mix Itself Is Genuine.'" Review of *Love and Theft: Blackface Minstrelsy and the American Working Class*, by Eric Lott. *Wide Angle* 18, no. 3 (1996): 107–12.

Lawton, Kim. "Bono Unplugged." *Religion and Ethics Newsweekly*, February 3, 2006. http://www.pbs.org/wnet/religionandethics/2006/02/03 /february32006bonounplugged/18832.

Lealand, Geoff. "American Popular Culture and Emerging Nationalism in New Zealand." *National Forum* 74, no. 4 (1994): 34–37.

LeBlanc, Douglas. "Honest Prayer, Beautiful Grace: The Messianic and Passionate U2 Sounds Like Itself Again." *Christianity Today*, February 5, 2011. http://www.christianitytoday.com/ct/2001/002/39.77.html.

Leonard, Bill J. *Baptists in America.* New York: Columbia University Press, 2005.

Lewis, Michael. *Boomerang: Travels in the New Third World.* New York: W. W. Norton, 2011.

Lhamon, W. T., Jr. *Raising Cain: Blackface Performance from Jim Crow to Hip Hop.* Cambridge: Harvard University Press, 1998.

Lodge, Tom. "An 'Boks Amach': The Irish Anti-Apartheid Movement." *History Ireland*, July–August 2006. https://www.historyireland.com/20thcentury contemporaryhistory/anboksamachtheirishantiapartheidmovement.

Lofton, Kathryn. "Considering the Neoliberal in American Religion." In *Religion and the Marketplace in the United States*, edited by Jan Stievermann, Philip Goff, and Detlef Junker, 269–88. New York: Oxford University Press, 2015.

———. *Consuming Religion.* Chicago: University of Chicago Press, 2017.

———. "I Don't Want to Fake You Out: Bob Dylan and the Search for Belief in History." In *Cultural Icons and Cultural Leadership*, edited by Peter Iver Kaufman and Kristin M. S. Bezio, 152–66. Cheltenham: Edward Elgar, 2017.

———. *Oprah: The Gospel of an Icon.* Berkeley: University of California Press, 2011.

———. "The Preacher Paradigm: Promotional Biographies and the Modern-Made Evangelist." *Religion and American Culture* 16, no. 1 (2006): 95–123.

———. "Response: The Sign of the Armageddon." Symposium on *America's Pastor Billy Graham and the Shaping of a Nation*, by Grant Wacker. *Syndicate*, May 16, 2016. https://syndicate.network/symposia/theology/americas pastor.

Logan, Dana. "The Lean Closet: Asceticism in Postindustrial Consumer Culture." *Journal of the American Academy of Religion* 85, no. 3 (2017): 600–628.

Lott, Eric. *Love and Theft: Blackface Minstrelsy and the American Working Class.* New York: Oxford University Press, 1993.

Ludwig, Mike. "Monsanto and Gates Foundation Push GE Crops on Africa." Truthout, July 12, 2011. http://www.truthout.org/news/item/2105:monsanto andgatesfoundationpushgecropsonafrica.

Lynch, Michael W. "Road Show: The Rock Star and the Treasury Secretary Demonstrate the Limits to Aid." *Reason* (August–September 2002). http:// reason.com/archives/2002/08/01/roadshow.

Magubane, Zine. "The (Product) Red Man's Burden: Charity, Celebrity, and the Contradictions of Coevalness." *Journal of Pan African Studies* 2, no. 6 (2008). http:// www.jpanafrican.org/docs/vol2no6/2.6_Red_Mans _Burden.pdf.

Mahar, William. *Behind the Burnt Cork Mask: Early Blackface Minstrelsy and Antebellum American Popular Culture.* Urbana: University of Illinois Press, 1999.

Maitra, Saikat. "Laboring to Create Magic: The New Worker in the Emerging Retail Industries of Kolkata." PhD diss., University of Texas at Austin, 2013.

Mann, Gregory. *From Empires to NGOs in the West African Sahel: The Road to Nongov-ernmentality.* New York: Cambridge University Press, 2015.

Marsh, Clive, and Vaughan S. Roberts. "Soundtracks of Acrobatic Selves: Fan-Site Religion in the Reception and Use of the Music of U2." *Journal of Contemporary Religion* 26 (2011): 417–30.

Marshall, Peter. *Heretics and Believers: A History of the English Reformation.* New Haven: Yale University Press, 2017.

Mathews, Donald G. *Religion in the Old South.* Chicago: University of Chicago Press, 1977.

———. "The Second Great Awakening as an Organizing Process, 1780–1830: An Hypothesis." *American Quarterly* 21, no. 1 (1969): 23–43.

———. "The Southern Rite of Human Sacrifice: Lynching and Religion in the South, 1875–1940." *Journal of Southern Religion* 3 (2000). http://jsr.fsu.edu/mathews.htm.

Mauss, Marcel. *The Gift: The Form and Reason for Exchange in Archaic Societies.* Translated by W. D. Halls. New York: W. W. Norton, 1990.

McAlister, Melanie. *The Kingdom of God Has No Borders: A Global History of American Evangelicalism.* New York: Oxford University Press, 2018.

McClendon, David. "Sub-Saharan Africa Will Be Home to Growing Shares of the World's Christians and Muslims." Pew Research Center, April 19, 2017. https://www.pewresearch.org/facttank/2017/04/19/subsaharanafrica willbehometogrowingsharesoftheworldschristiansandmuslims.

McGee, Matt. *U2: A Diary.* London: Omnibus Press, 2011.

McKittrick, David, and David McVea. *Making Sense of the Troubles: The Story of the Conflict in Northern Ireland.* Chicago: New Amsterdam Books, 2002.

Mclaughlin, Lisa. "Bono and U2: Can Rock 'n' Roll Save the World?" *Time* magazine, September 15, 2001. http://content.time.com/time/magazine/article/0,9171,1000786,00.html.

McLaughlin, Noel. "Bono! Do You Ever Take Those Wretched Sunglasses Off? U2 and the Performance of Irishness." *Popular Music History* 4, no. 3 (2009). https://doi.org/10.1558/pomh.v4i3.309.

McLaughlin, Noel, and Martin McLoone. *Rock and Popular Music in Ireland: Before and After U2.* Dublin: Irish Academic Press, 2012.

McLoughlin, William G. "Awakenings as Revitalizations of Culture." In *Revivals, Awakenings, and Reform,* 1–23. Chicago: University of Chicago Press, 1978.

McPherson, Alan. *The World and U2: One Band's Remaking of Global Activism.* Lanham, Md.: Rowman and Littlefield, 2015.

Mills, C. Wright. *The Power Elite.* 1956. New York: Oxford University Press, 2000.

Mintz, Sidney. "Introduction." In *The Myth of the Negro Past,* by Melville Herskovits. Boston: Beacon Press, 1941.

Moin, Azfar. "Cosmos and Power: A Comparative Dialogue on Astrology, Divination, and Politics in Pre-Modern Eurasia." *Medieval History* 19, no. 1 (2016): 122–29.

Molosankwe, Botho. "Power Cut Leaves Paralysed Boy Immobile." *Star* (Gauteng, South Africa), September 13, 2010.

Morely, Veronica, and Katrinka Somdahl-Sands. "Music with a Message: U2's Rock Concerts as Spectacular Spaces of Politics." *Aether: The Journal of Media Geography* (Winter 2011): 58–74.

Moritz, Joshua M. "Beyond Strategy, Towards the Kingdom of God: The Post-Critical Reconstructionist Mission of the Emerging Church." *Dialog: A Journal of Theology* 47, no. 1 (2008): 27–36.

Morvaridi, Behrooz. "Capitalist Philanthropy and Hegemonic Partnerships." *Third World Quarterly* 33, no. 7 (2012): 1191–210.

Munck, Ronaldo. "Neoliberalism, Necessitarianism, and Alternatives in Latin America: There Is No Alternative (TINA)?" *Third World Quarterly* 24, no. 3 (2010): 495–511.

Nash, Kate. "Global Citizenship as Show Business: The Cultural Politics of Make Poverty History." *Media, Culture, and Society* 30, no. 2 (2008): 167–81.

Niequist, Aaron. "Too Much Bono in the Church?" *Liturgy* 32, no. 1 (2017): 42–45.

Noble, Ruth Jackson. "The Changing Face of Irish Christianity: The Evangelical Christian Movement in the Republic." In *Ireland's New Religious Movements*, edited by Olivia Cosgrove, Laurence Cox, and Carmen Kuhling, 131–46. Newcastle upon Tyne: Cambridge Scholars, 2011.

Noll, Mark A. *American Evangelical Christianity: An Introduction.* Oxford: Blackwell, 2001.

Nudd, Tim, Aaron Baar, David Kaplan, and Andrew McMains. "Stuck in a Moment: The Week Panel Gets an Earful from Bono." *Adweek* (New England edition), October 7, 2002, 40–44.

Olsen, Niklas. *The Sovereign Consumer: A New Intellectual History of Neoliberalism.* Cham, Switzerland: Palgrave Macmillan, 2019.

O'Neill, Kevin Lewis. *Secure the Soul: Christian Piety and Gang Prevention in Guatemala.* Berkeley: University of California Press, 2015.

Onkey, Lauren. "Ray Charles on Hyndford Street: Van Morrison's Caledonian Soul." In *The Irish in Us: Irishness, Performativity, and Popular Culture*, edited by Diane Negra, 161–95. Durham: Duke University Press, 2006.

Over, William. *Human Rights in the International Public Sphere: Civic Discourse for the Twenty-First Century.* Stamford, Conn.: Ablex, 1999.

Paarlberg, Robert. *Starved for Science: How Biotechnology Is Being Kept Out of Africa.* Cambridge: Harvard University Press, 2008.

Parsons, Talcott. "Religion in Postindustrial America: The Problem of Secularization." *Social Research* 41, no. 2 (1974): 193–225.

Paseta, Senia. *Modern Ireland: A Very Short Introduction.* New York: Oxford University Press, 2003.

Pew Research Center. "Global Christianity: A Report on the Size and Distribution of the World's Christian Population." December 19, 2011. http://www.pewforum.org/2011/12/19/globalchristianityexec.

——. "Growing Share of Muslims Expected to Live in Sub-Saharan Africa." April 3, 2011. http://www.pewresearch.org/fact-tank/2017/04/19/subsaharanafricawillbehometogrowingsharesoftheworldschristiansandmuslims/ft_170417_regionsmuslim.

———. "Religious Landscape Study." N.d. https://www.pewforum.org/religious landscapestudy.

Pillay, Udesh, and Orli Bass. "Mega-Events as a Response to Poverty Reduction: The 2010 FIFA World Cup and Its Urban Development." *Urban Forum* (September 2008). https://link.springer.com/article/10.1007/s12132 00890349.

Polanyi, Karl. *The Great Transformation: The Political and Economic Origins of Our Time.* 1944. Boston: Beacon Press, 1957.

Ponte, Stefano, Lisa Ann Richey, and Mike Baab. "Bono's Product (RED) Initiative: Corporate Social Responsibility That Solves the Problems of 'Distant Others.'" *Third World Quarterly* 30, no. 2 (2010): 301–17.

Portes, Alejandro. "Globalization from Below: The Rise of Transnational Communities." In *The Ends of Globalization: Bringing Society Back In*, edited by Don Kalb, 253–72. Lanham, Md.: Rowman and Littlefield, 2000.

Queen, Edward L., II, Stephen R. Prothero, and Gardiner H. Shattuck Jr. *The Encyclopedia of American Religious History.* New York: Facts on File, 1996.

Quinn, Steven. "U2 and the Performance of (a Numb) Resistance." *Social Semiotics* 9, no. 1 (1999): 67–83.

Ramer, Lynn. "A Century Apart: The Personality Performances of Oscar Wilde in the 1890s and U2's Bono in the 1990s." *Popular Music and Society* 32, no. 4 (2009): 447–60.

Reganold, John. "Can We Feed 10 Billion People on Organic Farming Alone?" *Guardian*, August 14, 2016.

Reid, Richard J. *A History of Modern Africa: 1800 to the Present.* Hoboken: John Wiley and Sons, 2011.

Reuters. "U2's Bono, U.S. Treasury Secretary to Tour Africa." April 23, 2002. https://www.atu2.com/news/u2sbonoustreasurysecretarytotourafrica.html.

Reynolds, Simon, and Joy Press. *The Sex Revolts: Gender, Rebellion, and Rock 'n' Roll.* London: Serpent's Tail, 1995.

Richey, Lisa Ann, and Stefano Ponte. *Brand Aid: Shopping Well to Save the World.* Minneapolis: University of Minnesota Press, 2011.

Roberts, Brian. *Blackface Nation: Race, Reform, and Identity in American Popular Music, 1812–1925.* Chicago: University of Chicago Press, 2017.

Rodrigues, Chris. "South Africa's World Cup Is a Disgrace." *Guardian*, May 6, 2010.

Rothman, Joshua. "The Church of U2." *New Yorker*, September 16, 2014. https://www.newyorker.com/culture/culturalcomment/churchu2.

Roy, Ananya. *Poverty Capital: Microfinance and the Making of Development.* New York: Routledge, 2010.

Roy, Arundhati. *Capitalism: A Ghost Story.* Chicago: Haymarket Books, 2014.

Sachs, Jeffrey. *The End of Poverty: Economic Possibilities of Our Time.* New York: Penguin Press, 2005.

Sassen, Saskia. *Globalization and Its Discontents: Essays on the New Mobility of People and Money.* New York: New Press, 1998.

———. *Losing Control? Sovereignty in an Age of Globalization.* New York: Columbia University Press, 1996.

Scharen, Christian. *One Step Closer: Why U2 Matters to Those Seeking God*. Grand Rapids: Brazos Press, 2006.

Schmidt, Leigh. *Restless Souls: The Making of American Spirituality from Emerson to Oprah*. New York: HarperCollins, 2005.

Schwartz, David R. *Moral Minority: The Evangelical Left in an Age of Conservatism*. Philadelphia: University of Pennsylvania Press, 2012.

Scott, David. *Omens of Adversity: Tragedy, Time, Memory, Justice*. Durham: Duke University Press, 2014.

Seales, Chad. "Race and Religion in *O Brother, Where Art Thou?*" In *Coen: Framing Religion in Amoral Order*, edited by Elijah Siegler, 109–23. Waco: Baylor University Press, 2016.

———. *The Secular Spectacle: Performing Religion in a Southern Town*. Oxford: Oxford University Press, 2013.

Seligman, Adam B., Robert P. Weller, and Bennett Simon. *Ritual and Its Consequences: An Essay on the Limits of Sincerity*. New York: Oxford University Press, 2008.

Sharlet, Jeff. *The Family: The Secret Fundamentalism at the Heart of American Power*. New York: HarperCollins, 2008.

Shepherd, Jack. "U2: 'People Don't Hate Us Enough.'" *Independent*, May 4, 2018.

Smith, Andrew William. "Hugging Bono, Engaging Marsh, and Wishing 'The Frontman' a Happy Birthday." *Sojourners*, May 13, 2013. https:// sojo.net/articles/huggingbono-engagingcriticsandwishingfrontmanhappybirthday.

Smith, Christian. *Christian America? What Evangelicals Really Want*. Berkeley: University of California Press, 2000.

Smith, Ted. *The New Measures: A Theological History of Democratic Practice*. Cambridge: Cambridge University Press, 2007.

Snow, Matt. *U2: Revolution*. New York: Race Point, 2014.

Sounes, Howard. *Down the Highway: The Life of Bob Dylan*. New York: Grove Press, 2011.

Stamp, Gavin. "Neighbours Across the Sea: A Brief History of Anglo-Irish Relations." *BBC News*, April 8, 2014. http://www.bbc.com/news/ukpolitics 26883211.

Stein, Atara. "*Epipsychidion, Achtung Baby*, and the Teaching of Romanticism." *Popular Culture Review* 6 (1995): 29–44.

Stephens, Randall J. *The Devil's Music: How Christians Inspired, Condemned, and Embraced Rock 'n' Roll*. Cambridge: Harvard University Press, 2018.

Stockman, Steve. *Walk On: The Spiritual Journey of U2*. Orlando, Fla.: Relevant Books, 2005.

Stokes, Niall, ed. *U2: In the Name of Love; A History from Ireland's Hot Press Magazine*. New York: Harmony Books, 1985.

Sutton, Matthew Avery. *American Apocalypse: A History of Modern Evangelicalism*. Cambridge: Harvard University Press, 2014.

Taylor, Jeff, and Chad Israelson. *The Political World of Bob Dylan: Freedom and Justice, Power and Sin*. New York: Palgrave Macmillan, 2015.

Thielke, Thilo. "Spiegel Interview with African Economics Expert." *Der Spiegel*, July 4, 2005. http://www.spiegel.de/international/spiegel/spiegel

interviewwithafricaneconomicsexpertforgodssakepleasestoptheaida 363663.html.

Thompson, John J. "Remembering Larry Norman." *CCM Magazine*, April 1, 2008. https://www.ccmmagazine.com/features/rememberinglarrynorman.

Tipton, Steven M. *Getting Saved from the Sixties: Moral Meaning in Conversion and Cultural Change*. Berkeley: University of California Press, 1984.

Trost, Theodore Louis. "Transgressive Theology: The Sacred and the Profane at U2's PopMart." In *U2: Above, Across, and Beyond; Interdisciplinary Assessments*, edited by Scott D. Calhoun, 91–104. Lanham, Md.: Lexington Books, 2015.

Tyrangiel, Josh. "The Constant Charmer." *Time* magazine, December 26, 2005, 46–62.

Umraw, Amil. "Just How Much Trouble Is Eskom In? Quite a Lot, and It's Complicated." *Huffington Post*, June 15, 2018. https://www.huffingtonpost.co.za /2018/06/15/justhowmuchtroubleiseskominquitealotanditscomplicated _a_23459713.

Urbanski, Dave. *The Man Comes Around: The Spiritual Journey of Johnny Cash*. Lake Mary, Fla.: Relevant Books, 2003.

Vagacs, Robert G. *Religious Nuts, Political Fanatics: U2 in Theological Perspective*. Eugene: Wipf & Stock, 2005.

Walker, Pamela. *Growing Good Things to Eat in Texas: Profiles of Organic Farmers and Ranchers Across the State*. College Station: Texas A&M University Press, 2009.

Wallis, Jim. "Bono's Best Sermon Yet." *Sojourners*, February 3, 2006. https://www .atu2.com/news/bonosbestsermonyet.html.

Wasike, Alfred. "Largest Plane Brings Xmas Gifts." Africa News Service, December 16, 2002. http://www.u2world.com/news/article.php3?id_article=9.

Waters, John. *Race of Angels: The Genesis of U2*. London: Fourth Estate, 1994.

Weber, Max. *From Max Weber: Essays in Sociology*. Edited by Hans H. Gerth and C. Wright Mills. New York: Oxford University Press, 1946.

——. *The Protestant Ethic and the Spirit of Capitalism*. New York: Charles Scriber's Sons, 1958.

——. *The Sociology of Religion*. Translated by Talcott Parsons. Boston: Beacon Press, 1993.

Welch, Marshall. "We Get to Carry Each Other: Using the Musical Activism of U2 as Framework for an Engaged Spirituality and Community Engagement Course." *Engaging Pedagogies in Catholic Higher Education* 1, no. 1 (2015). https://www.academia.edu/23769546.

Wells, Spencer. "Out of Africa." *Vanity Fair*, July 2007. https://www.vanityfair.com /news/2007/07/genographic200707.

Whiteley, Raewynne J., and Beth Maynard. *Get Up Off Your Knees: Preaching the U2 Catalog*. Cambridge, Mass.: Cowley Publications, 2003.

Williams, Michael. "'One but Not the Same': U2 Concerts and Cultural Identity." In *Identity Discourses and Communities in International Events, Festivals, and Spectacles*, edited by Udo Merkel, 242–59. New York: Palgrave Macmillan, 2015.

Wilson, Japhy. "The Shock of the Real: The Neoliberal Neurosis in the Life and Times of Jeffrey Sachs." *Antipode* 46, no. 1 (2014): 301–21.

Wilson, Jim. "Bono: Appeal to America's Greatness to Aid Africa." *USA Today*, September 16, 2003.

Wolterstorff, Nicholas. "The Christian Humanism of John Calvin." In *Re-Envisioning Christian Humanism: Education and the Restoration of Humanity*, edited by Jens Zimmermann, 77–94. New York: Oxford University Press, 2017.

Worthen, Molly. *Apostles of Reason: The Crisis of Authority in American Evangelicalism*. New York: Oxford University Press, 2014.

Wuthnow, Robert. *The Restructuring of American Religions: Society and Faith Since World War II*. Princeton: Princeton University Press, 1988.

Yrjölä, Riina. "The Invisible Violence of Celebrity Humanitarianism: Soft Images and Hard Words in the Making and Unmaking of Africa." *World Political Science Review* 5, no. 1 (2009): 1–23.

INDEX

Endnotes are referenced with "n" followed by the note number.

Bono
  as advocate for Africa, 22, 31–33, 63,
    67, 70–72, 77–79, 81–94, 144–48
  and African music, 38, 132–34, 137,
    140–41 (*see also* African Ameri-
    can music; African music)
  and blackness, 135
  as capitalist, 74–75, 88–89
  and commercialism, 56–57, 67
  and consumer consciousness, 43, 57
    (*see also* ONE.org; Product Red)
  conversion experience, 27
  and corporatism, 71–72
  and Elevation Partners, 56
  and evangelicalism, 9, 12, 15–18,
    25–28, 31–32, 35–42, 66–67, 75,
    83, 125
  on foreign aid, 115–16, 125, 131–2
    (*see also* foreign aid)
  on homosexuality, 47–48 (*see also*
    gay rights)
  and "Irishness," 8, 23, 25, 68, 80,
    133 (*see also* Irishness)
  and Live Aid, 79–82 (*see also* Live Aid)
  and loss of his mother, 27
  and Marshall Plan, 91–94
  musical influences on, 39
  neoliberal convictions of,
    78–80, 90, 97–98 (*see also*
    neoliberalism)
  as political actor/advocate, 72,
    87–88, 90–92
  and prophetic authority, 21–23,
    31–33, 41, 49, 50, 56–57, 62,
    79–80, 87–88, 141
  and religion, 13–14, 21–22, 25–27,
    35, 40–44, 54, 146–47 (*see also*
    Shalom Christian Fellowship)
  revival techniques of, 28–34, 37–38
  and secular spirituality, 53, 56, 89
    (*see also* secularism; U2: and
    secular spirituality)
  and taxes, 68 (*see also* "Paradise
    Papers," the)
  upbringing, 26
Bush, George W., 71, 77, 91, 100, 110,
  125

CAAT, 110
Campus Crusade for Christ, 27

Campaign Against Arms Trade (CAAT),
  110
capital/capitalism, 1, 37, 44–48, 78,
  84–86, 98–104, 108–15, 120–21
  Bono's statements about, 2, 36–37,
    46, 56
  vs. communism, 111–12 (*see also*
    communism)
  democratic or democratizing, 1, 4,
    10, 126–28
  and entrepreneurship, 47, 86, 94,
    101–4, 116
  and evangelicals, 19, 113
  and market deregulation, 78, 108,
    111–13 (*see also* TINA doctrine)
  millennial, 2, 9, 18–19, 46, 68,
    147–52
  neoliberal, 2, 23, 70, 75 (*see also*
    religion, neoliberal)
  poverty (*see* poverty capital
  reform of, 1
  and Weber, 86
Cash, Johnny, 41–42, 48
  as evangelical, 41
Catholicism, 14, 23–26, 35, 55, 83, 123
  and blackface, 166n12
celebrity, 72, 75, 99, 103
  and advocacy, 70–75, 129
  as charisma, 22
  moral, 69, 75
Celtic Tiger. *See* Ireland: and Celtic Tiger
class, 9–11, 45, 99, 103, 144–52
  and evangelicals, 113
  and globalization, 128
  and neoliberal religion, 11–12
  and Product Red, 148–52
  and race, 113, 136, 148–49
  and revivalism, 34
  and U2's fan base, 50–54
Clayton, Adam, 27, 97
Clinton, Bill, 33, 71, 87, 150
Colbert, Stephen, 101
Cold War, 70, 75, 91
colonialism, 24, 82, 149–51
  and capitalism, 149
  and colonized bodies, 144
  and cultural difference, 8–9, 134
communism, 1, 91–95, 120
  vs capitalism, 112
  See also capitalism

consumerism, 11, 32, 43, 53, 57, 108
  See also capitalism
conversion, 114–15
  Bono's conversion techniques,
    31–33, 87
  and consent, 115
conversionism. See evangelicalism: and
    Bebbington Quadrilateral
crucicentrism. See evangelicalism: and
    Bebbington Quadrilateral

DATA (Debt AIDS Trade Africa), 88,
    90, 105, 109, 113, 126, 151,
    163n54
  and Bono, 73–74, 79, 84, 93–94,
    146
  and Bill and Melinda Gates Foun-
    dation, 88
  and the Marshall Plan, 91–92
  purpose of, 79, 90–91
deregulation, 2, 78, 108, 111–12
  See also capitalism, and market
    deregulation and TINA
    doctrine
Drop the Debt Campaign, 79, 83, 90,
    151
Dylan, Bob, 41, 43, 81, 142–43, 145

Edge, the, 27–28, 33, 41, 59, 80, 97–98,
    158n1
Edwards, Jonathan, 30
  See also Great Awakenings
Elevation Partners, 56
entrepreneurship, 46, 78, 101–2,
    110–11, 116, 125
Eskom Holdings, 3–5
  deregulation of, 3–4
  six "universal principles" of, 4
  and 2010 World Cup, 3–4
  See also under capital/capitalism
ethics of disgrace. See under poverty
    capital
Ethiopia, 81–84.
  See also U2: songs of: "Don't They
    Know It's Christmas?"
evangelicalism, 1–2, 13–16, 21–50, 67,
    77, 118–22, 154n20, 159n29
  in Africa, 107–8, 113–14
  and Bebbington Quadrilateral, 36
    (see also Bebbington, David)

and Bono (see Bono: and
    evangelicalism)
and business, 113–14
definitions of, 14, 29
and fundamentalism, 15
and globalization, 83–84 (see also
    globalization)
history of, 29–30, 113–14 (see also
    Great Awakenings)
and humanitarianism, 52 (see also
    World Vision)
and libertarianism, 113
and moral authority, 75
and neoliberalism, 47, 83,
    107–8, 122–24, 161n7, 163n2
    (see also neoliberalism; religion:
    neoliberal)
premillennial, 44
and religious Right, 15
and revivalism (see revivalism)
and secularism, 57, 61
and self-identification, 16, 38
and whiteness, 8, 61
See also evangelicals
Evans, David Howell. See Edge, the

Falwell, Jerry, 38
Finney, Charles, 29–34, 95
  and the "anxious bench," 33
  See also revivalism
foreign aid, 33, 74, 90–91, 102–3,
    107–16, 131
  negative views of, 115, 110–13,
    115–16
  as Western coercion, 109–11,
    115–16

G8, 74, 109–10, 117
  and foreign aid, 109–10
Gates, Bill, 55, 88, 102, 108, 117
  See also Bill and Melinda Gates
    Foundation
Gates, Melinda, 55, 88
  See also Bill and Melinda Gates
    Foundation
gender. See muscular Christianity
"genetic" Africans, 133
gay rights, 47
genetically modified organisms,
    117–19, 122

globalization, 1, 8, 46, 83–85, 89–94, 107–11
  and Africa, 3–4, 107–8, 128–29
  agricultural, 122
  Bono on, 84–85, 89, 107
  and class, 128–29
  evangelicalism and, 1, 84–85
  and foreign aid, 108–9, 111
  and "millennial capitalism," 46 (*see also* capitalism, millenial
  vs. nationalism, 91–93, 98
glossolalia, 44
  See also Pentecostalism
Graham, Billy, 26, 31, 36, 75, 94, 155n9
  anticommunist message of, 94–95
  and the Cold War, 70
  and evangelical moralism, 94
Graham, Franklin, 88
Great Awakenings, 29–30
  and Edwards, Jonathan, 30
  See also revivalism
Gutiérrez, Gustavo, 46

Harlem Gospel Choir, 35, 38, 145
Helms, Jesse, 33, 87, 150
Heritage Foundation, 112
Hewson, Paul. *See* Bono
HIV/AIDS, 32–33, 90, 109, 154n17
  epidemic in Africa, 32, 47, 62, 72, 95, 99, 110, 125–28, 146

IRA. *See* Irish Republican Army
Ireland, 23–25, 68–69
  and British rule, 24–25
  Catholicism in, 23, 82
  and Celtic Tiger, 69
  conflict in, 22 (*see also* Ireland, and the Troubles)
  division of, 24–25
  and economic collapse of 2007–8, 69
  evangelicalism in, 26
  Republic of, 24
  and taxes, 68
  and the Troubles, 24–25, 39
  See also Irishness
Irishness, 25, 68
  and blackness, 8, 82, 132–34, 142–44
  and Bono, 8, 25, 68, 82, 142

  muscular, 8
  and "white niggers," 134
Irish Republican Army, 24
Islam, 31, 91
Islamic extremism, 91–92, 124
  See also, September 11, 2001
Israel, 47, 90

Jazz Singer, the, 136, 138, 141
Jefferson, Thomas, 98
Johannesburg, 3, 69, 79–80, 145
John Paul II, 79, 88
Jubilee 2000 movement, 77, 79, 83, 88, 95, 119, 163n64
  See also foreign aid

King, B. B., 38, 145
King, Jr., Martin Luther, 36, 46, 61, 88–89, 98, 144, 152

Lhasa Club, 51–52, 66–67
libertarianism, 111–14
Live 8, 109
Live Aid, 23, 80–82, 84, 109

Mandela, Nelson, 3, 88, 90, 126, 146, 152
Marshall, George. *See* Marshall Plan
Marshall Plan, 92
Marshall Plan for Africa, 91–95, 124
McGuinness, Paul, 28
Message, The, 60–61
microfinance, 1, 4, 120–21, 126
millennial capitalism. *See* capitalism: millennial
missionaries (Christian), 67–70, 114–15, 123–24, 151
  Catholic, 82–83
  evangelical, 83–84, 114, 123
monotheism, 105–5
  the price of, 104
Monsanto, 55, 110, 117–21
Moody, Dwight L., 31–35
muscular Christianity, 19, 37, 48–50, 156n34
  and Bono, 8–9 (*see also* Irishness: muscular)

neoliberalism, 2–3, 77–105, 116–18, 127–30, 161n5, 161n7
  and Bono, 23, 46, 85, 90

and Eskom utility company (*see* Eskom Holdings)
Gospel Choir (*see* Soweto Gospel Choir)
Soweto Electric Crisis Committee, 3–4, 153n4
Soweto Gospel Choir, 2–4, 132
soteriology, 22, 129
    secularized, 86–87 (*see also* Max Weber)
"spiritual but not religious," 53–54, 57, 60, 76
Sunday, Billy, 31–32, 35, 39

Thatcher, Margaret, 78, 98
    and TINA, 161n9 (*see also* TINA doctrine)
Thief in the Night, A, 43
TINA doctrine, 78, 118
Troubles, the, 24–25
    See also Ireland
Truman, Harry, 93–94
Trump, Donald, 32, 53, 95–105
    Bono on 96–99
Tutu, Desmond, 39, 88, 145, 152
Tylor, E. B., 141, 151

U2
    albums of: *Achtung Baby*, 35, 55, 145; *All That You Can't Leave Behind*, 146; *The Bluest Eye*, 7; *The Joshua Tree*, 5, 32, 59, 139; *Pop*, 56, 146; *October*, 27, 59; *Rattle and Hum*, 7–8, 32, 149, 144–5, 150; *Zooropa*, 145
    and Lhasa Club (*see* Lhasa Club)
    and religion, 27–28, 52, 65–66 (see *also* U2charist)
    and secular spirituality, 41, 52–53, 56–57, 60, 139 (*see also* secularism, and U2)
    songs of: "40," 40, 58; "Acrobat," 35; "Bad," 80; "Bullet the Blue Sky," 31–33, 39, 46, 87, 96; "Don't They Know It's Christmas?" 82; "Gloria," 40; "I Still Haven't Found What I'm Looking For," 6, 35, 56; "Love and Peace or Else," 31; "Love Rescue Me," 40; "Magnificent," 1, 5, 40, 59; "Miss Sarajevo," 31; "No Line on the Horizon," 40; "Pride (In the Name of Love)," 34, 89; "Running to Stand Still," 89; "Stuck in a Moment," 62; "Sunday Bloody Sunday," 39; "Wake up Dead Man," 40; "Where the Streets Have No Name," 3, 5, 16, 34, 38, 64, 89; "With or Without You," 39; See also *Sankey-Moody Hymn-book*, compared to U2 catalog and U2charist (*see* U2charist)
U2charist, 26, 66–67
United Nations, 33, 43, 73, 88–89, 162n38
    Millennium Development Goals, 73

Vietnam War, 82

Water Efficient Maize for Africa project, 117
    See also agricultural reform; genetically modified organisms
Weber, Max, 16, 45, 86–87
    and "myth of the redeemer," 93, 95
    and *The Protestant Ethic and the Spirit of Capitalism*, 16
WEMA. *See* Water Efficient Maize for Africa
Whitefield, George, 29
whiteness, 51, 101, 133
    and Bono, 8, 133, 142–44
    and slavery, 101, 135
    See also blackness; Irishness
World Vision, 27, 51–52, 67, 83–84
World War II, 52, 68, 91–93, 95

RELIGION AROUND

BOOKS IN THE SERIES: